THE
GARDENER
AND THE
CARPENTER

ALSO BY ALISON GOPNIK

*The Philosophical Baby: What Children's Minds Tell Us
About Truth, Love, and the Meaning of Life*

The Scientist in the Crib: What Early Learning Tells Us About the Mind
(with Andrew N. Meltzoff and Patricia K. Kuhl)

Words, Thoughts, and Theories (with Andrew N. Meltzoff)

THE
GARDENER
AND THE
CARPENTER

What the New Science of
Child Development Tells Us
about the Relationship
Between Parents and Children

ALISON GOPNIK

THE BODLEY HEAD
LONDON

1 3 5 7 9 10 8 6 4 2

The Bodley Head, an imprint of Vintage,
20 Vauxhall Bridge Road,
London SW1V 2SA

The Bodley Head is part of the Penguin Random House group of companies
whose addresses can be found at global.penguinrandomhouse.com

Penguin
Random House
UK

First published by The Bodley Head in 2016
(First published in the United States by Farrar, Straus and Giroux in 2016)

penguin.co.uk/vintage

A CIP catalogue record for this book is available from the British Library

Hardback ISBN 9781847921611

Book design by Abby Kagan

Printed and bound in Great Britain by Clays LTD, St Ives PLC

Penguin Random House is committed to a sustainable future
for our business, our readers and our planet. This book is made
from Forest Stewardship Council® certified paper.

MIX
Paper from
responsible sources
FSC
www.fsc.org   FSC® C018179

For Pa Boot
and Augustus, Georgiana, and Atticus,
my late-life loves

Contents

Introduction: The Parent Paradoxes   3

From Parenting to Being a Parent   8

The Paradoxes   11

The Paradoxes of Love   11

The Paradoxes of Learning   13

The Uniqueness of Childhood   16

The Child Garden   18

1. Against Parenting   21

In Praise of Mess   26

The Ideas That Die in Our Stead   29

Exploring vs. Exploiting   30

Protective Parents   35

2. The Evolution of Childhood   37

Two Pictures   38

Beyond Just-So Stories   42

The Paradox of Immaturity   45

Learning, Culture, and Feedback Loops   51

Variability: The Unknown Unknowns   54

Back to Parenting   55

3. The Evolution of Love   57

Pair-Bonding: It's Complicated   60

Varieties of Love   68

Grandmothers   71

Alloparents   74

The Commitment Puzzle   76

The Roots of Commitment   83

The Costs of Commitment   85

Love and Parenting   86

4. Learning Through Looking   88

The Little Actors   90

The Myth of Mirror Neurons   92

The Birth of Imitation   96

Learning About the World   97

When Children Are Better Than Adults   102

Overimitation   105

Rituals   107

Imitation Across Cultures   111

Doing Things Together   112

5. Learning Through Listening   115

Learning from Testimony   117

Being Sure of Yourself   119

Who You Gonna Believe?   120

Telling Stories   123

Questions and Explanations   130

Why Ask Why? 134

The Essential Question 137

Letting the Dude Figure It Out 144

6. The Work of Play 148

Rough-and-Tumble Rats 151

Getting Into Everything 154

Pop-Beads and Popper 158

Making Believe 161

Bayesian Babies 163

Kinds of Minds 168

Dancing Robots 170

Beyond Miss Havisham 173

7. Growing Up 179

Apprenticeship 184

Scholastic Skills 187

Thinking Differently 190

Attention Deficit Disorder 193

Schooling and Learning 196

The People in the Playground 197

The Two Systems of Adolescence 201

8. The Future and the Past: Children and Technology 211

The Reading Brain 216

The World of Screens 222

Eden and *Mad Max* 223

The Technological Ratchet 225

The City of the Web 229

What to Do? 230

9. The Value of Children 233

Private Ties and Public Policy 240

Finding the Money   241

The Old and the Young   247

Work, Play, Art, Science   250

Conclusion   252

Notes   257

Bibliography   267

Acknowledgments   291

Index   293

THE
GARDENER
AND THE
CARPENTER

Introduction: The Parent Paradoxes

Why be a parent? Taking care of children is demanding and exhausting, and yet for most of us it is also profoundly satisfying. Why? What makes it all worthwhile?

A common answer, especially for middle-class fathers and mothers today, is that you are a parent so that you can do something called "parenting." "To parent" is a goal-directed verb; it describes a job, a kind of work. The goal is to somehow turn your child into a better or happier or more successful adult—better than they would be otherwise, or (though we whisper this) better than the children next door. The right kind of parenting will produce the right kind of child, who in turn will become the right kind of adult.

Of course, people sometimes use the word "parenting" just to describe what parents actually do. But more often, especially now, "parenting" means something that parents *should* do. In this book, I'll argue that this prescriptive parenting picture is fundamentally misguided, from a scientific, philosophical, and political point of view, as well as a personal one. It's the wrong way to understand how parents and children actually think and act, and it's equally wrong as a vision of how they should think and act. It's actually made life worse for children and parents, not better.

The parenting idea is so pervasive and seductive that it might seem self-evident, incontrovertible, and obvious. But at the same time that parents, most definitely including the parent writing this book, feel the pull of the parenting model, they also feel, often in an inchoate way, that there is something wrong about it. We simultaneously worry that our children are not doing well enough in school, and that they are suffering from the pressure to make them do well in school. We compare our children with the children of our friends and then feel despicable for doing it. We click on the latest headline praising or attacking some new parenting prescription and then say, perhaps a little too loudly, that we are actually just going to act on instinct after all.

Working to achieve a particular outcome *is* a good model for many crucial human enterprises. It's the right model for carpenters or writers or businessmen. You can judge whether you are a good carpenter or writer or CEO by the quality of your chairs, your books, or your bottom line. In the parenting picture, parenting follows the same model. A parent is a kind of carpenter; however, the goal is not to produce a particular kind of product, like a chair, but a particular kind of person.

In work, expertise leads to success. The promise of parenting is that there is some set of techniques, some particular expertise, that parents could acquire that would help them accomplish the goal of shaping their children's lives. And a sizable industry has emerged that promises to provide exactly that expertise. Some sixty thousand books are in the parenting section on Amazon, and most of them have "How to" somewhere in the title.

Many of the parenting how-to books, of course, simply give practical advice about being a parent. But many more promise that if parents just practice the right techniques, they can make a substantial difference in the way their child turns out.

The parenting model isn't just something you find in how-to books, though. It shapes how people think about children's development in general. I'm a developmental psychologist—I try to figure out what children's minds are like and why they are like that. Even so, practically everyone who has ever interviewed me about the science of childhood has some question about what parents should do, and what the long-term effect of what they do will be.

The parenting idea is also a major source of grief for parents—especially mothers. It helps fuel the never-ending "mommy wars." If you accept the idea that parenting is a kind of work, then you must choose between that kind of work and other kinds of work (such as, for example, work). Mothers in particular become endlessly defensive and conflicted about whether it is possible to both successfully parent and successfully work at other jobs, and they feel forced to choose between de-emphasizing the importance of motherhood and forgoing their careers. But the same dilemmas affect fathers, all the more intensely because they are less acknowledged.

Partly as a result there is a countervailing impulse to devalue the importance of being a parent—hence all the wry memoirs in which women self-consciously confess to their ambivalence about motherhood. After all, if being a parent is a kind of work aimed at creating a successful adult, it's a pretty lousy job—long hours, nonexistent pay and benefits, and lots of heavy lifting. And for twenty years you have no idea if you've done it well, a fact that in and of itself would make the job nerve-racking and guilt-inducing. But if it isn't a kind of work, why do we do it? If the point is not to create a particular kind of adult, what is the point?

I'm one of those anxious, middle-class working parents myself, and all my life I've felt both the pull of the parenting model and the reaction against it. My three sons are all grown up, reasonably happy and successful, and starting to have children of their own. But I have also found myself perpetually assessing my responsibility—or should that be credit?—for the ups and downs of their lives. Was I overprotective when I walked my youngest son to school every day when he was eight years old? Or was I neglectful when I didn't do the same when he turned nine? I wanted my children to follow their own paths and discover their own gifts. But should I have insisted that my oldest child finish college instead of trying to become a musician? I believed—and still do—that good public schools are best for all children. But when my older kids were suffering at the local public high school, should I have sent them to a fancy private school in the suburbs, as I did with my youngest son? Should I have forced my youngest to turn off the computer and read, or should I have let him master coding? How could I have made sure that my "gifted" middle child had lots of free time to play, and did his homework, and at the same time went to an advanced math tutor and ballet classes? Hardest of all, I got divorced when my youngest child finished high school. Should I have done it sooner or later or not at all?

My professional expertise and knowledge about development has brought me no closer to answers than anybody else. Looking back on my nearly forty years as a parent, I suspect the best answer is that these are just the wrong questions.

Reflecting on your own experience as a parent may make you skeptical about parenting. But reflecting on other parents and children makes the parenting model look unsatisfactory, too. After all, the members of my generation, the happily cocooned and prosperous baby boomers, aren't actually a dramatic improvement on our Greatest Generation parents who grew up in the miseries of depression and war. And we all know people with terrible childhoods who grow up to become wonderful grown-ups and loving parents themselves, and good parents who end up with tragically unhappy children.

The most telling, heartbreaking counter to the parenting model comes when we think about the parents of children who will never reach adulthood. In 2011, Emily Rapp wrote an immensely moving and much circulated article about her son, Ronan, who she knew would die of Tay-Sachs disease before he turned three. That made no difference to the intensity of the love she felt for him. Her son would never become an adult at all, and yet we feel that Emily Rapp and others like her are the most profound examples of what it means to be a parent.

Is it important to figure out why being a parent is worthwhile? Worrying about parents and children is often relegated to the Lifestyle section and the Mommy blogs. But I'll argue in this book that, in fact, those everyday worries reflect genuine and deep aspects of the human condition itself—tensions that are built into who we are as human beings. From a biological point of view, our exceptionally long and helpless human childhood, and the enormous investment in children that goes with it, is a crucial part of what makes us human. What purpose does that investment serve? Why did it evolve?

Figuring out why being a parent is worthwhile isn't just a personal or biological question, but a social and political one, too. Caring for children has never, in all of human history, just been the role of biological mothers and fathers. From the very beginning it's been a central project for any community of human beings. This is still true. Education, for example, is simply caring for children broadly conceived.

As with other social institutions, the way that we care for children has changed in the past and will continue to change in the future. If we want to make good decisions about those changes, we need to think deliberately about what caring for children is all about in the first place. What should preschool look like? How can we reform public schools? Who gets to make decisions about a child's welfare? How should we deal with new technologies? Caring for children is a political subject as well as a scientific and personal one, and the tensions and paradoxes emerge at greater as well as smaller scales.

There must be a way of thinking about children that goes beyond "how-to" on the one hand or wry memoir on the other. Taking the long view offered by science and philosophy might help. But I've recently become a grandmother, and maybe that view can give an even better perspective. Grandmothering provides a more empathetic kind of distance, both from the mistakes and triumphs of the young mother you once were (who couldn't tell the two apart at the time) and from the struggles of your own children.

So this book will be the work of a grandmother as well as a scientist and philosopher—a bubbe, as my own Jewish grandmother would have said—but a bubbe at Berkeley, a grandmother who runs a cognitive science laboratory and writes philosophy papers in between telling stories of the olden days and making blueberry pancakes. Grandmother scientists and philosophers have been rather thin on the ground in the past, so perhaps combining both perspectives can help us understand the value of being a parent in a way that takes us beyond parenting.

From Parenting to Being a Parent

If parenting is the wrong model, what's the right one? "Parent" is not actually a verb, not a form of work, and it isn't and shouldn't be directed toward the goal of sculpting a child into a particular kind of adult. Instead, to be a parent—to care for a child—is to be part of a profound and unique human relationship, to engage in a particular kind of love. Work is central to human life; we couldn't do without it. But as Freud and Elvis both remarked, apocryphally at least, work *and* love are the two things that make life worthwhile.

The particular love that goes with caring for children is not just restricted to biological mothers and fathers, but includes all the people whom academics call caregivers and the British, more elegantly, just refer to as carers. It's a form of love that is not limited to biological parents, but is at least potentially part of the lives of us all.

We recognize the difference between work and other relationships, other kinds of love. To be a wife is not to engage in "wifing," to be a friend is not to "friend," even on Facebook, and we don't "child" our mothers and fathers. Yet these relationships are central to who we are. Any human being living a fully satisfying life is immersed in such social connections. And this is not only a philosophical truth about human beings, but one that is deeply rooted in our very biology.

Talking about love, especially the love of parents for children, may sound sentimental and mushy, and also simple and obvious. But like all human relationships, the love of children is at once a part of the everyday texture of our lives—ubiquitous, inescapable, and in the background of everything we do—and enormously complicated, variable, and even paradoxical.

We can aspire to love better without thinking of love as a kind of work. We might say that we try hard to be a good wife or husband, or that it's important to us to be a good friend or a better child. But I would not evaluate the success of my marriage by measuring whether my husband's character had improved in the years since we wed. I would not evaluate the quality of an old friendship by whether my friend was happier or more successful than when we first met—indeed, we all know that friendships show their quality most in the darkest days. Nevertheless, this is the implicit picture of parenting—that your qualities as a parent can be, and even should be, judged by the child you create.

If being a parent, especially a parent of young children, is a pretty awful kind of work, it's a pretty great kind of love, at least for most of us. The love we feel for our young children and the love they feel for us is simultaneously unconditional and intimate, morally profound and sensually immediate. The most important rewards of being a parent aren't your children's grades and trophies—or even their graduations and weddings. They come from the moment-by-moment physical and psychological joy of being with this particular child, and in that child's moment-by-moment joy in being with you.

Love doesn't have goals or benchmarks or blueprints, but it does have a purpose. The purpose is not to change the people we love, but to give them what they need to thrive. Love's purpose is not to shape our beloved's destiny, but to help them shape their own. It isn't to show them the way, but to help them find a path for themselves, even if the path they take isn't one we would choose ourselves, or even one we would choose for them.

The purpose of loving children, in particular, is to give those helpless young human beings a rich, stable, safe environment—an environment in which variation, innovation, and novelty can blossom. This is true both from a biological and evolutionary point of view and from a personal and political one. Loving children doesn't give them a destination; it gives them sustenance for the journey.

The Paradoxes

So being a parent is simply about loving children. Except that love is never simple. Volumes have been thought, spoken, written, sung, and sometimes screamed about the paradoxes, complexities, and unique craziness of erotic love. Our love for children is just as intense, just as paradoxical and complex, just as uniquely crazy. But the discussion of relations between parents and children, particularly young children, is almost entirely confined to the how-to books or the memoirs.

In this book I'll focus on two kinds of paradoxes: paradoxes of love and paradoxes of learning. These paradoxes are built into the evolutionary nature of childhood itself. The parenting model just can't deal with them. They emerge when we think about childhood scientifically as well as personally. In fact, the most recent scientific research makes these paradoxes especially vivid.

But they aren't just abstract scientific and philosophical questions. They're instantiated in the real-life tensions and dilemmas that bedevil the lives of parents. And they're at the root of the difficult moral and political decisions that arise when we try to care for children as a society.

The Paradoxes of Love

The first dilemma comes from the tension between dependence and independence. Parents and other caregivers must take complete responsibility for that most utterly dependent of creatures, the human baby. But they must also transform that utterly dependent creature into a completely independent and autonomous adult. We start out feeding and changing diapers and physically holding our children most of the day, and doing all this with surprising satisfaction and even happiness. We end up, if we're lucky, with the occasional affectionate text message from a distant city. A marriage or friendship that was like either end of our lives as parents would be peculiar, if not down-right pathological. Children move from a dependence that is far greater than that of the neediest lover to an independence that is far greater than the most distant and detached one.

In the early part of a child's life we have more control over the details of their lives than they do themselves. Most of what happens to a baby happens through a parent or caregiver. But if I've been a good parent, I'll have no control at all over my child's adult life.

This tension becomes particularly striking during adolescence. Not only are our children independent and autonomous from us, they are also part of a new generation that is independent and autonomous from the previous one. Infancy and intimacy go together—we hold our babies close, literally and metaphorically. Our adult children are and should be foreigners—inhabitants of the future.

A second tension comes from the specificity of our love for children. I care about *my* children in a special way. We feel that the welfare of our own children is more important than just about anything else, even the welfare of other children or our own happiness. We can be—we even should be—ruthless about advancing it. Think about a poor mom in a terrible neighborhood who scrimps and saves to send her child to a good private school, a school out of reach for most of the other kids around. She's heroic, not selfish or foolish.

But it's a unique kind of heroism. The classical ways of thinking about politics and morality turn on the idea that moral and political principles should be universal. Fairness, equality, justice—these ideas are supposed to apply to everybody. The very idea of a law, for example, is that some principle applies equally to all. But I care about and am responsible for my own specific children, far more than children in general. And so I should be.

Where does this specific commitment come from? It isn't just a matter of genetic affinity. Almost anyone who cares for a child will come to love just that specific, special miracle. How can we accommodate the dramatic specificity of our love for children within a broader politics of child-rearing? And what would this mean for public policy?

The Paradoxes of Learning

A second set of paradoxes concerns the ways that children learn from adults. In a world where schooling determines success, a lot of parenting focuses on getting children to learn more, learn better, and learn faster. The parenting model is also the default model for much of education. The idea is that adults teach children what they should know and so determine how they think and act. Again, the idea may seem obvious, but both science and history suggest otherwise.

A first paradox concerns play and work. It's a truism that children learn through play. But how do they do it, and why? By definition, play is an act of spontaneous exuberance that isn't designed to accomplish much of anything in particular. And yet the ubiquity of play in childhood suggests that it must be serving some special function.

In fact, just about everybody thinks that children should have time to play. But playtime is one of the first things to go when we start legislating children's lives. Recess is replaced by reading drills, and wall ball and hopscotch give way to soccer practice.

The parenting model gives us a long list of activities that children should do. From Mandarin classes to Kumon math practice to SAT prep, there simply isn't much time left over for kids to just play. We feel bad about it, but we don't quite know what to do.

Conventional moral and political systems are all about the stern and earnest business of human work. They are about how individuals and societies should think, plan, and act in order to accomplish particular goals. But children and childhood are all about play. Why do children play? And how should we value play, not only personally, but morally and politically, too?

Just as children must move from being the most dependent of creatures to the most autonomous ones, they must also move from being people who (mostly) play to people who (mostly) work. This transformation requires profound changes in children's minds and brains. Parents, caregivers, and teachers must somehow manage this transition in a way that both preserves the benefits of play and enables the benefits of work. Schools, the main institutions we use to manage this transition, arguably do a pretty terrible job on both fronts. Is it possible to do it better?

A second tension concerns tradition and innovation. The great twenty-first-century battle of the screens and the books is just the latest skirmish in a long war. We humans have always been caught between preserving the old and ringing in the new. This tension has gone on for a very long time—it isn't just a feature of our technological culture, but a part of our evolutionary program. Children have always, by their very nature, been on the front lines of that war.

Many moral and political views, particularly classical, conservative ones, emphasize the importance of preserving traditions and histories. Continuing a past cultural identity, placing yourself in a tradition, is a deep and satisfying part of human life. Caregivers pass on traditions just in the course of nurturing babies.

At the same time one of the basic functions of childhood is allowing for innovation and change. Indeed, paradoxically there would be no specific cultures and traditions to pass on if past human beings hadn't done something new. Without unprecedented new events there would be no history. By adolescence, children characteristically invent new ways of dressing, dancing, talking, and even thinking. How can we value and pass on our own culture and traditions, yet also allow and encourage our children to invent entirely new ones?

Science speaks to these paradoxes of love and learning, and I'll outline new scientific research that helps us understand just how love and learning work. Research in evolutionary biology is elucidating the origins of our love for children, and the ways that dependence and independence, the specific and the universal, play out in that love.

In cognitive science, there are new approaches to learning, and a new line of research about how children learn from the people who care for them. Even babies and very young children are sensitive to social norms and traditions and quickly adopt them from their caregivers.

But equally, one of the great discoveries of the past few years has been that even very young children can imagine new possibilities and consider new ways they themselves, or the world around them, could be. And new studies actually demonstrate and explain the ways that play contributes to learning.

In developmental neuroscience, we are starting to understand how young brains are different from old brains. And we are starting to understand how the transformation from early play-based learning to later, more focused goal-directed planning takes place neurologically.

All this scientific research points in the same direction: Childhood is designed to be a period of variability and possibility, exploration and innovation, learning and imagination. This is especially true of our exceptionally long human childhood. But our remarkable human capacities for learning and imagination come at a cost. There is a trade-off between exploration and exploitation, learning and planning, imagining and acting.

The evolutionary solution to that trade-off is to give each new human being protectors—people who make sure that the child can thrive, learn, and imagine, in spite of being so vulnerable. Those protectors also pass on the knowledge that previous generations have accumulated. And they can provide each child with the opportunity to create new kinds of knowledge. Those protectors are parents, of course, but they are also grandparents and uncles and friends and caregivers. Human caregivers must both fiercely protect each individual child and give that child up when they become an adult; they must allow play and enable work; they must pass on traditions and encourage innovations. The parent paradoxes are the consequence of fundamental biological facts.

The Uniqueness of Childhood

I won't suggest a simple resolution to these paradoxes or a simple solution to the personal and political dilemmas that stem from them. There just isn't a simple way to deal with the transformation from profound dependence to equally profound independence. There is no formula to resolve the tension between the fact that we love just this one child but still have to make policy decisions about children in general. There is no simple algorithm to weigh the values of work and play, or of tradition and innovation.

But at least we can try to recognize these paradoxes and acknowledge that they go far beyond the scope of the usual parenting discussion. We need to go beyond thinking about whether a particular parenting technique will have good or bad outcomes. Thinking about childhood in a more abstract way, from a more universal and general perspective, can help to make our discussion of parents and children more thoughtful and less divisive, more complex and less tortured, more nuanced and less simplistic.

I do think, though, that there is a good way of approaching the paradoxes, even if we can't resolve them. We should not only recognize that being a parent—caring for children—is a relationship, but recognize that it is a relationship unlike any other. We need to recognize that caring for children just isn't like the other kinds of human activities that are our usual models. Raising children is special, and it needs and deserves its own brand of scientific and personal thinking, and its own set of political and economic institutions.

In fact, the distinctive example of caring for children may help us solve other difficult moral and political questions. The tensions between dependence and independence, specificity and universality, work and play, and tradition and innovation are at their clearest in childhood, but they lie behind intractable adult questions, too. They influence how we understand everything from abortion to aging to art, and the insights we gain from understanding children may help us to solve grown-up problems, too.

We can start thinking about caring for children in a way that escapes the morass of guilt and resignation, of parenting manuals and personal stories, and of codified political divisions that make up most of the current discussions of children and parents. We can recognize that relations between children and the people who care for them are among the most important and most distinctive of all human relationships.

The Child Garden

Perhaps the best metaphor of all for understanding our distinctive relationship to children is an old one. Caring for children is like tending a garden, and being a parent is like being a gardener.

In the parenting model, being a parent is like being a carpenter. You should pay some attention to the kind of material you are working with, and it may have some influence on what you try to do. But essentially your job is to shape that material into a final product that will fit the scheme you had in mind to begin with. And you can assess how good a job you've done by looking at the finished product. Are the doors true? Are the chairs steady? Messiness and variability are a carpenter's enemies; precision and control are her allies. Measure twice, cut once.

When we garden, on the other hand, we create a protected and nurturing space for plants to flourish. It takes hard labor and the sweat of our brows, with a lot of exhausted digging and wallowing in manure. And as any gardener knows, our specific plans are always thwarted. The poppy comes up neon orange instead of pale pink, the rose that was supposed to climb the fence stubbornly remains a foot from the ground, black spot and rust and aphids can never be defeated.

And yet the compensation is that our greatest horticultural triumphs and joys also come when the garden escapes our control, when the weedy white Queen Anne's lace unexpectedly shows up in just the right place in front of the dark yew tree, when the forgotten daffodil travels to the other side of the garden and bursts out among the blue forget-me-nots, when the grapevine that was supposed to stay demurely hitched to the arbor runs scarlet riot through the trees.

In fact, there is a deeper sense in which such accidents are a hallmark of good gardening. There are admittedly some kinds of gardening where the aim is a particular outcome, such as growing hothouse orchids or training bonsai trees. Those kinds of gardening demand the same sort of admirable expertise and skill as fine carpentry. In England, that land of gardeners, they use the term "hothousing" to refer to the kind of anxious middle-class parenting that Americans call helicoptering.

But consider creating a meadow or a hedgerow or a cottage garden. The glory of a meadow is its messiness—the different grasses and flowers may flourish or perish as circumstances alter, and there is no guarantee that any individual plant will become the tallest, or fairest, or most long-blooming. The good gardener works to create fertile soil that can sustain a whole ecosystem of different plants with different strengths and beauties—and with different weaknesses and difficulties, too. Unlike a good chair, a good garden is constantly changing, as it adapts to the changing circumstances of the weather and the seasons. And in the long run, that kind of varied, flexible, complex, dynamic system will be more robust and adaptable than the most carefully tended hothouse bloom.

Being a good parent won't transform children into smart or happy or successful adults. But it can help create a new generation that is robust and adaptable and resilient, better able to deal with the inevitable, unpredictable changes that face them in the future.

Gardening is risky and often heartbreaking. Every gardener knows the pain of watching that most promising of sprouts wither unexpectedly. But the only garden that didn't have those risks, that wasn't attended with that pain, would be one made of Astroturf studded with plastic daisies.

The story of Eden is a good allegory for childhood. We grow as children in a garden of love and care, a garden at its best so rich and stable that, as children, we don't even recognize the work and thought that lie behind it. As adolescents we enter both the world of knowledge and responsibility and the world of labor and pain, including the literal and metaphorical labor pains of bringing another generation of children into the world. Our lives wouldn't be fully human without both phases—Eden and the Fall, innocence and experience.

Of course, although our young children often think we are omnipotent and omniscient, we parents are all too painfully aware that we utterly lack anything approaching divine power and authority. Still, parents—both literal, biological parents and everybody who cares for children—are both witnesses and protagonists of this most compelling part of the human story. And that makes being a parent worthwhile all by itself.

So our job as parents is not to make a particular kind of child. Instead, our job is to provide a protected space of love, safety, and stability in which children of many unpredictable kinds can flourish. Our job is not to shape our children's minds; it's to let those minds explore all the possibilities that the world allows. Our job is not to tell children how to play; it's to give them the toys and pick the toys up again after the kids are done. We can't make children learn, but we can let them learn.

1. Against Parenting

A curious thing happened to mothers and fathers and children in the late twentieth century. It was called parenting.

As long as there have been animals, there have been mothers and fathers and their young. And as long as they have been *Homo sapiens*, human mothers and human fathers, and others as well, have taken special care of children. "Mother" and "father" are as old as English itself, and "parent" has been around since at least the fourteenth century. But the word "parenting," now so ubiquitous, first emerged in America in 1958, and became common only in the 1970s.

Where did parenting come from? The parenting model has become particularly influential because of a series of distinctive social changes that took place in twentieth-century America, changes that made being—and especially becoming—a parent very different than it had ever been before. Smaller families, greater mobility, and older first-time parents radically altered the learning curve. For most of human history, people grew up in large extended families with many children. Most parents had extensive experience of taking care of children before they had children themselves. And they had extensive opportunities to watch other people, not just their own parents, but grandmothers and grandfathers, aunts and uncles and older cousins, take care of children. Those traditional sources of wisdom and competence—not quite the same as expertise—have largely disappeared. Parenting how-to books, websites, and speakers are appealing because they seem to fill that gap.

At the same time that families got smaller and more scattered, and people had children later, middle-class parents spent more and more time working and going to school. Most middle-class parents spend years taking classes and pursuing careers before they have children. It's not surprising, then, that going to school and working are today's parents' models for taking care of children—you go to school and work with a goal in mind, and you can be taught to do better at school and work.

So there's a reason the parenting model is popular. But it's a poor fit to the scientific reality. From an evolutionary perspective, the relations between human children and the adults who care for them are crucially and profoundly important; indeed, they are a large part of what defines us as human beings. Our most distinctive and important human abilities—our capacities for learning, invention, and innovation; and for tradition, culture, and morality—are rooted in relations between parents and children.

These relations are profoundly important for human evolution. But they are fundamentally unlike the picture that is invoked by the word "parenting." Parents are not designed to shape their children's lives. Instead, parents and other caregivers are designed to provide the next generation with a protected space in which they can produce new ways of thinking and acting that, for better or worse, are entirely unlike any that we would have anticipated beforehand. This is the picture that comes from evolutionary biology, and it is also the picture that comes from empirical studies of child development, like the ones we do in my lab.

This doesn't mean that parents and other caring adults have no influence on children. On the contrary, that influence is deep and necessary. Providing a safe, stable context that lets children thrive is important, not to mention hard. After all, being a parent, even a bad one, involves a greater investment of time, energy, and attention than any other human relationship, by a sizable margin. I say hello to my husband in the morning, leave him alone all day, cook him dinner, and spend an hour or two talking to him sympathetically in the evening. He does the same for me (and actually cleans up the kitchen, which is tougher than cooking). That makes me a pretty good wife, but it would be criminal child abuse if he were my literal, rather than metaphorical, baby. Caring adults don't just influence children's lives—without them, children wouldn't have lives at all.

But it is very difficult to find any reliable, empirical relation between the small variations in what parents do—the variations that are the focus of parenting—and the resulting adult traits of their children. There is very little evidence that conscious decisions about co-sleeping or not, letting your children "cry it out" or holding them till they fall asleep, or forcing them to do extra homework or letting them play have reliable and predictable long-term effects on who those children become. From an empirical perspective, parenting is a mug's game.

Those scientific facts might not matter, of course. Our human evolutionary inheritance crucially includes the ability to overthrow or revise that very inheritance. Even if parenting is a very recent cultural invention, it might be a good or useful one. Even if it is terribly difficult to do well, and only has marginal effects, we might still feel that the attempt is worthwhile. Democracy, another recent cultural invention, is, after all, the worst form of government, except for all the others, and the ubiquity of divorce doesn't make us doubt the value of marriage (well, not much, anyway). The criterion should be whether parenting has helped people thrive.

But, in fact, parenting is a terrible invention. It hasn't improved the lives of children and parents, and in some ways it's arguably made them worse. For middle-class parents, trying to shape their children into worthy adults becomes the source of endless anxiety and guilt coupled with frustration. And for their children, parenting leads to an oppressive cloud of hovering expectations.

Middle-class parents are consumed by the pressure to acquire parenting expertise. They spend literally billions of dollars on parenting advice and equipment. But at the same time, the social institutions of the United States, the great originator and epicenter of parenting, provide less support to children than those of any other developed country. The United States, where all those parenting books are sold, also has the highest rates of infant mortality and child poverty in the developed world.

The rise of parenting is a lot like what happened to food in America at about the same time, what Michael Pollan has called "the omnivore's dilemma." In the past we learned how to eat by participating in cooking traditions. We ate pie, pasta, or pot stickers because our mothers cooked them, and they cooked that way because their mothers did before them. Those many and varied traditions all led to reasonably healthy outcomes. In the twentieth century, especially the American middle-class twentieth century, the erosion of those traditions led to a culture of "nutrition" and "dieting" that has a lot in common with the culture of parenting.

In both cases traditions have been replaced by prescriptions. What was once a matter of experience has become a matter of expertise. What was once simply a way of being, what the philosopher Ludwig Wittgenstein called a form of life, became a form of work. An act of spontaneous and loving care became, instead, a management plan.

Evolutionary scientists argue that cooking is as crucial to human survival as child-rearing. And yet, both evolutionary considerations and scientific research show that conscious decisions to "diet," to control what we cook or eat, have a marginal effect at best. In fact, the explosion of dieting and nutrition advice coincided with an explosion in obesity.

The fundamental paradox is similar. Cooking and caring for children are both essentially and distinctively human—we couldn't survive as a species without them. But the more we intentionally and deliberately cook and eat in order to become healthy, or raise children in order to make them happy and successful adults, the less healthy and happy we and our children seem to become.

The preponderance of parenting books, like the preponderance of diet books, should, just by itself, be a sign of their futility; if any of them actually worked, that success ought to put the rest of them out of business. And the gap between private goals and public policy, vivid enough in the case of food, is a yawning chasm in the case of caring for children. A society that is obsessed with dieting has the highest obesity rate—a society obsessed with parenting has the highest child poverty rate.

The problem is that we can't put the genie back in the bottle. Once the continuity of traditions has been broken, there is no way to simply restore it. We can't merely unself-consciously cook, or raise our children, as our parents and grandparents did. Nor should we. In fact, as a grandmother, I'm grateful that I can put electrically pumped frozen breast milk back in the bottle—it's a wonderful new child-care invention. Mobility, variety, and choice are unquestionable goods in their own right. I certainly wouldn't want to give up sushi or tortillas or frozen yogurt and return to my grandmother's overcooked brisket and bow ties—or our Pleistocene ancestor's roots and berries, for that matter. Nor would I give up breast pumps or my career as a scientist just because those possibilities didn't exist for previous generations.

In Praise of Mess

But if the details of caregiving don't actually determine how children turn out, why should we invest so much time, energy, and emotion—and just plain money—in raising our children? Why embark on such a demanding, difficult, and uncertain relationship at all?

This is both a personal and political question, and an evolutionary and scientific one. We might just say that evolution makes us care—our genes try to reproduce themselves. But then, why don't we simply become self-sufficient shortly after we are born, as many animals do? Why do children require so much intensive care? And why should adults provide that care if it doesn't make a predictable difference?

The central scientific idea of this book is that the answer lies in disorder. Children are incontrovertibly and undeniably messy. Whatever the rewards of being a parent may be, tidiness is not one of them. In fact, in the perpetual academic search for funding, I've wondered whether I could get the military to consider weaponizing toddler chaos. Unleash it on an opposing army, and they would hardly be able to get out of the house in the morning, let alone coordinate a battle.

Scientists have other words for mess: variability, stochasticity, noise, entropy, randomness. A long tradition, going back to the Greek rationalist philosophers, sees these forces of disorder as the enemies of knowledge, progress, and civilization. But another tradition, going back to the nineteenth-century Romantics, sees disorder as the wellspring of freedom, innovation, and creativity. The Romantics also celebrated childhood; for them, children were the quintessential example of the virtues of chaos.

New science provides some ammunition for the Romantic view. From brains to babies to robots to scientists, mess has merits. A system that shifts and varies, even randomly, can adapt to a changing world in a more intelligent and flexible way.

Evolution by natural selection is one of the best examples of the merits of mess, of course. Random biological variation leads to adaptation. But biologists are also increasingly interested in the idea of "evolvability," that some organisms may be better than others at generating new alternative forms, forms that can then be preserved or abandoned by natural selection. There is some evidence that evolvability can itself evolve; some species may actually have evolved to produce more varied individuals.

For example, the bacteria that cause Lyme disease are very good at producing new variants that can resist antibodies—that's why Lyme disease is hard to treat. If you expose the bacteria to a lot of new antibodies, they become even more variable. The new potential defenses aren't necessarily effective against the particular antibodies attacking the bacteria now, but they make it more likely that the bacteria will survive another attack from different antibodies in the future.

Human beings produce a particularly wide, variable, and unpredictable mix of children, each with unique temperament and abilities, strengths and weaknesses, types of knowledge and varieties of skill. This provides us with the same kind of advantage as the "evolvable" Lyme bacteria. It lets us adapt to an unpredictable changing culture and environment.

Think about risk-taking. We know that from the time they are very small, some children are timid while others are adventurous. Alexei, my oldest son, always got to the top of the jungle gym, but never went up a rung without checking that he had a way down again. Nicholas, my middle son, went hell-bent for the top without looking back. As for me, I wouldn't have gotten anywhere near those high rungs, in any circumstances.

The parents of a risk-taking child may live with their hearts in their mouths, with good reason. If risk-taking people really *are* more at risk, why wouldn't natural selection have eliminated those traits long ago? Alternatively, if the rewards outweighed the risks, why didn't the more timid children disappear?

When things are predictable, a more conservative, safety-first strategy will be more successful. When things change, risk-taking becomes important. The same strategies that once served you in the old environment will no longer do. And of course you can't tell in advance whether unpredictable change will happen—that's what makes it unpredictable.

So having a mix of people around, some timid and some adventurous, means that each individual person is more likely to survive. The conservative folk ensure that risk-takers get the advantage of security when things are predictable, and the bold allow the timid to get the advantages of innovation when things change.

Nicholas, the child who went straight for the top rung, ended up being very successful in a career where he has to make risky decisions involving millions of dollars—just thinking about it makes me anxious. My parenting certainly would never have had the goal of creating an adult with a life full of risk and uncertainty. But that turned out to be just the life for Nick.

Here's another example. Hunting was an important part of our evolutionary past. When you hunt, you need to pay attention to everything at once and remain constantly on the alert for even subtle changes in the environment. So you might think that back when hunting was crucial to our survival, everybody would have developed those traits. People who just paid attention to one thing at a time and screened out everything else might have provided some other benefits, but they would have been less valuable overall.

However, people with this sort of focused attention turned out to be very valuable when circumstances changed. Once schooling, rather than hunting, became the dominant way of life, focused attention became an advantage. Now it's the children with a wide focus who have trouble adapting.

The Ideas That Die in Our Stead

There is still controversy about how evolvability works, and there is still a lot of scientific work to do to discover just how evolution produces variable creatures in response to variable environments. But there is no question that human learning and culture produce a kind of evolvability that works at much faster time scales than biological evolution.

Instead of waiting for natural selection to turn us into more well-adapted creatures, we adapt on our own by trying out many different pictures of the world (different theories), keeping the ones that fit the data and eliminating the ones that don't. The philosopher Karl Popper said that science lets our theories die in our stead.

This also applies to cultural progress. We can try out different pictures of what the world is like, but we can also actually try to make different kinds of worlds. We can do this either through new tools and technology or through new political and social arrangements—new laws, customs, and institutions. Then we can see which technologies and institutions help us thrive.

So the strategy for human success has two parts. We begin by generating many different possibilities, at least partly at random. Then we preserve the ones that work. However, we don't entirely eliminate the alternatives. Instead, we keep generating alternative possibilities to keep in reserve to deal with a new environment or an unexpected set of problems.

Exploring vs. Exploiting

This strategy has a weakness, however. As all parents know, there is an intrinsic tension between messiness and effectiveness; that's why weaponized toddler chaos would be so devastating. There is a trade-off between generating many alternatives that might be useful in the future and having a lean, mean, fast, efficient system right now. Computer scientists and neuroscientists call it the tension between exploration and exploitation.

Exploring possibilities, whether they are possible personalities, theories, technologies, or cultures, allows for innovation. It gives you alternatives in the face of a new environment. But, of course, you also have to act, right now, in this environment. Exploration won't help you then—you don't want to be considering all the options for dealing with a mastodon when one is barreling toward you. Great generals and executives don't think through every possible plan and pick the absolutely best one; they pick one that is good enough and execute it confidently and decisively. Even dithery scientists like me eventually have to choose from among all the possible experiments, and go ahead with just one.

One way to solve this problem is to alternate between periods of exploration and exploitation. A particularly effective strategy is to start out exploring, and then proceed to exploit. You begin by randomly generating lots of variation and then zero in on what works.

The problem, of course, is that you have to stay alive while you explore. How can you fend off that mastodon while you're still considering whether a slingshot or a spear would be most effective? Or while you're still learning how to use slingshots and spears in the first place?

One answer is "Call Mom and Dad!" A protected period of childhood is one solution to the explore/exploit dilemma. We are allowed to explore when we are children so that we can exploit when we are adults. Childhood and caregiving are two sides of the same coin; children can't exist without care. By giving an animal a protected early period, a period when its needs are met in a reliable, stable, and unconditional way, you can provide space for mess, variability, and exploration.

Human beings are arguably the most exploratory species. Other species are exquisitely adapted to their particular environments. We are, and always have been, nomadic, wandering from environment to environment and dealing with what we discover there. We can be found everywhere, from forest to veldt, from Arctic waste to Saharan desert. And unlike any other species, we create our own new environments. The lights of the great cities illuminate Earth even from space. Imagination and creativity are essential to our success. We have to imagine how the new places we explore, and the new places we build, will work.

It's no coincidence that we also have a much longer childhood—a much longer period of protected immaturity—than any other species. This long childhood gives us our chance to explore.

If children are designed to explore, it would make sense that they are so much messier than adults. In fact, new scientific discoveries suggest that the messiness of children makes a special contribution to human evolvability. Variability and exploration are at their height during childhood.

One of the most striking discoveries involves the variety of early childhood temperaments. Small subtle genetic variations can interact with experience and lead to differences in children's personalities. The difference between the timid and the bold has been linked to some of this genetic variation. But there are many other early strengths and weaknesses, vulnerabilities and resiliencies.

The mechanisms of mess, though, extend far beyond variability in the genes themselves. In early childhood, complex interactions between genes and environments lead to even more variability.

One of the most exciting scientific developments in recent years has occurred in a field called epigenetics. There is a long, winding path that connects our genes to the shapes our bodies and minds finally take. One important part of that path is called gene expression. Genes can be turned on or off in childhood, and that process leads to important changes in what adults are like. Research in epigenetics shows how features of the environment, even quite subtle ones such as the quality of caregiving, can make genes active or inactive. For example, mice who are stressed early in life express certain genes differently. The same thing happens in human children. Genes vary, but children's experiences also vary, and this influences how those genes are expressed.

It's not just that children have different genes and different experiences, and that genes and experiences interact—it's even more complicated than that. Some genetic factors make children more or less sensitive to their environments. Some children are resilient; they come out pretty well in both good and bad circumstances. They are like dandelions that flourish just about anywhere. Other children are more sensitive to differences in their surroundings; they do especially well in rich circumstances, but do especially badly in impoverished ones. They are more like orchids, flourishing with elaborate care and rich feeding, withering without them. So these children not only are different from one another—they also react differently to their surroundings.

Behavioral genetics researchers try to disentangle how genes and the environment contribute to development. They analyze the similarities and differences between identical and fraternal twins, among siblings, and between birth children and adopted children, and compare them with their parents. Twins, for example, are a kind of natural experiment in nature and nurture. But rather than discovering some simple partition of genes and environment, studies have shown just how complex and unpredictable the interactions between nature and nurture really are.

For one thing, children influence the way their parents behave as much as parents influence children. In fact, much of what looks like the effect of genes may really be the result of the way genes feed back on the environment. If you have a child with a small genetic tendency toward risk-taking, you will probably treat him very differently, even just unconsciously, than you treat his more timid brother, and that difference in nurture will greatly amplify the difference in nature.

One of the most striking findings concerns what is called the nonshared environment. If the parenting view was right, you might expect that siblings, who share most of their genes and also have the same parents, would be very similar to each other. In fact, behavioral geneticists find that siblings are much more different from one another than you would expect. The nonshared environment is simply a way of describing all the factors that influence children other than genes and the shared experiences they have as members of the same family, including parenting. Those factors may range from prenatal influences to epigenetic variation, to birth-order differences, to sheer random events like accidents or illnesses. They even include differences in exactly how children interpret their parents' actions. Put the risk-taking baby in the bouncy swing and he's exhilarated; put his timid brother in the swing and he's terrified.

In behavioral genetics studies, the nonshared environment seems to have a surprisingly large influence on how children turn out. Another way of saying this is that even siblings turn out very differently from one another, and there is no way to predict just what those differences will be. So this line of research also shows that diversity and variability is the rule in human development.

When we study children's learning, we see the same early variability. Children begin by considering a very wide range of ideas about how the world might work, and they often shift unpredictably from one idea to another. Ask preschoolers exactly the same question several times and you're likely to get a slightly different answer each time. This kind of apparently random variability originally made writers such as Jean Piaget think that children were irrational—after all, it does seem irrational to answer a question one way one moment and another the next. But more recent studies suggest that this may be exactly what lets children learn so much.

We can even see this in the developing brain. Young brains are much more "plastic" than older brains; they make more new connections, and they're much more flexible. In fact, a one-year-old brain has twice as many neural connections as your brain does. A young brain makes many more links than an older one; there are many more possible connections, and the connections change more quickly and easily in the light of new experiences. But each of those links is relatively weak. Young brains can re-arrange themselves effortlessly as new experiences pour in.

As we grow older, the brain connections that we use a lot

become swifter and more efficient, and they cover longer distances. But connections that we don't use get "pruned" and disappear. Older brains are much less flexible. Their structure has changed from meandering, narrow pathways to straight-ahead, long-distance information superhighways. As we get older our brains can still change, but they are more likely to change only under pressure, and with effort and attention.

Young brains are designed to explore; old brains are designed to exploit.

Protective Parents

Each new generation of children is a shot of noise, a little dose of disorder, shaking up the stable patterns of the previous generation and allowing for new possibilities. But this means that being a parent takes on a new meaning. Being a parent is very different from being somebody who "parents," though it's just as hard.

The unconditional, individual commitment we feel for each child we care for, no matter what their individual temperament or personality may be, gives a chance for wide variation to continue for the future. We love our children whether they're bold or timid, whether they filter out the whole world to focus on just one thing or are open to everything, whether they're an orchid or a dandelion.

That dedicated love also gives children a chance to be intellectually messy, to explore before they have to exploit, and to let their ideas die in their stead. If children are like Popper's scientists, we're like the universities and funding agencies. We give children the resources, tools, and infrastructure they need to solve problems we haven't even thought of yet. And as with science, we'll get much better results by supporting a thousand different programs of basic research than by putting all our money and energy into just one.

We can also literally and metaphorically provide children with space for exploration. The rise of parenting has accompanied the decline of the street, the public playground, the neighborhood, even recess. In the world before parenting, even toddlers could explore the environment they would grow up in—the village or the farm, the workshop or the kitchen. Middle-class American children now spend much of their lives in highly structured settings; poor children's environments are even more narrowly constrained. Ironically, in a society that values creativity and innovation more and more, we provide fewer and fewer unfettered opportunities for children to explore.

The caregiver's job isn't just to give children a protected space in which to explore, learn, and make a mess. It is also to guide the child's transition from this exploratory disorder into a new kind of control—a new variety of order that comes with a new set of adult competencies. But we can't precisely anticipate what that new order will be; that's the whole point of the generational human reboot.

2. The Evolution of Childhood

Knowing where something comes from always helps you to understand it. Our evolutionary history should help explain how our brains and minds work, just as it helps explain how our stomachs and skeletons work. If we want to deepen our understanding of the relationships between children and parents, thinking about how those relationships evolved is one way to do it.

What do we know about how human children and parents evolved? What can that tell us about the way they act and think now? In this chapter, I'll talk about the big evolutionary picture and the links between childhood, love, and learning. In the next chapter I'll talk in more detail about how that link led to the special kind of love that we feel for our kids. The model of parents and children that will emerge is very different from the parenting model.

Two Pictures

The scene is familiar from hundreds of movies, textbook illustrations, and natural history museum dioramas. A group of bearded men dressed in skins, with jutting jaws, furrowed brows, and intense expressions, tracks a giant woolly mammoth. Suddenly, the great beast, with his intimidating ten-foot tusks and shaggy coat, rears up in front of the diminutive and vulnerable hunters. But in spite of their puny size the humans are clever, and react as a team. The leader gestures to some of the men to move behind the monster and pelt him with rocks, and drive him closer and closer to the one great hunter, who bravely brandishes his spear and brings the beast toppling down with a crash. The happy crew carves out giant steaks and ribs and drags them home to the rest of the tribe.

Contrast this picture of the Hunt Primeval, with nature red in tooth and claw, to the peaceable, gentle, not to say effete, Tuesday afternoons when I used to take my one-year-old grandson Augustus to the farmers' market.

Augie had big blue eyes, wispy gold curls, and chubby pink cheeks, but his greatest attraction was a shy smile, which he judiciously flashed at passersby. According to his uncles, he was a proven chick magnet.

In the farmers' market scene, old ladies with shopping baskets stop by the stroller to remark, "He's so adorable!" A pretty little girl kneels down to talk to him—"Oh, look at the baaaby!"—in a high-pitched motherly voice. And he doesn't just charm girls; the pasta guy smiles, too, and offers him a piece of hazelnut-and-dried-cherry biscotto.

I, his proud grandmom, hoist him onto one hip and point to

the sunflowers: "Look at the pretty flower, Augie!" Augie's reaction is to pay close attention to the flower, grab it, and take a big bite out of it, so I shriek, "No, Augie, no, yucch!" and gave him tastes of peach and tomato instead. Augie is just as intent on pointing out the interesting sights to me—"That!" "Balloon!" "Doggie!" (Gretzky, the dog, named after the great hockey player in honor of our Canadian heritage, is one of the most important figures in Augie's life.)

We stop at the (vegan, organic) sorbet stand, and Augie, enthusiastically, though not very effectively, digs in to a cup with a wooden spoon, trying to imitate his grandfather. On the corner, a young man is playing the cello for spare change, and Augie sits transfixed, his eyes tracking every motion of the bow. A woman starts to dance, and Augie grooves along, waving his little bare feet in perfect rhythm to her aging baby boomer boogie.

His grandfather keeps him distracted with the music while I finish getting food. Then his father and uncle arrive and they toss him back and forth, to his infinite delight. Finally, we all go home, his beloved mother nurses him, and worn out from all the excitement, he settles in for a nap.

Remarkably, the most recent work in anthropology says that this second picture actually captures our evolutionary past better than the familiar story of the hunt. This is not to say that hunting wasn't important or that it played no role in the development of uniquely human intelligence. But the most significant changes in our evolution may well have had more to do with the relations between bubbes and babies than those between men and mammoths.

The market is where I forage for fruits and roots and nuts, much like my early human ancestors (though admittedly the advent of cars and cash makes this process a lot easier for me). Many of our early cognitive advantages depended on our skill at "extractive foraging." Early humans found ingenious ways to defeat the natural defenses of potential food sources, from the shells of nuts to the bitter toxins of manioc, and to sort out the potentially edible from the incorrigibly poisonous. Recent work argues that those skills may have contributed as much to human success as hunting—although in the Pleistocene they involved extracting delicious organic termites from trees rather than extracting delicious organic sorbet from a recycled paper cup. Sharing that food with the helpless young was equally important. So was teaching them just how to extractively forage for themselves, how to know which fruits and roots to cherish and which to avoid.

That hazelnut-and-cherry biscotto also illustrates just what our cooking, nut-cracking, grain-extracting, grinding, preserving, and processing skills could do to get the calories needed to keep a baby like Augie beautifully plump in the first place. Recent studies show that early *Homo sapiens*, and possibly *H. neanderthalensis*, was already grinding and cooking starches. Bringing home the biscotti, or at least the ground cattail roots, was as important as bringing home the bacon.

But bringing up baby was the most important skill of all. The everyday scene at the farmers' market also illustrates many distinctive facets of the way humans take care of children. We take these things for granted—what else would you do with kids?—but they played a crucial role in our evolutionary history. The cluster of parents, grandparents, older children, and passersby (and even pet dogs) who are all engaged with the baby is a distinctively human phenomenon. So is the fact that so many people share the work of caring for children—a cooperative enterprise that can be just as challenging as bringing down a mammoth.

Grandmothers may seem especially ancient (it certainly feels that way sometimes), but from an evolutionary point of view they are a recent invention. We're the only primate that continues to live, thrive, and take care of children well past the age when we can no longer bear children ourselves.

Human babies are exceptionally slow to develop and are helpless compared with the babies of other primates. Augie still had to be carried at an age when a chimp baby would be adept at getting around on his own. But human babies do seem designed to be especially good at using their inimitable charm to engage other people in their care and to get other people to teach them what they need to know. Even as a baby, Augie can understand something about what goes on in the minds of other people, what they see and what they want. He draws my attention to what he sees, and pays attention to what I see. He can tell that I think eating peaches is a great idea and eating sunflowers is more dubious.

Human children are also remarkably effective social learners. To a much greater extent than any other animal, they immediately observe and imitate the tools that people use—you can see that Augie was convinced that if he could just get his hands on that cello bow he would be dishing up Bach as well as he dishes up sorbet with his wooden spoon.

Using a spoon to extract sorbet has an obvious practical outcome. But humans also have shared rituals. We act in ways that have no obvious practical outcome—indeed that often have no outcome at all—but are still important in identifying who we are and establishing solidarity. Dancing is a good example. When we dance with another person we establish that they are like us and we are like them, and for humans that intangible affinity may be more important than any immediate practical benefit. Although he was only a year old, Augie was already tuned in to gestures and rituals, like dancing, as well as actions and tools.

Human children are distinctively adapted to learn, and especially to learn from other people, and human grown-ups are distinctively adapted to care for and teach them at the same time. Many biologists think those facts played a major role in our evolutionary success.

Beyond Just-So Stories

But before we go any further, we need to ask the most important question of all about the evolution of the human mind: If our origins are lost in the prehistoric past, how could we possibly know just how we evolved?

Biologists have methods that let them make precise and testable claims about evolutionary history. They can compare many closely related species, and see how particular traits help them to adapt and increase survival and reproduction. They can show how black peppered moths won out over white ones in the sooty environment of industrial Northern England. They can count the bones of different kinds of mice in an owl's belly to see which species were most likely to be eaten and which were more likely to survive. They can study whether stickleback fish with redder spots mate more often than those with duller ones. They can insert a new gene into mice and see how the animals develop and how well they survive.

Psychologists who study humans can't do any of that. Humans are the only surviving species of the *Homo* genus, so we can't compare them with other closely related variants. We can't compare the *Homo sapiens* and Neanderthal bones in a saber-toothed tiger belly, or insert a new gene into a baby's DNA and examine the result.

There's another problem. To a much greater extent than any other animal, we humans act to achieve our goals. We do this individually and collectively, in our own lifetimes and across generations. We learn, make things happen, and try to get things to change for the better.

That means that whenever we think of an evolutionary explanation for some human trait—say, that women are attracted to older men because they will provide more resources for their children—there is always an alternative explanation in terms of learning and culture. Women may simply learn that older men are good providers and so know that it would be good to be attracted to them. Or they may take on the wisdom (or otherwise) of earlier generations of women who concluded the same thing. Cultural evolution influences human actions more than those of any other animal, and that adds a whole extra layer of complexity.

All this has led to the entirely justified criticism that the explanations in "evolutionary psychology," especially popularized versions of evolutionary psychology, are "just-so" stories. You can't explain why people act the way they do by just saying that that action might have helped them survive back in the Pleistocene.

But it is possible to make more careful and scientific hypotheses about evolution and psychology. We do have some real evidence about the evolution of human psychology, and that evidence can help explain human child-rearing.

Humans may not have close living relatives, but we can develop general principles by studying a wide variety of species and environments. For example, we can appeal to general correlations across species between longer childhoods and larger brains, or between more helpless children and more monogamous parents.

With a great deal of care, we can use the fossil record of our immediate human ancestors, *Homo habilis*, *H. erectus*, *H. neanderthalensis*, and the rest. Fossil jaws tell us that Neanderthal children got their adult teeth earlier than Augie will. And we can examine the bits and pieces that remain of our ancestors' culture, the fragments of axe and ocher. The claim that early humans made flour comes from the discovery of traces of cereal on Neolithic grinding stones.

We can compare human behavior with that of our closest primate relatives, the great apes, though we should always remember that they also have gone through millions of years of evolution since we shared a common ancestor. Although chimpanzees can learn from their elders, they don't produce the kind of fine-grained imitation that Augie does.

We can study people who live in ways that are similar to those of our human ancestors, like the !Kung in Africa or the Ache of the Amazon. These groups are very different from each other, but they do share a common way of life: they rely on wild food rather than agriculture. Anthropologists used to call them hunter-gatherer cultures, but more recently they have called them foraging cultures, since collecting wild foods such as tubers and nuts is actually even more important for these people than hunting. !Kung and Ache grandmothers play a major role in child care, and this suggests that grandmothering may have played an important role in our evolution.

We can construct mathematical models of evolutionary change under different assumptions. For example, we can see how altruistic acts, such as taking care of someone else's baby, might emerge biologically in a population of closely related organisms who depend on one another for survival. And we can make similar models of cultural evolution: we can explore how a set of gestures, such as waving hello, might be preserved or transformed as it is transmitted from one generation to another.

And finally, we can look at the development of human children. This gives us a way to actually track the contributions of learning and culture and to untangle how they interact with the innate endowments from our evolutionary heritage. The fact that one-year-old Augie is already so adept at understanding and imitating other people suggests that these are foundational human abilities.

Every one of these ways of figuring out our evolutionary heritage comes with many complexities and caveats. It's no wonder, then, that hypotheses about our evolutionary origins so often seem like academic Rorschach tests. It's hard not to smile a little when, at an evolutionary psychology meeting, ferocious professorial silverbacks furiously argue that small-group warfare is the origin of everything most important about us. And it is surely no coincidence that as more women have become involved in the science, we've learned that gathering is as important as hunting, and the complexities of cooperative child care are as interesting as the politics of competition and deception.

The truth is that many factors interact in human evolution, and we can't point to just one key adaptation that made *Homo sapiens*. But there is a growing consensus that changes in what biologists call our life history, the way we develop, were especially important.

The Paradox of Immaturity

Why do we have children at all? OK, we all know the immediate cause, but where do babies come from in an evolutionary sense? Childhood is the stage of life in which animals depend on others, especially their parents, for their most basic needs. Babies seem useless, maybe even worse than useless, because adults have to put so much time and energy into just keeping them alive.

The obvious explanation for this parental altruism is that children carry on their parents' genes. But that still leaves a puzzle. If an organism has the potential to be competent and productive, why not just reach that stage immediately? In fact, many animals—most fish, for example—do have a very brief childhood, emerging almost fully formed with very little need for parental care. Why don't all animals do that? As even the most devoted parent will sometimes ask, why don't we do that?

This is an especially important and puzzling question, because one incontrovertible point about human evolution is that human childhood actually got substantially longer. Mammals already have a longer childhood than invertebrates and fish, and primates already have a longer childhood than most other mammals. But even chimpanzees and bonobos, our nearest relatives, have a much shorter childhood than we do.

Chimpanzees are mobile at three or four months, are sexually mature at about eight or nine years old, and have their first babies at ten or eleven. Human beings, especially foragers, don't typically have babies until they are eighteen or so. Overall, human children are dependent for at least one and a half times as long as chimpanzee children. (That's in forager societies; let's not even talk about house down payments.) Young chimps bring in as much food as they consume from the time they are about seven. Forager children don't do that until they are about fifteen. (Let's not even talk about medical school tuition.)

We also live longer overall than other primates. Even with perfect health care, chimpanzees don't live past fifty or so, while human foragers can live into their eighties. And human women, unlike the females of any other primate species, systematically outlive their fertility—menopause is distinctively human. It's as if the whole human developmental program somehow got stretched out.

There is one interesting exception to this pattern. Human beings typically wean our babies earlier than chimpanzee mothers do. Even in forager societies babies are weaned at two or three instead of at four or five. Partly as a result, we have babies more often than other primates, every three years instead of every six.

Nevertheless, after our babies are weaned they remain dependent on others for food—recall that hazelnut biscotto. As a consequence, we actually end up having more, and more needy, babies than our primate relatives.

You may have heard that we have a longer childhood because, once we walked upright, women had smaller pelvises, and at the same time our babies had bigger heads to hold all those brains. To get the bigger heads through the smaller openings, babies had to be born earlier. That may have played a role but it's hardly the crucial part of the story. The extension of childhood includes not only a prolonged infancy, but also an extended longer period of middle childhood and adolescence.

On top of that, childhood became longer as humans evolved. Early humans such as *Homo erectus* already stood upright, but they didn't have the extended childhood that today's humans do. There is even recent evidence from fossil teeth patterns that Neanderthal children matured slightly more quickly than those of *Homo sapiens*.

Why would this be? Species with a "life history" that includes a long period of immaturity tend to have other characteristics. Longer immaturity is correlated with larger size and a longer life span overall. Immaturity is also correlated, logically enough, with more parental care and investment. When babies are immature, parents have to devote more resources to caring for them.

Animals with a longer childhood also have fewer babies at one time. We take it for granted that we usually have just one baby per pregnancy. But, of course, most mammals have litters. A long childhood also correlates with a higher survival rate. Fish produce thousands of eggs, but only a few survive; primates and humans produce only a few babies but they are more likely to become adults. When more babies are likely to make it through to adulthood, you can afford to invest more in supporting each one.

Finally, and most important for human beings, immaturity also correlates specifically with larger brains, and with increased intelligence, flexibility, and learning abilities.

These correlations even include odd creatures such as the marsupials—animals like kangaroos and wallabies that grow their babies in a pouch instead of a womb. Take the charmingly named quokka, a small catlike animal that lives on a few islands off Western Australia. You can compare the quokka with the more familiar American marsupial the Virginia opossum. Both animals weigh about the same amount. But the quokka babies live in the mother's pouch for much longer, and their parents invest much more time and energy into their care. And the quokkas' brains are much larger than the possums'.

The poster animals for this correlation are birds. Ornithologists—not thinking about humans at all—long ago distinguished between what they called altricial and precocial birds. Precocial species, such as chickens, geese, and turkeys, are quick to mature and rapidly become independent of their parents. They are also not very bright. Or rather they are very good at doing a few important things—like pecking grain—but are not very good at learning new skills.

In contrast, altricial birds such as crows and parrots are exceptionally intelligent. Crows can wield and even create tools, and in some ways are even smarter than chimps. Crows and parrots take much longer to fledge—to become independent of their parents—than do chickens, ducks, or turkeys.

One particular variety of crow lives on an island east of Australia called New Caledonia. The crows are so intelligent that they not only use tools, but design and make them. (You can find amazing videos of them on YouTube, and for once, those cute animal videos really do seem to mesh with what the scientists see in controlled experiments.) They take the branches of a local palm tree, strip the leaves off the stems, leaving barbed edges, and then trim the stems into a digging tool. They poke this tool into a tree full of insects, stir it around so that the insects stick to the barbs, and then pull out a delicious termite shish kebab.

New Caledonian crows are immature and depend on adults for food for as long as two years—a very long time in the life of a bird. If you look at videos of the young, the reason for this becomes clear. The amazing skills of the adults depend on a long, painful, and almost comically clumsy learning period. The young crows drop the stems, put them in with the wrong side up, pick them up by the wrong end. If they had to depend on their tool-using skills, they would quickly starve. The parent crows patiently let the youngsters practice with the branches they've discarded, and they keep feeding their children the insects they've dug out themselves.

Because many different features of an animal's life history tend to hang together, it can be hard to be sure about causal relationships. For example, it could be that developing a longer life span or a larger body size helped humans, and the longer immaturity of the babies just came along for the ride.

And, of course, the causal forces of evolution often run in both directions. Brains, like so many other useful computing gadgets, are expensive. They use up a great deal of energy. But a larger brain helps ensure that more members of the species survive, which means that you can afford to grow a larger brain, and that you can afford to invest more in a longer childhood, which helps you develop a still larger brain, and so on.

On all these measures, human beings are on the far end of the spectrum. We have a much longer immaturity, a much larger relative brain size, and a much greater ability to learn than any other creature. And human adults invest a remarkably large amount of time and energy into taking care of children.

It's possible that our long immaturity simply reflects the time it takes to grow a large brain. But it is very unlikely that's the whole story. From the moment they're born, human children are exceptional learners. We take the extra time to program our brains, not just to grow them.

In fact, our brains are most active, and hungriest, in the first few years of life. Even as adults, our brains use a lot of energy: when you just sit still, about 20 percent of your calories go to your brain. One-year-olds use much more than that, and by four, fully 66 percent of calories go to the brain, more than at any other period of development. In fact, the physical growth of children slows down in early childhood to compensate for the explosive activity of their brains.

Augie is really a creature out of the science-fiction series *Doctor Who*: a giant hungry brain in a skinny little body, very good at hypnotizing other people into serving his every need.

All of these features of humans—large brain, long childhood, greater parental investment—seem to have developed in concert and at about the same time in our evolutionary history.

The videos of young crows may explain why. The problem with relying on learning is that you need to have time to learn, and while you develop the skills you need, you may be vulnerable. We all know that we learn from failure, from mistakes, miscalculations, risks, and experiments. But failure leaves you exposed. You don't want to have to figure out how to deal with an approaching tiger when the tiger is charging. (For that matter, you don't want to have to learn how to deal with a miserable baby when the baby is crying; an inconsolable baby can seem even scarier than a charging tiger.)

It would be better if you figured it out beforehand. And it would certainly be better if other people who were already competent were there to take care of you while you did. It would be better still if the people who took care of you could also help you to solve problems. And it would be best of all if you could combine your own intelligence with the accumulated insights of everyone who had gone before you. That seems to be the human solution.

Childhood is *for* learning—that's what children are designed to do, and that's why adults and children have such a special relationship. But children's learning goes far beyond just listening to what their parents say or doing what their parents want.

Learning, Culture, and Feedback Loops

What do our specially evolved learning abilities look like? In the past, evolutionary psychologists often talked about specific, innate "modules"—particular cognitive skills that evolved to serve particular purposes. The psychologists would often describe the mind as a sort of Swiss Army knife, with specialized devices designed to solve particular problems. More recently, that view has shifted. More and more theorists point to the evolution of wide-ranging and broad-based kinds of learning and cultural transmission. Those abilities can help us to develop many different, new, and often unprecedented cognitive skills.

The evolutionary theorist Eva Jablonka has suggested that the human mind is more like a hand than a Swiss Army knife. A human hand isn't designed to do any one thing in particular. But it is an exceptionally flexible and effective device for doing many things, including things we might never have imagined. When I carry Augie, he can hold on to my shoulder with one hand, as generations of primate babies before him have done, while he plies my iPhone with the other, as no generation has ever done before. The mind of a human child working in concert with the minds of the people caring for him is the most flexible and powerful learning device in the known universe.

Broad changes in learning and cultural transmission can lead to the emergence of brand-new skills in a wide range of areas. Early humans developed better methods for cooking, foraging and hunting, cooperating, competing, and nurturing children. Becoming better at learning and at passing on what they'd already learned made humans better at just about everything else.

But learning and cultural transmission are also especially important because they allow—in fact, encourage—feedback loops. Minute changes in our ability to learn or teach can turn into massive changes in what we do and how we think. For example, consider what it's like to learn how to use a new tool. Whether it's a wooden spoon or a cello bow, a grinding stone or a baby sling, this kind of learning involves watching others use the tool, and understanding the new possibilities that tool offers.

Imagine one group of early human children who are just a bit better at learning to use tools than another group. Those children will have more and better tools when they grow up, both because they can quickly learn to use the tools that have already been invented, and because they can figure out how to tweak and improve them. These tools will help them hunt and forage, cook, and raise children more successfully than the children who weren't quite so good at learning.

But now think about the children of those slightly more clever children. Not only will they have inherited their parent's quickness, but they will have even more tools to learn about and improve than their own parents did. This generation won't just be as good as their grandparents at using tools—they'll be much better. And as those techniques allow this next generation to be more effective foragers, hunters, and nurturers, they can afford to have more children who spend a longer time learning about tools.

As each generation passes on information to the next generation there will be a qualitative advance in the kinds of things they can do. Initially small differences in social learning can rapidly snowball to make enormous differences in minds and lives.

There is an interesting proviso here, though. We would never make any progress if each generation slavishly copied exactly what the previous generation did. At some point, and preferably at many points, someone in the new generation has to innovate, and other people have to work out that the innovator is the one to follow. Just how evolutionary forces, both biological and cultural, can best determine the balance between innovation and imitation is a really tricky question that we're only just starting to understand.

This new view also speaks to some of the central puzzles of human evolution. We share almost all our genes with chimpanzees and bonobos; there has been much less genetic change in our descent from our common ancestor than we might have thought. And *Homo sapiens* diverged in only a few hundred thousand years, an eye-blink in evolutionary time. Somehow small genetic differences led to the dramatic changes in the ways we think, act, and live now.

And there is another puzzle. Anatomically modern humans, humans with the same skeletons we have, evolved some two hundred thousand years ago. But psychologically modern humans, humans who acted like us—who buried their dead, painted their caves, made sewing needles and throwing spears, and used makeup and glue—emerged in force only in the past fifty thousand years or so.

You might think that there was some subtle genetic change, some new gadget on the Swiss Army knife. But new studies show that this probably wasn't the case. Many of the distinctive human cultural innovations, such as using pigments and burying the dead, did show up earlier in the human record, but only locally and sporadically. They just didn't seem to "take" until about fifty thousand years ago.

Both these puzzles make more sense if human evolution, both biological and cultural, involves the kinds of dynamic feedback loops that I just described. Small changes can lead to big differences, and if conditions are right those changes can "take off" to become even more substantial changes.

Variability: The Unknown Unknowns

What triggered the dramatic and rapid changes that led to human evolution? What were we adapting to? The change we adapted to was change itself.

First, the climate changed. It wasn't just that the weather got colder or hotter, wetter or drier. Instead, the climate became more variable and more unpredictable; it was harder to tell just what sort of weather humans would face, both within and across generations. Climate change caused humans long before humans caused climate change.

A second source of variability came from our nomadic lives. From very early on, humans moved. Our great ape relatives still live in more or less the same places where they originally evolved. But humans spread out from forest to veldt to ice field to desert, moving, quite literally, across oceans and over mountains. Wanderlust seems to be built into our genes. This nomadic strategy meant that we were constantly confronting new environments.

Our social environments varied, too. One of our human strengths is that we can construct different kinds of social organization to suit different circumstances. The invention of agriculture radically changed human social structure. People began to stay in one place and accumulate resources, instead of traveling from place to place and living on what they could forage that day. That transformed the very same humans with the very same DNA into what looks almost like a different species. Before long, we went from living in relatively egalitarian small groups to living in cities with strict hierarchies and radical power inequalities. And industrialization transformed the way we lived once more.

How do you deal with variability and change? Mathematical models (and common sense) suggest that you meet variability with variability. By varying what individual children are like, how they think and develop, and what they learn from others, all those children stand a better chance of survival when things change. As a result we can expect a great deal of apparently random variability in the temperament and development of children, and in the behavior of adults.

The fact that so many different people take care of human children also ensures that children are exposed to a wide variety of information and models. The variability of each child's own temperament, ability, and developmental course adds an additional measure of complexity and uncertainty. And historic variability and change adds even more complexity. Each generation of human beings both grows up in and creates a slightly different world than the generation that preceded them. It's a mess. But it's a good mess, a mess that allows human beings to thrive in a staggering array of constantly changing environments.

Back to Parenting

By now, it should be obvious why, from an evolutionary perspective, parenting isn't a good model for parents and children. Caring for children, nurturing them and investing in them, is absolutely crucial for human thriving. Teaching children implicitly and explicitly is certainly important. But, from the point of view of evolution, trying to consciously shape how your children will turn out is both futile and self-defeating.

Even if we humans could precisely shape our children's behavior to suit our own goals and ideals, it would be counterproductive to do it. We can't know beforehand what unprecedented challenges the children of the future will face. Shaping them in our own image, or in the image of our current ideals, might actually keep them from adapting to changes in the future.

You might reply, "Well, who cares about the evolutionary perspective?" Even if relations between children and parents worked a particular way in the Pleistocene, and even if those relations were responsible for our success as a species then, there is no reason to believe that they should continue to be that way. Many adaptations we made to past environments, such as our fondness for sugar and animal fat, don't help us in our current environment.

It is true that we no longer face an environment where termites and mammoths are major protein sources. But our central adaptation—the adaptation to change itself—is more crucial now than ever. The ability to learn flexibly, to adjust to new circumstances, to alter social structures imaginatively—all those abilities are more important than they ever were before. And the relations between parents and children are still the key to solving those challenges, even if parenting isn't.

3. The Evolution of Love

I f caring for children is not a kind of work, as the parenting picture suggests, but a kind of love, just what kind of love is it? Can we say anything more specific beyond the bromide that, of course, we love our kids? I'll argue in this chapter that our human love of children is actually very distinctive, shaped by a striking and particular evolutionary history. And that love of children informs and shapes other kinds of human love.

Nearly twenty years ago, when I was writing my first book, I began one chapter with a description of the overwhelming experience of pregnancy and birth. There are the nine months of physical transformation, the incredibly strange feeling of sharing your body with another being, and then the combination of total absorption and marathon effort that is labor. There is the bizarre but compelling sensation of the baby moving through your vagina, the surge of euphoria producing chemicals in your brain, and then the lovely warmth of the small body pressed against yours. It might have seemed that this distinctive set of sensations, emotions, and chemical changes in biological mothers was *the* quintessence of how it feels to love a baby.

Now, though, I have to report on a different and in some ways even stranger experience. On October 8, 2012, when Augie was born and I held him for the first time, I was exactly the same person I was on October 7. There were no hormonal changes, no baby kicking, no radical transformations of body and mind. And yet without any of that preparation, I've experienced something similar. There is the same specific intense love, the sense that *this* baby, in particular, is someone I would give my life for.

In fact, I can pinpoint when that emotion fully kicked in more exactly. It was during a difficult afternoon with a fussy two-week-old. After a long stretch of holding and soothing and rocking, he fell asleep on my shoulder, still sobbing slightly. The familiar, throat-tightening sense of both the terrible fragility and the overwhelming importance of this tiny, helpless creature coursed through me. I already had lots of abstract reasons to love my first grandchild, of course. But the very fact of successfully soothing the baby seemed to consolidate all those abstract thoughts into a powerful and immediate feeling, a sensation, even without pregnancy and labor and the rest. It's a bit like the difference between falling in love as an adolescent and in middle age. At fifteen lust leads to love, at fifty-five love leads to lust. For grandmothers, our commitments drive our emotions rather than the other way around.

The idea that biological motherhood is connected with the impulse to care for children is certainly right in some ways. But, as we'll see, the systems that underpin motherly love have often been co-opted by evolution to promote other kinds of love. These biological patterns also become reshaped by knowledge and culture. And, especially for human beings, biological motherly love is only one of the many kinds of love involved in caring for children.

In the years since I wrote that paragraph about birth, evolu-tionary anthropologists such as Sarah Blaffer Hrdy and Kristen Hawkes have emphasized the depth and the breadth of our human care for children, care that goes way beyond biological mothers.

We humans have a care "triple threat" that distinguishes us from even our closest primate relatives. First, we pair-bond. Men and women love each other as well as the children we make, and fathers as well as mothers care for children. In fact, those bonds can form between women and women and men and men. Second, we grandmother. Uniquely among primates, human females live past menopause and provide care for their children's children as well as their own. And third, we alloparent. We care for other people's children as well as our own.

These kinds of care are all linked to the extended immaturity and increased demands of human children. We may have devel-oped the "triple threat" in partial response to those demands, or it may be that the development of networks of care actually allowed us the indulgence of extended immaturity. Most likely, the two developments interacted in a coevolutionary way. Each increase in care allowed an increase in large-brained learning, which created more resources, in turn allowing for more care.

So for human beings, the scope of care is drastically expanded. And care for children becomes part of caring for one another. The very demands of cooperatively caring for children lead to bonds of care and love among those who do this work. In fact, "cooperative breeding," as our collective investment is unroman-tically called, may have helped lead to other kinds of care—to human altruism and cooperation, in general.

Evolution may have given us the instinct to value children and the goal of helping them thrive. But it's important to remember that we also have the distinctively human ability to reinvent our social arrangements to help achieve that goal. The initial motivation to care for children may come from evolution, but we can implement it in all sorts of brand-new ways.

Over history we have invented ways to care for children that go far beyond the "triple threat"—from wet nurses to universal preschool. When I lobby the legislature for better child care or fight for better family leave policies at my university, there is (believe me) no rush of warmth and joy. The chemical soup of indignation and frustration I feel while I'm lobbying hardly resembles the profound pleasure of cradling a sleeping baby, but ultimately it's grounded in the same deeply held values.

Pair-Bonding: It's Complicated

The first and most obvious bond that helps ensure care for children is the one between the men and women who create them. Of course, that bond is as mysterious, complex, and troubled as any aspect of human nature. Still, we might want to ask what evolution can tell us about romantic love and its relationship to parental love. Here's a simple question that has probably occurred to most of us at some time or other, with emotions that range from the curious to the tortured. Is monogamy due to our nature or nurture? Is it a natural human impulse rooted in our biology? Or is it a human social construction maintained only by law and convention?

The evolutionary answer, as you can probably guess, is, well, it's complicated. It depends what you mean by monogamy. Many very different animal behaviors have been lumped together under the term, and things get even more confusing when you try to relate those behaviors to the institutionalized ideals of human culture.

Here's the bad news (depending on your point of view, of

course). No species is sexually monogamous, not even swans. New studies of DNA show that almost all animals have sex with multiple partners. But here's the good news (also depending). For at least some animals, there is a distinctive link between mating and caring. Biologists call it pair-bonding. Many birds pair-bond, but there are only a few pair-bonding mammals, including just one other ape, the gibbon. And then there's us.

Pair-bonding means that a pair of animals who have sex with each other also share their lives and care for the young together. In birds this can mean everything from sharing a nest to cocreating a song. Pair-bonding may not last for life, but it lasts for longer than a mating season or two. And for many animals pair-bonding can sometimes involve same-sex as well as opposite-sex partners, like the famous gay penguin couple at the Central Park Zoo.

In human cultures we focus on the social, institutional, and legal differences between monogamy and polygamy. But from a biological point of view, the important thing is not so much whether you have one partner or several. It's the very idea of partnership at all—the idea that you live with and care for at least some of those you have sex with, that you do it for a long time, and that you also care for children together.

Along with our extended childhood, pair-bonding is one of the most distinctive evolutionary features of human beings, one we share with very few other mammals. Other primates have a strikingly varied array of different sexual and social arrangements. Many monkeys, such as macaques, are simply promiscuous: males and females both have sex with whoever's available. Orangutans are largely solitary. The males live with their mothers until they are mature, and eventually peel off to find their own solitary domains. Then they venture out to mate with equally solitary females. Chimpanzees have a very fluid and dynamic set of sexual and social relationships. Females move in and out of different groups and mate with a wide range of males. Bonobos famously use sex very generally as a way of defusing tension, creating alliances, and enjoying themselves, all independently of reproduction. Lesbian sex in particular is ubiquitous. And among gorillas, a single male lives with a group of females and their children, but the males do relatively little to care for the children. Instead they put their energy into controlling the females and warding off other males.

Among the apes, only gibbons exhibit something like pair-bonding. Gibbon males and females aren't entirely sexually monogamous, but they coordinate songs and defend territories together. There is something charming about the role that singing duets seems to play for so many pair-bonded species—music leads the way to romance, for gibbons as well as Fred Astaire and Ginger Rogers.

We humans also organize our sex lives in a wide variety of ways. And as with so many human projects, we do this by creating ideals that we then struggle to achieve. At various times and places those sexual ideals have ranged from lifelong sexual fidelity to polygamy to free love. The one clear universal seems to be that no matter what the ideal is, the reality is messier.

The great ethologist and anthropologist Irenäus Eibl-Eibesfeldt once told me about a "first contact" with a remote tribe. After all his inquiries about the ways of the tribe, he asked if they had any questions for him. "Yes," they said, and asked, "Does it ever happen among your people that someone who is married to one person has sex with someone else?" It kept on happening to them, in spite of the fact that it made everybody miserable, so had Eibl-Eibesfeldt's tribe come across this problem, and did they have any good suggestions?

The problem isn't just with monogamy, either. In the ancient Japanese novel *The Tale of Genji*, the hero muses regretfully over the social obligation to have several paramours when just one wife would be so much simpler. The bonobo option isn't all that much more satisfactory. Every generation or so the idea of guiltless sex reemerges with a hopeful new name—free love or open marriage or now polyamory—and with the same hopeless old problems of insecurity and jealousy.

Nevertheless, among all these many and varied sexual arrangements, the idea of a link between sex and love, between mating and caring, is a deeply ingrained and widespread part of human culture. Both sexual love and some form of marriage appear to be as close to human universals as anything is. We may take this for granted, but the evolutionary picture suggests that it is actually very unusual. In fact, less than than 5 percent of all mammal species act this way.

Why do some animals pair-bond when most do not? And why would humans, in particular, have developed pair-bonding, in such a strong contrast to the sexual arrangements of our closest primate relatives? As always in evolution, pair-bonding can serve many functions and come from many sources. But pair-bonding is highly correlated with "paternal investment"—with fathers who help take care of their babies. And that, logically enough, is related to the total investment—the total amount of work, resources, and care—that you need to raise a baby in the first place.

Although pair-bonding and paternal investment go hand in hand, there is some debate about just how much fathers actually contributed to their babies' welfare in our early human history. And there are the usual evolutionary chicken-and-egg questions about which came first. But there is little dispute that even in forager societies human fathers invest much more in their children than gorilla or chimpanzee fathers do. And there is clear evidence that this investment and care helps children thrive in both modern and ancient societies.

If paternal investment helps babies so much, why is it still relatively uncommon among animals? There is a puzzle about how paternal investment could evolve. As many traditional evolutionary psychologists have pointed out, there is an asymmetry in the reproductive interests of men and women. In principle, men could distribute their genes among many different women, fathering many babies and so increasing the chances that their genes will replicate. Females, on the other hand, face the pregnancy bottleneck. It's more efficient to care for the babies you already have than to try to have as many as possible.

This male screwing-around strategy would be especially effective for males who could use their extra size, strength, and aggressiveness to displace other males and keep females from mating with them. They could even just have more aggressive sperm that are more effective at impregnating females. This is the strategy of most male primates. How could you move from that to pair-bonding?

One idea is that females will pass on their own genes more effectively if they develop a preference for males who are less aggressive and make greater paternal investments. Women need those resources for their own bottleneck babies, and the needier the babies are, the more sense this strategy makes. Once women start to develop these preferences, men who engage in paternal investment will also have a genetic advantage. Eventually, males who display this pattern of behavior, and females who develop this pattern of preferences, could dominate over the earlier pattern.

Parental investment also makes more sense for males when babies are especially needy. The more care and resources a child needs to survive and thrive, the more the male trade-offs shift. Fathering many babies who share your genes may actually not be such a good strategy if the babies all die young. Better to turn out fewer babies and provide them with the resources they need.

But this strategy will be most effective for males when there is at least a strong probability that the babies they invest in are actually theirs. Pair-bonding is a kind of genetic compact between males and females. The particular attachment between men and women helps make it more likely that men are investing in babies who carry their genes. At the same time the addition of paternal care means that the babies carrying women's genes are more likely to thrive and can afford a long period of immaturity.

Pair-bonded species develop distinctive physical characteristics as sexual aggression is replaced by sexual cooperation. In pair-bonded species there is less of a size difference between males and females than in what biologists call polygynous ones, like gorillas. Males no longer have to rely on their superior strength to ward off other males and control females. Pair-bonded males have smaller testicles, since there is less sperm competition. There are even differences in finger length, which are associated with the amount of testosterone babies are exposed to in the womb.

Human men have smaller testicles than other great apes, are only a little larger than human women, and have relatively higher finger-length ratios. By measuring fossilized remains, scientists have tracked how these changes gradually emerged as human beings evolved. This research suggests that the development of pair-bonding was related to other distinctive changes that make human beings special, particularly our long childhood.

One way to understand the complications of human erotic lives is to consider the possibility that we have the genetic potential for pair-bonding along with other primate sexual patterns. A single set of genes can produce a wide variety of physical or psychological traits in different environments. Humans appear to have the potential for many of the sexual patterns we see in our primate relatives, from the promiscuous "free love" of bonobos and chimps, to polygynous gorilla harems, to gibbon pair-bonding.

Human fathers, for example, are what biologists call facultative caregivers. Depending on the circumstances they can be utterly devoted or completely indifferent. For fathers especially, what seems to matter is the actual experience of care. If fathers are put in a situation in which they have to actively care for a baby themselves, they are more likely to develop a bond with the baby, which leads them to engage in more care. But fathers also seem more likely than mothers to just leave the job of caring to someone else.

Different environments may also encourage the expression of one sexual pattern over another. For example, there was a transformative moment in human history with the invention of agriculture. For hundreds of thousands of years humans lived in small, egalitarian forager groups. But around twelve thousand years ago when we invented agriculture, we also started living in large, complex, and hierarchical societies.

The rise of agriculture is puzzling because the same humans with the same genetic inheritance began to act in ways that were radically different from the ways they had acted before, and this applied to sexuality, too. Forager groups generally seem to have some kind of pair-bonding with relative equality between men and women. With the rise of agriculture and larger and more unequal societies, a more polygynous, gorilla-like pattern emerged—with harems of many subordinate wives for one man. In the industrial and postindustrial world this pattern changed once again, back to something more like egalitarian pair-bonding.

I would speculate that some of the historical tensions of feminism may stem from this conflict between different sexual patterns. Since at least the eighteenth century, feminists have gone back and forth between celebrating and distrusting sexuality. For women, sexuality can go along with commitment, love, and nurturance—pair-bonding—or it can go with male aggression, competition, and domination—polygyny—or it can just be a simple pleasure. Our inclinations toward gibbon-ish, gorilla-ish, or bonobo-ish sex lives can color our view of how sexuality should be shaped by culture, tradition, and law.

At least for this feminist, the phenomenology of sex does seem to reflect this set of tensions. Our contemporary sexual ideal is close to the pair-bonding vision—an egalitarian, committed, and loving partnership. But it is hard to deny, as much as one may want to, the links between power and aggression and sexual attraction, even in a relatively harmless form such as bodice-ripper romance novels or *Fifty Shades of Grey*. (There is a joke that women spend their first thirty years looking for Heathcliff and the next thirty trying to get rid of him.) And as a woman who had the great good fortune to grow up in the late sixties, in that glorious five minutes after the pill and before AIDS, I find that the vision of free love and uncomplicated sexual pleasure still has its charms.

No matter how much we are shaped by our biology, we also have the ability to rationally shape our own environments. Although we may not be able to liberate ourselves entirely from our evolutionary heritage, we can at least construct environments that call out the best versions of that heritage. Harems may have deeper evolutionary roots than gay marriages; nevertheless, laws that discourage one and encourage the other can help create sexual and family lives that help humans thrive.

Varieties of Love

The evolutionary background suggests that pair-bonding is distinctively human, and that it emerged in concert with the greater demands of human children. But even if pair-bonding is a good idea in principle, evolution has to provide a mechanism. There has to be something in the brains and minds of men and women that can actually make pair-bonding happen. Many researchers have suggested that some of the same psychological and even physiological processes that underpin the love between parents and children also underpin pair-bonding. Sexual love and the love of children are closely intertwined in yet another way.

The anthropologist and biologist Helen Fisher distinguishes among three kinds of biological processes that underpin sexual love—lust, intense romantic attraction, and long-term attachment. Those distinctions make intuitive sense, too. Sheer sexual lust propels all species. But romantic love and long-term attachment are the emotions of pair-bonding.

Clearly something has gone badly wrong if lust is directed at children. But there do seem to be similarities between the other two kinds of love and the love we feel for children. The almost hallucinogenic, altered consciousness that comes with romantic love is very much like the way we feel when we fall in love with a baby. (When Augie is in the room it's hard for me to see anybody else.) And there is the sheer physicality of our love for babies and small children, much like the physicality of romantic love—that sense of the beauty and deliciousness of the beloved. Like Maurice Sendak's wild things, most lovers of babies have proclaimed, at least internally, "I'll eat you up, I love you so!"

In fact, scientific studies support the idea that we love babies partly because of the way they look—they are just so damn *cute*. The distinctive physical features of babies—their large heads and eyes and small chins and noses—trigger affectionate and protective behavior even when they don't belong to actual babies. That "awww" reaction seems to be a very deeply rooted human emotion. Even a sufficiently babylike, scaly gray alien like E.T. can call it out, let alone a cuddly baby seal.

But, as we all sadly know, intense romantic love is transitory. The real pair-bonding emotion is the less storied but more durable one of partnership—the emotion of marriage rather than courtship. And, from a biological point of view, that kind of conjugal love is most similar to our love for children and plays the largest role in our care for them.

For at least some creatures, voles, for instance, we actually can trace the biological bases of pair-bonding in some detail. Those studies do indeed suggest that the chemical bases of bonding are similar for parents and partners.

Prairie voles are pair-bonded mammals, while the closely related meadow voles are promiscuous. The monogamous male prairie voles produce exceptionally high levels of the neurotransmitters oxytocin and vasopressin—the meadow voles don't.

Scientists can actually change the voles' genes. Some of the prairie voles' genes make oxytocin. Meadow voles have the same genes, but they typically aren't turned on. When scientists activate those genes, the promiscuous meadow voles change their behavior. They pair-bond like the prairie voles.

Oxytocin is sometimes described as the "tend and befriend" hormone, in contrast to "fight or flight" chemicals such as adrenaline. In human beings as well as voles, oxytocin appears to be closely related to feelings of trust, commitment, and attachment.

Women are flooded with oxytocin in labor. And administering oxytocin to people seems to make them more trusting, more willing to share and cooperate.

At least in the voles, genetic differences lead to differences in brain chemicals and so to differences in behavior. But it is important to point out that the reverse is also true. That is, caring behaviors—grooming or mating if you're a vole, kissing and hugging if you're a human—themselves produces oxytocin and related chemicals. And those chemicals, in turn, produce more affectionate behavior.

There is no simple equation between love and oxytocin and vasopressin, even in voles. The chemicals have different effects on males and females, and there are very complex patterns of interaction between the brain, genes, neurotransmitters, and experiences. But it does seem clear that there is an overarching connection between pair-bonding and baby-bonding, between the biology of our attachment to our lovers and our children.

Our love for our partners is like our love for children, both biologically and as a matter of lived experience. It also seems evolutionarily rooted in the demands of caregiving. Of course, none of this implies that either type of love is automatic, that there is some nuclear family "natural law" that links the two. In fact, the birth of children, at least in our society, typically puts great strains on the relations between partners.

Nevertheless, if we want to understand the love between parents and children more deeply, we need to appreciate its intimate biological and evolutionary connection to sexual love. For human beings, the love between fathers and their children (paternal investment) and between fathers and mothers (pair-bonding) are part of the same evolutionary package.

Grandmothers

I'm an evolutionary riddle. Why are menopausal women like me alive at all? Human menopause is another of those phenomena, like pair-bonding, that we all take for granted. But from an evolutionary perspective, it's actually even more unusual and mysterious. As far as we know, killer whales are the only other mammals who go through menopause. Chimpanzees die in their fifties, at about the same time that they stop being fertile. Why do human women live on for twenty or thirty years more?

The answer might just be that a longer life comes with good nutrition and medical care. But actually, fossil records and studies of forager cultures show that some women have always lived long past menopause. Our modern average life expectancy is longer because fewer people die during childhood. Once we get through childhood, the difference is much less dramatic—in forager societies a woman who makes it past thirty is quite likely to live past sixty. And chimpanzees die much earlier than human women even in zoos and sanctuaries, where they are well-fed and get good medical treatment.

Of course, this longer life span also means that there are more human grandfathers, but they are less puzzling. Older men can continue to reproduce their genes directly by fathering more children, as well as indirectly by supporting their grandchildren. Menopause is the really puzzling phenomenon.

The anthropologist Kristen Hawkes has suggested what she calls the grandmother hypothesis. Her idea is that grandmothers contributed substantially to the welfare of early human children. This contribution was great enough that menopause made evolutionary sense. When babies are especially needy, helping the grandchildren who share your genes may be a better strategy than producing more children yourself.

In fact, mathematical models show that in a world of needy babies, evolution will produce postmenopausal grandmothers. If just a few women live past menopause and use that time to care for their grandchildren, their genes will be more likely to spread. Eventually, grandmothering becomes the norm rather than the exception.

Hawkes has done amazingly detailed studies of forager groups, recording exactly how many calories each member of the group produced and consumed. She discovered that grandmothers may actually contribute more high-calorie food to the group than hunters do, especially through the "extractive foraging" of delicious and nutritious foods such as nuts and honey (not to mention termites).

In different groups, the balance between hunting and gathering, and between the contributions of men and women, young and old, may vary, of course. Grandfathers, like fathers, may make a substantial contribution too. But grandmothers seem to make a particularly significant difference to their grandchildren's survival.

In particular, grandmothers may have made it possible for humans to have lots of children and still be able to care for those children for an extended amount of time. We often bring new babies into the world at a time when their older siblings are still very needy toddlers. Hawkes found that infants were more likely to thrive if their mothers had more resources—not surprising. But for toddlers what mattered was how many resources Grandmom had. Grandmom stepped in at the critical juncture when a new baby appeared.

Grandparents can help out with child care more directly, too. Given the demands of human childhood, the more caregivers there are, the better. And, from an evolutionary point of view, grandparents clearly benefit from caring for their own genetic offspring. The geneticist J. B. S. Haldane, discussing the evolution of altruism, said that he would be willing to give his life for two brothers or eight cousins—thus ensuring that his genetic material would continue to be preserved. As I point out to my sons, on Haldane's principle it would really make much more evolutionary sense for me to give my life for four grandbabies than just two or three.

There is other support for the grandmother hypothesis. Human mothers and daughters are likely to live in the same place. That makes humans very different from chimps—chimpanzee females typically leave their own group when they are sexually mature and go join another group. Human females can do this, too, but they are more likely to stay in their original group. Grandmotherhood wouldn't be much use if your grandchildren were off on the other side of the forest, without even Skype to unite you.

Grandmothers have other virtues. Hawkes emphasizes the material contributions that grandmothers make, but they can contribute intellectual resources, too. Just keeping babies out of trouble is difficult enough for modern mothers. You can imagine how much harder it would be in a world of open fires, poisonous berries, and hungry saber-toothed tigers. Even for modern humans, grandmothers are a rich reserve of child-rearing experience and practical advice. Not only can they help care for babies themselves, they can also teach mothers and fathers how to care more effectively.

Finally, human beings are, most of all, a cultural species. Our long human childhood allows us to be especially attuned to culture. We can learn from all the generations that have gone before us. Grandmothers and grandfathers provide a rich trove of cultural information. They connect children to two generations' worth of experience and knowledge. Songs, stories, spells, recipes, even old wives' tales—we learn them all at the feet of our grandmothers. In the days before writing, grandparents were the most potent link to the historical past.

Alloparents

We take it for granted that human fathers contribute to the welfare of their children. We recognize that extended families—grandmothers and grandfathers—play a role too. But human beings seem to be designed to care for children even when they aren't related to them. In fact, this may have shaped human evolution in important ways.

The idea comes from Sarah Blaffer Hrdy, the distinguished biologist and primate scholar. Hrdy argues that human evolution involved a move toward "cooperative breeding." We have "alloparents"—other people in a group who take on the responsibilities of child care. These allomothers and fathers may not even be directly related to the babies they care for.

There is relatively little alloparenting among our closest primate relatives. Chimpanzee mothers, for example, hold ferociously tight to their babies—protesting loudly if anyone else gets near them. But go farther afield in the primate world and you find much more cooperation. Alloparenting is common among lemurs and langurs. These primates may be more distant from us genetically, but we share some of the same child-care issues. Unlike chimps and gorillas, but like us, these primates live on the savanna instead of in the forest. Also like us they are long-distance travelers, with heavy babies in tow.

Among lemurs and langurs, mothers often share caregiving duties. Some adults help take care of babies even when they aren't directly related to them. Juvenile females are especially helpful—the lemur equivalent of teenage babysitters. Young langurs are spontaneously attracted to babies and take care of them without any immediate reward.

Like pair-bonding, allomothering is common in birds but relatively unusual among mammals. It isn't found just in primates, though—elephants allomother and even share breast-feeding duties.

Allomothering plays an important role in contemporary foraging societies. These groups rely not only on grandmothers, but also on older brothers and sisters, cousins and aunts, and even other mothers (and fathers) in the community—the proverbial village that it takes to raise a child.

A recent study shows that in foraging societies women often breast-feed other moms' babies. Even grandmothers can pitch in. Babies in these societies often start out sucking on their grandmothers' breasts—grandmothers are sort of big pacifiers—but that can actually lead the grandmothers to "relactate" and start producing milk again.

It may make evolutionary sense for older siblings to look after little ones—recall Haldane's dictum about giving your life for two brothers. But the contribution of other adults, like other forms of altruism, is paradoxical. Why would I put in all this effort to further another mother's genes?

There are several answers, and all of them involve the basic helplessness and dependency of human babies. Recall that human daughters tend to stay in the same group instead of moving away, so human communities tend to share many genes even when they aren't directly related to one another. Helping all the babies to thrive enables the genes of the whole group to perpetuate. And since our babies are so very helpless, we may not survive at all as a group unless we engage in reciprocal altruism. If I take care of your baby while you go off and forage, I can rely on you to do the same for mine. We all benefit.

Alloparenting may also be an important learning experience, especially for young females. Experience with other babies may be very helpful when you eventually have your own babies to deal with. For many primates, humans included, first-time mothers are more vulnerable and are more likely to reject their babies or fail to nurture them. Alloparenting not only gives mothers a break, it gives young women and young men a chance to practice caring for children.

Hrdy argues that allomothering developed quite early in the course of human evolution. When we moved to the savannas and started giving birth to relatively large babies, we needed help. Cooperative breeding started out as a way to deal with carrying big babies over long distances. But once cooperative breeding was in place it allowed other developments. In particular, it allowed for longer immaturity, larger brain size, and advanced learning. Hawkes has a similar picture of grandmothers, and others have made similar arguments about pair-bonding.

You can see how the development of helpless babies and the drive to care for them go hand in hand. Our extended love for children is visible in faithful and devoted fathers; lively, garrulous, if rather gnarled old grandmoms; and cooing teenage babysitters. All of these forms of care let babies take full advantage of their long, protected immaturity and the learning it allows.

The Commitment Puzzle

Before Augie was born I said—possibly a little too loudly to be convincing—that I wasn't actually sure how I'd feel about a grandchild. I'd loved taking care of children for twenty-five years, but I was very happy with my new life without them. At last I had the liberty to work all night or make love all day, and I had a tidy house to boot. So I was none too convinced that I wanted to go back to caregiving, even part-time.

And, in fact, as I point out to the many family members who treated this stated indifference with extreme skepticism, I was right. I'm not crazy about "a grandchild." I'm crazy about "*this* grandchild"—this particular blue-eyed, curly-haired miracle. And this is no less true even though I know that I would almost certainly have felt the same way about all the other possible miracles my son could have produced.

The miraculous quality of this commitment became even more vivid with the birth of Georgiana, my second grandchild. The intricate process that transforms a few strands of DNA into a living creature is the product of blind biological forces. It can go wrong.

Georgie is a bright, pretty, exceptionally sweet and happy little girl. But a small random mutation in one of her genes means she has a rare condition called congenital melanocytic nevus, or CMN. The most notable symptom is a giant mole, or nevus, that covers much of Georgie's back. But CMN can also invade children's brains and cause developmental problems, and it puts them at greater risk for potentially fatal skin cancers. (The thought of a baby with melanoma should remove any doubt that the universe is indifferent to human concerns.)

We've been lucky. At two years old, Georgie is just fine. But the remarkable thing is that this condition, with all its attendant anxieties and potential demands, has made absolutely no difference to the way I feel about her or the way that Georgie's parents and uncles and aunts and grandfathers feel. What could be more precious than Georgie's wispy blond hair, the cleft in her chin, her charming laugh, her passion for animals, and her tremendous pleasure in life?

And this is true, of course, for parents of children with much more disruptive and difficult conditions as well.

This unconditional specific commitment to a particular person is one of the things that makes love strange, and makes loving children especially strange. It's at the heart of one of the most profound of the paradoxes. After all, you might think, as generations of economists have, that social relationships depend on what the other person actually does—on the mutual exchange of benefits and responsibilities. It's remarkable that a mere accident of circumstance should make this one particular very small person loom so large.

You might imagine that only mothers and fathers would feel this way. And certainly, my feeling for Augie and Georgie, however profound, doesn't have the same depth, weight, passion, cost, and obsession as their mother and father's feeling. Or you might think, since caring for human children does extend beyond biological mothers, that we would all value children, in general, rather than just *this* child, in particular.

But the specificity seems to go along with the very fact of care itself. At the same time that I became a grandmother, four other students and colleagues at Berkeley had babies, too. (Our lab may not produce the most papers, but we do produce a lot of babies.) They are all extremely cute and sweet and bright, and I'm more than happy to hold them and coo at them. But they aren't my Augie and my Georgie.

Of course, we take this specificity for granted; it's integral to the experience of caring for children—the very way it feels. Like the inhabitants of Lake Wobegon, that microcosm of human nature, all our children are above average. (It can, of course, make talking about children a bit annoying. As a scientist who studies children, I've spent years on the receiving end of parents who turn every discussion of Children into a discussion of My Child. So as a new grandmother I bite my tongue, though admittedly not very hard, when I'm tempted to extoll all of Augie's and Georgie's particular virtues.)

But there is also something mysterious about it. Why does our love for children feel this way? Why love just this baby and not all the rest? For biological mothers the answer might seem obvious—this baby carries the mother's genes. But as we've seen, human babies are cared for by many people beyond biological mothers, including many people who are not directly related to them. Even human fathers and paternal grandmothers can't tell for sure that the baby they care for is genetically theirs. For most of the people who care for babies, the act of caring itself creates the bond.

Once again, there is a link to the similar mystery of romantic love. As much as we may know, abstractly, that if it hadn't been him or her, it would have been somebody else, the phenomenology of romantic love is that of Fate, Twin Souls, Destiny. But at least with romantic love we have the illusion of choice. We can tell ourselves that we love him because of his kindness or intelligence or just the way that he laughs.

But the paradox of babies and children is deeper. In spite of the fact that we have no choice about the children we bear, or even the children we end up caring for, we love just those children. In fact, we love those particular children even when they're blind, deaf, or disabled—fussy, sickly, or even dying. We would never trade them for another.

Before Georgie was born, I found myself worrying, just as I

did when I was a mother, about how I would find it possible to love a second child the way I loved the first, even though I had every reason to believe that my commitment to that particular miracle, when it came, would be just as strong as it had been for the first one.

Sometimes, of course, this profound attachment and commitment doesn't happen at all, and it often takes a while to develop. We shouldn't blame parents who take care of their children but, for whatever reason, don't have these emotions of unconditional attachment. But we can say that these cases are the exception, and that they are sad and difficult for both parents and children.

That ineffable, existential sense of commitment, strange as it seems, may reflect a rather abstract mathematical strategy in response to a technical problem in evolutionary theory. The technical problem comes from one of the central mysteries of human evolution. Why do we cooperate? Where does altruism come from? How can it ever pay for one organism, driven by nothing nobler than the replication of its genetic code, to care about another?

The classic statement of the problem is the famous "prisoner's dilemma." Imagine that Bonnie and Clyde, two suspected bank robbers, get arrested. The cops offer each of them a deal. If you turn the other guy in and plead guilty yourself, you get five years. If you remain silent and the other guy cops a plea, you get twenty years. If you both remain silent, however, they won't be able to convict either of you and you'll both get off scot-free. Suppose both Bonnie and Clyde think there's a better than even chance that the other will rat. Rationally, thinking only of themselves (or their genes from an evolutionary point of view), they each should make the decision to talk. But, of course, if both of them talk they'll both end up with a much worse outcome than they would have if they had kept faith.

Our lives are full of dilemmas like these. It may be in the interests of each individual driver to add carbon to the air, but the accumulated effects will end up being disastrous for everybody. Each piece of trash tossed in a national park hardly counts; together they can be devastating. Each sheep grazed on the common field eats only a little grass, but collectively they leave a desert behind.

Altruism and cooperation are ways of escaping those dilemmas. They allow us to thrive collectively. We can already see the beginnings of altruism and cooperation in other primates. But the elaboration and development of our kind of cooperation is one of the greatest, distinctively human strengths. Indeed, you might argue that human history is a grand succession of increasingly ambitious attempts to solve the prisoner's dilemma through wider and wider cooperation.

But what would that solution look like in detail? How could evolution transform a community that wasn't altruistic into one that was? Whole subdisciplines of evolutionary theory have been devoted to working out how altruists can prevail in an evolutionary competition without being driven out by the cheaters and bullies.

One way to solve the prisoner's dilemma over the long run is for each individual prisoner to track whether the other prisoners have ratted them out in the past and to respond in kind in the future. For obvious reasons this strategy is called tit for tat. You can prove that if a group of animals follows this strategy, cooperation can emerge. It's easy to see why—a cheat will rapidly be frozen out by his fellow game players. The success of the tit-for-tat strategy has led to a Machiavellian picture of human evolution replete with mechanisms for the detection of cheaters and reciprocal punishment.

But tit for tat isn't the only or the most effective strategy to establish cooperation. In fact, constantly monitoring the behavior of others comes at a cost. And given the exigencies of human life, the tit-for-tat strategy comes with a constant temptation to defect. Commit just one betrayal and the whole collaborative project collapses. If there are moments of temptation for everyone, the whole structure of collaboration will crumble.

An alternative strategy is, instead, to identify those individual people who you are willing to collaborate with and who are willing to collaborate with you, and then stick to those collaborators through thick and thin. But while it is easy to identify this as a good strategy from the empyrean heights of evolution, how could we implement it in actual human minds? One idea is that our emotions of commitment and attachment—the particularity of our love for one another—give us a way to resolve the prisoner's dilemma more effectively and over a longer time scale than would be possible otherwise.

The deep satisfactions of love, whether of child or partner, are notoriously independent of the immediate benefits that love provides. The great writer Alice Munro once drily noted, "Love does not contribute to happiness in any reliable way." But we can't live without it. Somehow, love ties us to just this one individual person, so that we find deep satisfaction in their company independent of any benefits we may receive from them. We could think of these profoundly positive emotions of attachment and commitment as an evolutionary way to reward love itself.

Ironically, this sort of transcendent commitment can actually deliver better long-term outcomes for both parties than they would be able to achieve through a process of negotiation, back and forth, and tit for tat. If Bonnie loves Clyde so much that his welfare is as important to her as is her own, that will outweigh the temptation to defect, even when defection would be in her short-term interest. That sort of long-term cooperation allows the complex committed projects of human beings.

The Roots of Commitment

These emotions of specific commitment are nowhere more evi-
dent or more important than in the relations between caregivers
and children. A tit-for-tat strategy with our children would be
disastrous—there is such a profound asymmetry between what
we do for children and what they do for us, and such long lags
between our investment in children and our return. Our commitment to children extends beyond our individual lives and
into the future after we are gone.

A specific link between particular caregivers and particular
babies is important even for nonhuman animals. Many birds become attached to the first large moving object they see after birth.
We all know that ducklings follow their mothers, and there are
famous photographs of the great biologist Konrad Lorenz leading a long trail of goslings. For biological mothers and babies these
specific links make perfectly good genetic sense, and they can
easily be rooted in the actual experience and biology of birth itself. You can see how the experiences of pregnancy and birth
that I described at the start of this chapter could be linked to the
specific commitments of motherhood.

But human beings take care of our young for longer than
other animals, and more of us participate in this care. Since we are
committed to more children than just our own biological offspring, the relatively simple commitment strategies of nonhuman
parents and children—the first moving thing you see, the first
baby you touch—aren't sufficient for us. For many caregivers—
fathers, grandparents, and alloparents—the genetic link is much
less clear. Fathers and the rest can't use the simple test of "love
that same baby that was just inside you."

For fathers, grandparents, and alloparents, the emotions of

care are triggered by a social context, by our immersion in a web of love that connects partners, parents, and others, and by what we experience, believe, and learn. Even more than other animals, humans respond to the act of caring itself.

Taking care of a baby helps us love that baby, and that baby in particular. Holding and caring for babies increases our oxytocin levels—that warm feeling inside. And in fathers, caring for babies also decreases testosterone and its associated feelings of aggression and anger.

Even motherly love isn't just a matter of biology. We continue to be committed to our babies long after the physiology of birth has faded. Our commitment to children can be truly long-term. Raising human children is not just a commitment to next week or next year, but to the future.

So many people, not just mothers, feel these emotions of commitment and attachment to children. In turn, we may have extended those emotions still further, to include others beyond children. Again, the development of human altruism may, at least in part, involve co-opting these emotions of commitment from the context of children and applying them more generally.

Children are the purest example of specific long-term commitments and attachments. But human cooperation, in general, is rooted in these kinds of emotions; we also feel this way about our partners and friends and even our schools and cities and countries. I wouldn't say that I love my university, Berkeley, as much as I love Augie and Georgie, but there are similarities. Stanford and Harvard and those other universities are very nice, but they aren't *my* university.

The Costs of Commitment

Of course, the fact that emotions are evolutionarily grounded doesn't necessarily mean that they are right. Murderous sexual jealousy and ruthless persecution of other tribes may have helped us to survive in the past and yet still doom us in the future.

There are costs to commitment. People stay in destructive, painful relationships—with children or parents, lovers, partners, or friends—long after they should have cut their losses and moved on.

A more profound cost is that these emotions are related to our tendency to divide the world into in-groups and out-groups, us and them. The flip side of my commitment to those I love is the lack of a similar commitment to those I don't. Indeed, studies even show that the same oxytocin that helps us trust and love people inside our own group also makes us less tolerant of people outside it.

In the same way, the impulses that lead us to care so deeply about "our" children, even when those children aren't actually related to us, can lead us to be indifferent to the children of others. For contemporary parents, the public school system is a dramatic example of this. I may believe that it would be better for all children if all children went to public schools, but that it would be better for my children to go to private ones.

Although we may recognize abstractly that caring for everybody is important, in practice we favor the welfare of our own. Some philosophical traditions—certain kinds of utilitarianism, for example—argue that this specificity is intrinsically misguided and that we should have a broader concern for the welfare of all creatures.

But surely, overall, these emotions are both sound and right.

The problem of long-term cooperation would still be there for us to solve even if evolution hadn't given us a head start, and committing to particular partners would still be a good solution. The emotions of commitment are among the most significant and profoundly human feelings. The fact that we care about the people we love for their own sake, and not for our own, is one of the foundations of our moral and even spiritual lives.

In fact, many religious and spiritual traditions articulate a human ideal that centers on these emotions. The ideal is to extend the same specific committed love that we feel so naturally for our children to everyone else. The project of the bodhisattva or the saint, loving everybody as you love your children, may be no more attainable than the utilitarian philosopher's project of maximizing everyone's individual welfare. Nevertheless, it's an ideal that I, at least, find warmer and more appealing.

Love and Parenting

So what's the picture of the relations between children and caregivers that comes from all this evolutionary thinking? It's very different from the parenting picture. Human beings evolved a striking set of adaptations that led a much wider range of adults to care for and about children: pair-bonding, grandmothering, and alloparenting. The key to these relationships is that they are the consequences of caring itself.

These adaptations led to new kinds of emotions and connections not only between adults and children, but between husbands and wives, between grandmothers and grandfathers and grandchildren, and among the many alloparents who care for a child. These emotions have a striking specificity and involve a deep, long-term commitment.

These emotions are in tension with the parenting picture. If the purpose of being a parent is to shape a particular kind of child or a particular kind of life for a child, then it is difficult to see why just this child and no other would be the exclusive focus of our commitment and love. Surely, if our aim is to bring a particular kind of adult into the world, we should just look around for the children that are most likely to become such adults, and then teach and train them! What makes us love a child isn't something about the child—it's something about us. We don't care for children because we love them; we love them because we care for them.

4. Learning Through Looking

We take it for granted that children learn from their parents and other caregivers. The parenting picture implies something more—that parents can and should control this learning consciously. It also implies a model of learning that is much like school: a single adult directs special, carefully designed actions toward a particular child, actions that are designed to produce particular kinds of knowledge or skills. The child learns as a result.

But just what do children learn from their parents? And how do they learn it? The most recent research shows just how much even the youngest children learn from other people, and it's much more than we would ever have thought before. But the really striking result is that very little of that learning comes through conscious and deliberate teaching.

The biological picture I described in the previous two chapters suggests that there is a special relationship between children, caregiving, and human learning. Our extended, protected childhood allows for a long period of learning, in general. But the relations between children and caregivers are especially well designed to allow cultural learning, in particular.

Precisely because we have a long childhood, and a wide range of caregivers who are deeply invested in children, children can take advantage of the discoveries of the previous generation—especially those grandparents! But they can also combine that information with their own experiences and make new discoveries. The central paradox of learning is the tension between tradition and innovation.

We might expect, then, to see that children are equipped with particularly powerful devices for learning both from their own experiences and from other people. And that is just what a lot of exciting recent research suggests. From birth, babies and children are especially sensitive to information that they get from other people, particularly their caregivers.

But the story is more complicated than this. Children may be sensitive to the information they get from other people, but they are not passively shaped by others. Instead, they actively interpret and try to understand both what people do and why they do it. And they combine that information in sophisticated ways with the information that comes from their own experiences. In some circumstances they may even do this more effectively than adults do. Children come to understand both the physics of the world and the psychology and sociology of the people around them. And they are surprisingly, even disturbingly, accurate.

In some ways, at least, your children may actually know more about you than you do yourself. Children are tuned in to details of how parents act that you may not even notice. For example, preschoolers notice whether you say "Let's see what this does" or "Let me show you what this does."

Nowadays, when middle-class people become parents they

typically have had lots of experience with schooling but little experience with caregiving. So when parents or policy makers hear from scientists about how much children learn, they often conclude that we should teach them more, the way we teach them in school. But children actually learn more from the unconscious details of what caregivers do than from any of the conscious manipulations of parenting.

There is an interesting irony here. Schooling is a very modern and local invention; schools as we know them have been around for only a couple of hundred years. They were a very specific reaction to the rise of industrialization in nineteenth-century Europe.

But scientific studies suggest that other kinds of social learning are more sophisticated, and more fundamental. They are evolutionarily deeper, developmentally earlier, and more pervasive than schooling. They have been much more important across a wide range of historical periods and cultural traditions.

And yet, given the particular quirks of our culture, middle-class parents, and the parenting culture that surrounds them, know all about school, but don't know much about these other kinds of social learning until they have children themselves.

In this chapter and the next, I'll talk about two kinds of social learning that have been the focus of a lot of important research in the past few years. Children learn by watching and imitating the people around them. Psychologists call this observational learning. And they learn by listening to what other people say about how the world works—what psychologists call learning from testimony.

The Little Actors

See, at his feet, some little plan or chart,
Some fragment from his dream of human life,

Shaped by himself with newly-learnèd art;
A wedding or a festival,
A mourning or a funeral;
And this hath now his heart,
And unto this he frames his song:
Then will he fit his tongue
To dialogues of business, love, or strife;
But it will not be long
Ere this be thrown aside,
And with new joy and pride
The little Actor cons another part;
Filling from time to time his "humorous stage"
With all the Persons, down to palsied Age,
That Life brings with her in her equipage;
As if his whole vocation
Were endless imitation.

Wordsworth described the way even the youngest children mimic even the most trivial details of adult behavior. Augie helps whip egg whites for pancakes, replicating exactly my big "all in the wrist" gestures, with the unfortunate side effect of painting the kitchen in egg-white fresco. Or Georgie enthusiastically, if entirely ineffectively, insists on sweeping up the fallen pancake detritus with a much-too-large broom, just the way that Grandmom does. The family joke is that Grandmom's extravagant praise of her grandchildren always ends with "I say this as a scientist, objectively," and Augie's little voice gravely repeats in just the same tone, "objectively."

This kind of imitation is especially interesting from the perspective of cultural evolution. As we'll see, when children imitate their caregivers they show just how deeply they understand the purpose and meaning of their actions. But imitation isn't just about understanding what people do. It also involves taking on what other people do—putting an action into your repertoire and making it your own.

When we imitate other people, in a very real sense we become those people. Even adults experience "imposter syndrome"—that sense that you aren't really a competent grown-up but are only imitating the competent grown-ups around you. The funny thing about imposter syndrome, of course, is that even if you're just imitating, you actually behave as much like a competent grown-up as everybody else. In fact, the cure for imposter syndrome is to realize that all the other people are just convincing imposters, too.

Wordsworth says earlier in the poem that his infant imitator is a "six years darling." But when do children start to imitate? Back in 1978 the psychologist Andrew Meltzoff discovered that very young infants, even newborns, would imitate the facial expressions of other people—stick your tongue out at a newborn baby and they stick their tongue out at you; open your mouth and the baby will do the same. Dozens of studies since have replicated that startling result.

So some kinds of imitation are in place literally from the time we're born. But new work has also shown that learning from others can be extraordinarily complex and subtle.

The Myth of Mirror Neurons

Imitation can seem deceptively simple. You might think of imitation as an automatic process, something that simply happens without requiring much thought or knowledge. The imitator might somehow mindlessly reproduce what the other person did, without really understanding it, like birds in a flock.

A particularly popular and misleading version of this view

involves "mirror neurons." These are individual neurons that fire both when an animal acts and when the animal sees another animal acting in a similar way. The idea is that this simple neural mechanism is somehow responsible for sophisticated kinds of human behavior—from imitation to empathy to altruism to language. Somehow, the story goes, the fact that the mirror neuron fires connects us to other people.

To be fair, most of the scientists who work on mirror neurons realize just how complicated the neural underpinnings of imitation, empathy, and language really are. But the mirror neuron idea seems to have escaped from the scientific context and into popular culture. It's become a kind of neuroscience myth.

Like traditional myths, neuroscience myths capture our intuitions about the human condition through vivid metaphors. There are lots of these myths out there. The "left brain/right brain" idea is another example of this sort of scientific mythmaking. We have a very old feeling that there is a deep human conflict between intuition and reason, and we express that thought with imagery: Aphrodite versus Athena, the heart versus the mind, or the right brain versus the left. But this metaphor is only distantly related to the real, and really complicated, functional differences between the two hemispheres.

In the same way, we intuitively feel that we are specially connected to other people. Mirror neurons give us a single image for this connection—a neuron reaching its dendrites from one person to another. I'm sure their mellifluous name helps, too; Groucho Marx once said that "cellar door" was the most beautiful-sounding phrase in English, but "mirror neuron" must be a close second.

There are many things wrong with the idea that we are connected to others through our mirror neurons. Understanding just why they're wrong may not only help us think more clearly about imitation, it may also help us think more clearly about the relationship between the mind and the brain. The mirror neuron misconception is a good example of much wider popular misconceptions about neuroscience.

For one thing, there is a strong temptation to use the results of studies of mice or monkeys to draw conclusions about human beings. Many of the most important neuroscientific experiments are done on animals, because scientists can control the experiments more easily. For instance, you can ensure that all your mice subjects have exactly the same genes.

The evidence for individual mirror neurons originally came from studies of macaque monkeys. You can't find these cells without inserting electrodes directly (though painlessly) into individual neurons in the brains of living animals. This is not something you can usually do to people, though there have been some studies that looked at patients undergoing brain surgery.

The trouble is that macaques don't have anything like human language or culture, and they don't understand other monkeys' minds in the same way that we understand human minds. In fact, careful experiments show that they don't even systematically imitate the actions of other monkeys—and they certainly don't imitate in the prolific and detailed way that the youngest human children do. Even chimpanzees, who are much more cognitively sophisticated than macaques, show only limited abilities in these areas. Apes don't actually do much aping. The fact that macaques have mirror neurons actually demonstrates that these cells alone can't explain our social behavior.

Second, the myth suggests that brain structure is innate. It assumes that we're born with these special cells that allow us to connect with other people. Human imitation probably is innate, but finding mirror neurons in adult macaques doesn't prove that idea or even support it. To prove that imitation is innate, we have to turn to developmental studies of newborns—studies that showed innate imitation long before anyone had thought of a mirror neuron.

In fact, we know that almost everything in the brain, particularly the tuning of individual neurons, is shaped by experience. It's really true that every time we learn something, that learning physically changes our brains.

How could mirror neurons arise from a monkey's experience? When a monkey moves his hand, he almost always sees a hand moving in front of him (that is, he sees his own hand). This means the visual experience of seeing a hand move will be very strongly associated with the experience of actually moving a hand. Neurons learn by association—"cells that fire together wire together," as the saying goes. So that association between seeing and doing could itself lead to the emergence of mirror neurons—cells that fire when either one of these experiences takes place. If one of these cells then saw another animal's hand moving, we would also expect it to fire.

A third misconception is that a single type of cell, or even a single area of the brain, can be responsible for a single type of experience. In fact, experiences and behaviors are never going to be the result of just one kind of cell, or even several kinds. More than forty years ago, scientists used electrodes to record the activity of individual neurons in the visual system of cats. They found a group of cells that responded distinctively to certain kinds of shapes, and they called them edge detectors. You might think we see shapes because our edge detectors fire. But decades of research have shown that the real picture is much more complicated. Something as simple as seeing an object results from a very complex pattern of interactions among many different types of neurons.

Moreover, the most recent research shows that both individual neurons and brain areas actually change how they respond from moment to moment depending on the context. This is true even in the relatively simple and stable visual system. You can imagine how many types of interacting and changing neurons it takes to drive a social behavior such as imitation.

The intuition that we are deeply and specially connected to other people is certainly right. And there is absolutely no doubt that this is due to our brains, because everything about our experience is due to our brains. (It certainly isn't due to our big toes or our earlobes.) But the mirror-neuron advocates suggest that a single, very simple connection between inputs and outputs in a single cell could underpin the whole sophisticated range of human social behavior. And that's a substantial leap backward from a scientific perspective. Developmental studies have shown just the opposite—they've shown just how intelligent, complex, and subtle imitation can be, even in babies.

The Birth of Imitation

When babies and young children imitate others they are doing much more than automatically reproducing actions. Imitation helps children learn two important things. It lets them learn how objects work. And it lets them learn how people work.

What gave us our distinctive evolutionary advantage? There are two main hypotheses. One is that we learned to master physical tools, from digging sticks to baby slings. The other, sometimes called the Machiavellian hypothesis, is that we learned to master psychological tools, from a winning glance to a well-placed insult. Human beings had an evolutionary advantage because we learned to manipulate other things, or other people, or both. Other animals have turned out to be considerably better at both kinds of tool use than we previously thought; still, there is little doubt that we humans have developed strikingly along these two dimensions.

Tool use, whether physical or psychological, requires causal knowledge. It requires that you know how doing one thing makes another thing happen. This is one of the most fundamental and difficult kinds of knowledge to master. Imitation turns out to be a potent form of causal learning.

There are two ways to learn about cause and effect: by trial and error, and by observing other people or events. Learning through trial and error is the most fundamental way that all animals learn. Even the simplest of creatures—flies, slugs, and snails—will repeat an action that has led to a reward in the past. Trial and error lets you test how your actions cause events and learn how to make new things happen.

More-sophisticated animals, such as chimpanzees or crows, can sometimes learn by simply observing the actions of others without having to act themselves. But human beings rely on this kind of indirect, observational learning to an even greater extent than do other animals. And it's a particularly powerful way for children to learn from parents.

Learning About the World

Andy Meltzoff and Anna Waismeyer and I tried to see how twenty-four-month-olds might use imitation to figure out a simple machine. We showed them the setup in the picture on page 98. The children saw a toy car on a table with a box at either end and an exciting flashing toy in the middle. When the experimenter moved the car along the table and bumped it into one box, the toy lit up. When she moved it the other way and bumped the other box, nothing happened. She did both things several times.

The twenty-four-month-olds imitated the effective action but not the ineffective one—they immediately bumped the car against the right box themselves. What's more, even before the toy lit up they looked toward it, as if they expected it to light up. This may seem obvious, but it goes far beyond the kind of automatic response you'd expect from mirror neurons. The toddlers didn't imitate just anything. They imitated the action that would lead to the interesting result.

This kind of imitation goes beyond trial-and-error learning as well. The children didn't actually have to try moving the car both ways themselves—they immediately learned from the experimenter's successful and unsuccessful attempts.

But here's the most interesting part. We also showed the toddlers the same scenario, with the car moving and the toy flashing, but this time the car moved one way or another by itself, and then the toy flashed or didn't. In spite of the equally strong association between the moving car and the flashing toy, the twenty-four-month-olds in this experiment surprisingly didn't push the car at all. They just sat there, even when we asked them to make the toy flash. They didn't even look toward the toy when the car moved—it's as if they genuinely didn't get that the car would make the toy flash.

The children started out assuming that cause-and-effect relationships were always the result of what some other person did. Watching other people, and figuring out causal relationships from the outcomes of their actions, was the central way these children learned how to do things themselves. When exactly the same events just happened, without the experimenter's actions, children were much less likely to learn from them.

Children use imitation to figure out how tools work. They imitate effective actions but not ineffective ones. But they don't just imitate everything they see another person do, and they don't even imitate everything they see another person do that leads to an effect. They imitate only intentional actions. They try to reproduce what the actor wanted to do—not just the action itself.

Suppose you show the children someone either making something happen on purpose (pushing a button that makes a box open) or doing exactly the same thing by accident (brushing against the box and making contact with the button). One-year-olds are much more likely to imitate the intentional action than the unintentional one.

Children take the intentions of the person into account in other ways, too. For instance, suppose you show eighteen-month-old babies someone trying but failing to pull a two-part toy dumbbell apart, their fingers slipping off the ends each time. The children don't imitate the other person's slipping fingers. Instead, they do the intelligent thing and firmly pull the toy apart themselves.

But just as children won't learn from the car that moves by itself, they won't try to pull the toy apart if they see a robotic machine that brushes the toy ends with pincers, even if the machine does it in exactly the same way as the person did. It has to be a person.

Consider another experiment. An eighteen-month-old sees someone with her arms wrapped up in a blanket so she can't use her hands, and then sees her bang her head on a box to make it light up. Alternatively, they see someone with their hands free bang their head on top of the box in just the same way.

If the person has their hands wrapped up in the blanket then the children reach out and make the box light up with their own hands, instead of using their heads. As with the other experiments, these babies seem to read through to the goal of the person's actions. They seem to think: "Well, she couldn't use her hands, so she had to use her head instead, but since my hands are free that would be a more efficient way to make the box light up."

On the other hand, if her hands are free, the babies will imitate her exactly. They'll bang their heads on the box. Now they seem to think: "If she could have used her hands she would have, so there must be a reason she used her head."

As children grow older, this kind of reasoning becomes even more sophisticated. They combine what they learned from the other person with information they've learned from their own experience.

In one experiment three-year-olds tried to open a drawer. Either the drawer opened easily or it opened only with substantial difficulty. Then they saw that when another person pushed a button, the drawer immediately sprang open. The children were much more likely to imitate the other person's action when they'd had a hard time opening the drawer themselves than when they hadn't. So they not only took into account how efficient the other person was, they also considered how efficient different courses of action would be for them.

Skilled tool use often involves a combination of actions with many different details, both relevant and irrelevant. This can make learning from others especially difficult. When Augie sees me make a peanut-butter-and-jelly sandwich he has to figure out that you have to twist the jar top counterclockwise instead of clockwise.

But he also has to figure out that other details don't matter, like whether you put the peanut butter or the jelly on first, or that stopping to dip your finger and taste the delicious jelly is definitely optional.

In my lab, we did an experiment where we showed four-year-old children complex sequences of actions. The experimenter did three things to a toy: for example, she might shake it, squeeze it, and then pull a ring on one side of it. Afterward, the toy either played music or it didn't. She did this five times, each time with a different sequence of actions and a different outcome.

The experimenter always did three things, but sometimes it looked as if all three were necessary, and sometimes it looked as if you could have gotten the effect with just one or two actions. For instance, the toy might always work if the experimenter pulled the ring at the end, but not if she didn't, regardless of the other actions. That suggests that all you really need to do is pull the ring.

If children were paying attention to efficiency, as they did in the earlier experiments with the person wrapped in the blanket and with the difficult drawer, they should have preferred to reproduce just the necessary actions—to just pull the ring, for example. And that was just what they did.

There was another interesting twist to this experiment. We controlled exactly how likely it was that a particular combination of actions would work. Amazingly, the children seemed to unconsciously calculate the same probabilities. They produced each action or combination of actions more often if it was more likely to bring about the result.

All this means that even very young children aren't just directly reproducing what they see a caregiver do. Instead, they're reading through to the intention of the person—they're figuring out what the person was trying to accomplish. They imitate the goal of the action instead of the action itself. They assume that the experimenter is trying to be efficient. They adjust what they do to suit their own goals and purposes. And they take statistics and probability into account, too.

All that, in turn, makes imitation a particularly powerful and useful way to learn about how physical tools work, from a whisk to a broom to a weird car-bumping machine to an iPhone. And watching other people allows children to work out which actions are the most important to understand and master.

When Children Are Better Than Adults

In fact, in some circumstances children may actually be better at this kind of observational learning than adults are. We usually think that children are much worse at solving problems than we are. After all, they can't make lunch or tie their shoes, let alone figure out long division or ace the SATs. But, on the other hand, every parent finds herself exclaiming, "Where did *that* come from!" all day long.

A study from our lab shows that four-year-olds may sometimes actually learn better than grown-ups do. To do these experiments, we designed a machine we call the blicket detector, a box that lights up and plays music when you put certain combinations of blocks on it but not others. We show the children what happens when you put different blocks on the machine, and see what conclusions they draw about how it works. Like little scientists, children are remarkably good at analyzing statistical data and drawing causal conclusions, though they do this intuitively and unconsciously. They figure out which blocks are blickets and use them to make the machine go.

Chris Lucas, Tom Griffiths, Sophie Bridgers, and I used our blicket machine. Try it yourself. Imagine that you, a clever grown-up, see me put a round block (labeled D in the picture below) on the machine three times. Nothing happens. Same with a column-shaped block (E). But when I put a square block (F) on next to D, the round one, the machine lights up twice. So F, the square one, makes it go and D, the round one, doesn't, right?

"And" Training

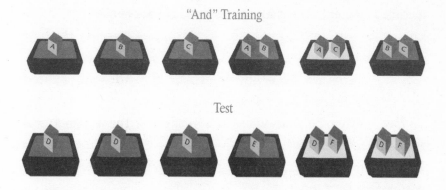

Test

Well, not necessarily. That's true if individual blocks have the power to activate the machine—so that D always activates the machine or never does. That's the obvious idea and the one that grown-ups always think of first. But the machine could also work in a more unusual way. It could be that it takes a combination of two blocks to make the machine go, the way that my annoying microwave will go only if you press both the "cook" button and the "start" button. Maybe the square and round blocks both contribute, but they have to go on together.

Suppose I also show you that a triangular block (A) does nothing and a rectangular one (C) does nothing, but the machine lights up when you put them on together, as in the "'And' Training" panel above. That should tell you that the machine follows the unusual combination rule instead of the obvious individual-block rule. Will that change how you think about the square and round blocks?

We showed patterns like these to kids aged four and five as well as to Berkeley undergraduates. First we showed them the triangle/rectangle "And" kind of pattern, which suggested that the machine might use the unusual combination rule. Then we showed them the ambiguous round/square kind of pattern.

The kids got it. They figured out that the machine might work in this unusual way—they called both blocks blickets and they knew that you should put both blocks on together. But the best and brightest students acted as if the machine would always follow the common and obvious rule, even when we showed them that it might work differently.

Does this go beyond blocks and machines? We've also found this pattern in several other experiments—younger learners are better than older ones at figuring out unlikely options. We think it might reflect a much more general difference between children and adults. Children might be especially good at thinking about unlikely possibilities. After all, grown-ups know a tremendous amount about how the world works. It makes sense that we mostly rely on what we already know.

This difference between children and adults reflects the "explore" versus "exploit" tension I talked about earlier. In "exploit" learning we try to quickly find the solution that is most likely to work right now. In "explore" learning we try out lots of possibilities, including unlikely ones, even if they may not have much immediate payoff. To thrive in a complicated world you need both kinds of learning.

Once again, childhood seems to be designed to produce innovation and creativity. Grown-ups stick with the tried-and-true; four-year-olds have the luxury of looking for the weird and wonderful.

Overimitation

In these studies, children are using observation to figure out how to make things happen efficiently and effectively, and they are strikingly creative. But other studies might seem to contradict this impression. The charm of young children's imitation comes from the fact that they don't just imitate the useful parts of what other people do. They also imitate all the frills and furbelows, the bells and whistles. Augie reproduces the exact exaggerated wristiness of my egg whisking, and the precise professorial tone of "objectively."

More systematic studies of children's imitation show this too. Children not only imitate, they overimitate. In a classic study, Victoria Horner and Andrew Whiten showed children and chimpanzees a puzzle box with some food inside and a stick you could use to open it. Some things you could do with the stick, such as pushing aside a door panel in front of the food, seemed obviously relevant to getting the food. But others, such as sticking the tool into a hole in the top of the box, seemed much less relevant.

The children and the chimps saw the experimenter perform the relevant action—pushing aside the door panel—but they also saw him perform a number of other irrelevant actions, actions like sticking the tool in the hole that actually weren't necessary to get the food. Children imitated everything the experimenter did rather than picking out just the relevant actions. The chimpanzees acted differently and in some ways more intelligently than the children did. They reproduced only the actions that led to the correct outcome.

Does this show that children really do just mindlessly and automatically reproduce the actions of others? Actually, it may show just the opposite. Overimitation may be a sign of how sophisticated children are. Sometimes, imitating all the unnecessary, fine details of someone else's actions makes sense.

For example, overimitating makes sense if the person you are observing is an expert trying to demonstrate precisely how to do something. When Grandmom dramatically whisks the egg whites high for the blueberry pancakes, she is trying to convey something important, and not at all obvious, about how to whisk eggs.

There is an underlying reason for this: whisking the eggs high incorporates more air. But in truth the reason Grandmom does it that way is mostly because Great-Grandmom did it that way too (though it ultimately tracks back to Julia Child rather than past generations of Gopniks, given Great-Great-Grandmom's culinary repertoire of pot roast and bow ties).

By attending to the fine details Augie is actually learning something that goes beyond what he already knows. He knows that if you stir eggs together the whites and yolks will combine. He doesn't yet know that if you whisk eggs, and especially whisk eggs high, they will become puffy.

So if you think an expert might be teaching you, then it makes sense to overimitate in this detailed way. I also do this when I try to imitate my son's iPhone texting technique, including gratuitous details that I find completely mystifying, and that often turn out to be embarrassingly unnecessary. But for Augie, at least for now, Grandmom still counts as an expert.

To test this idea, my lab redid the experiment I described before, the one with the three actions on the toy. This time, though, we varied whether the experimenter was an expert. In our original experiment the adult acted as if she were completely clueless and didn't know how the toy worked. She said, "How does this toy work? I don't know, it's weird, let's try this." In this version, instead, she said, "I know how this toy works, let me show you."

When the experimenter said that she had no idea how the toy worked, the children acted efficiently and intelligently and creatively; they imitated only the necessary actions. But when she indicated that she was an expert, they faithfully imitated every detail of her actions, whether they were necessary or not.

Of course, there's a kind of paradox here. The fact that the children were so sensitive to the teacher's intentions made them stupid, or at least stupider than they would have been otherwise. Or to put it another way, their intelligence about teaching, and their cleverness in figuring out just what the teacher wanted, made them worse at actually learning. (As any college professor knows, this isn't just restricted to three-year-olds.)

In fact, young children seem to assume that other people are out to teach them important things about the world unless they get direct evidence to the contrary. When we simply showed the children the experimenter acting on the toy without specifying whether she was trying to teach them, they also imitated the unnecessary actions. It's as if, by default, the children assumed that the adult had special expertise, which she was trying to pass on. This might explain why in the Horner and Whiten study, the children, unlike the chimps, reproduced irrelevant actions.

Rituals

Overimitation makes sense in another context, too. Human beings engage in rituals, from Sunday morning football to afternoon tea service to midnight mass. Rituals are actions that make little sense by themselves but serve important social functions. By performing very specific actions in a highly prescribed way, you can identify who you are or what group you belong to.

In fact, you can actually become a different kind of person by engaging in the right ritual. I became a wife by doing a bunch of elaborate things with rings and wearing a funny dress; I became a Ph.D. by walking slowly down a long aisle in an impressive Christopher Wren building in Oxford and being tapped on the head by a man in a funny dress. (Funny dresses seem to play an especially important role in rituals.)

The whole point of rituals is that they don't make ordinary causal sense. They are potent precisely because they're divorced from ordinary principles of efficiency—the kind that inform children's imitation in the experiments I've talked about so far. (I once made the grave mistake of attending a Japanese tea ceremony when I was thirsty and wanted tea—the ritualized beauty of the proceedings is much easier to appreciate when you're not counting on a useful causal outcome.)

If I use a stick to pick up my food, that simply means I know how to use a tool effectively. But I might, like most Arabs, use only my right hand and never my left. Or even more oddly, I might, like most Americans, eat with a fork only in my right hand, and also cut my food with the knife only in my right hand, thus having to transfer my fork and knife to different hands every time I cut my food.

The weird eating rituals don't help me get fed, but they do tell you something about who I am, about my ethnic, religious, or national affiliation, and about whether I know and follow the rules of my group or defy them. (In at least two movies I can think of, American spies are discovered because, unlike Europeans, they use the elaborate fork-and-knife ritual I just described. You may not even know consciously whether you do it, but it's something to remember the next time you're on a secret mission.)

Passing on rituals seems to be as important in cultural evolution as passing on technologies. In fact, you might argue that rituals *are* technologies. But they're social technologies instead of physical ones. When you use a tool you influence the physical world: putting your fork in the food gets it to your mouth. But when you use a ritual you influence the social world: swapping the fork from your left hand to your right tells other people that you are American. Rituals are designed especially to communicate to other people that you belong to a particular social group.

Even very young children are sensitive to rituals. In fact, children use the very absence of a causal outcome as a clue that an action is a ritual. In one experiment, children saw a grown-up perform a complicated sequence of actions that had a sensible outcome, such as waving a pen in the air, twirling it around, and then putting it in a box. The children themselves put the pen in the box fairly straightforwardly.

But when the action seemed purposeless—when, for example, the experimenter took the pen off the table and then after twirling it elaborately put it right back in the same place, the children were much more likely to insist on reproducing every fine detail of the action themselves.

When children imitate another person's actions in this way, they not only say "I see how this works" or "I see that you know about this," but also "I see that this is the kind of person you are."

For example, in one experiment with three-year-olds, two adults demonstrated how a puzzle box worked. One performed only relevant actions, and the other added irrelevant ones. The adults then left the room, and only one returned and gave the toy to the child. If the adult who performed the unnecessary actions gave the children the toy, the children imitated the unnecessary actions, too. But they didn't do so when the other, more efficient adult gave them the toy. They seemed to think: "Well, I know you don't have to do it that way, but I guess this is how she does it, so I'll humor her."

There is an apocryphal story about a queen (Victoria or

Elizabeth or Wilhelmina) being visited by an ignorant foreigner (African or American or Persian) who proceeded to drink from the finger bowls at dinner. The queen, seeing his faux pas, carefully drank from her own finger bowl, her action followed by all the rest of the court. The three-year-olds showed the same regal politeness.

Children are more likely to exactly imitate people who are like them. Remember the experiment with the person who banged her head on the box? In a similar study, fourteen-month-old babies first saw either that the person spoke the same language they did or that she spoke a different language. When the person spoke the same language, children used their heads; when she spoke a different language, they used their hands. The children seemed to think that they should imitate the exact actions only of the person who was like them.

Taken together, all these experiments suggest that even very young children are tuned in to the more symbolic, ritual aspects of what other people do, in addition to the more practical, useful aspects.

Children's imitation, far from being simple aping, is actually subtle, complex, and well designed to allow cultural learning. Very young children look to others for information about how the world works. They pay attention to causal relationships and probabilities. They can combine their own experiences with observations of others to make things happen in the most intelligent and efficient way. In fact, they actually learn in a more creative and innovative way than adults do.

They are also sensitive to the intentions, goals, and purposes of the person they're imitating. They pay attention to what the person wants, but they also pay attention to what the person knows, to whether the other person has expertise. All this means that children are in an excellent position to learn about the most significant tools and techniques of the previous generation, and to take advantage of the information that previous generations have discovered.

But at the same time that culture conveys information about the physical world, it also conveys information about the social world. We pass on information about the kind of people we are, the groups we belong to, the traditions we uphold, the rituals we engage in—how we hold our forks. Babies and young children are sensitive to social facts. They imitate differently depending on who they are with, and whether they think that person is like them.

Imitation Across Cultures

The children in the studies I've described so far were middle-class Americans and Europeans. They come from what psychologists have taken to calling WEIRD cultures (White, Educated, Industrial, Rich, and Developed). What about children in other cultures? The cross-cultural psychologist Barbara Rogoff has argued that children in other cultures and in past times were actually even more likely to learn through observation and imitation.

Rogoff studies people who live in small-scale agricultural villages where there is relatively little formal schooling, such as the Quiché Mayan Indians of Guatemala. She found that Quiché parents assume that even very young children can learn complex tasks by watching what other people do. And those parents seem to be right. The Mayan children attend to, imitate, and master difficult and dangerous adult skills such as making tortillas or using a machete, skills that we would never think of teaching young children.

Parents in these communities slow down and exaggerate their own actions, and act in a way that makes it easy for the children to join in. But they don't design special actions or do special things in order to teach the children—they act in order to get things done, and the children learn at the same time.

In fact, in systematic studies, Rogoff and her colleagues found that children from these communities were actually better at learning from observation and imitation than American children were. Five- to eleven-year-old children saw an adult teaching their sibling how to make an origami figure. The adult simply told the child that their turn would come next and that they should wait. The Indian children paid much more attention to what went on when the sibling was learning than the American children did. When their turn came, they had already learned a lot about making the figure and they learned the rest more quickly. The American children seemed to learn only when the teacher was paying attention to them individually, rather than when she was attending to another child.

In another experiment, three children learned from one teacher at the same time. The Indian children were more likely to be able to simultaneously pay attention to what they were doing, what the adult was doing, and what the other children were doing than the American children were.

Doing Things Together

What does all this mean for parents? The old injunction to do as I say and not as I do is unlikely to work with young children. Children not only do as you do, they do as you intend to do, as you really ought to have done, and as it would make most sense for you to do. They do as they ought to do if you knew what you were doing, or as they ought to do even if you had no idea. They do as you do when you're trying to perform rituals and be a good

American or be a good Arab. And they differentiate between all these subtly different ways of doing what you do.

A common practice of parenting instructors is to prescribe a series of actions that parents—or more usually, one parent, or even more usually, Mom—should perform when they are alone with the child. The parents are supposed to do something that is directed only at the child, something the parents would never do otherwise, like holding up cards and naming the objects on them. There are even apps that text such suggestions to parents.

But for children, observing and imitating their parents and others as they behave in skilled and useful ways is an education in itself. This is true whether those actions involve bashing cars or bumping your head, making tortillas or chopping wood, cooking or gardening, taking care of children or talking to grown-ups, drinking your tea or using your fork. And children learn not only from but about other people. Watching the range of ways that people act can teach children about how many kinds of people there are and can help them decide what kind of person to be themselves.

Of course, this is easier said than done, especially when, if you're like me, it sometimes seems that the only skilled action you actually get a chance to do is to peck letters on a keyboard. But even pathetic keyboard-pecking caregivers like me also cook and clean, walk and shop, and read and garden and sing and talk, and it isn't that hard to integrate babies and young children into these everyday activities, even if, as with the Mayan caregivers, it means slowing down a little. That would probably do us all some good anyway.

This picture of living with babies and young children echoes the point I made earlier about caregiving as a form of love, a relationship rather than a form of work. Imagine again the spousing or friending manual. Just as you wouldn't measure your marriage by its effects on your husband or wife, you also wouldn't set aside particular activities that you directed only at them, and then measure whether those activities had the desired effect. Not even the activities you're thinking about—even there, joint coordinated action is, after all, the whole point.

The key to love in practice is doing things together—whether it's working, child-rearing, lovemaking, taking a walk, or baking a cake—participating in the world in a way that accommodates the strengths and weaknesses of both of you.

Here's another way to think about caregiving that isn't like work or school. Some evolutionary theorists think that music and dancing emerged as a way of promoting social relationships. You can't simply make another person move in a particular way and call it dancing. Dancing involves a back-and-forth between the movements of one person and another—a fine coordination between what each person does.

The back-and-forth of observation and imitation is more like that kind of expert coordination than like a form of goal-directed activity. Like dancing, it's a form of love, not work.

5. Learning Through Listening

Nearly all animals, even slugs, can learn about the world through trial and error. Smart animals such as crows and primates can also learn by observing others. As we've seen, human children take learning through observation and imitation to a whole new level. They use imitation pervasively to figure out how the world, other people, and their cultures work. But children have an additional and uniquely human way of learning. Since we use language, we can teach other people by talking to them, and we can learn by listening.

In fact, much of what you know comes from listening, reading, or looking at a screen. You know about things that are too far away or too long ago, too big or too small, to observe directly. Paris is the capital of France; Columbus sailed the ocean blue in fourteen hundred and ninety-two; the world is round—these basic facts depend on the testimony of others.

Many kinds of knowledge can come *only* through language. Knowledge about language itself, such as knowing what words or sentences mean, has to come through this route. This is also the only way to acquire fictional, mythological, or religious knowledge. I know that Harry Potter has a lightning-shaped scar, but I had to find that out indirectly.

Learning from what other people say may seem simple, just as imitation may seem simple. But, when you think about it, it's actually very complicated. Some people are more reliable than others—better to listen to honest experts than to the shady and the shallow. And the same person may sometimes be knowledgeable and sometimes ignorant, or may be confident about some facts and dubious about others. What they say may fit with what we already know or may contradict it. And much of what we learn from language is indirect. We draw conclusions from the details of the person's intonation, gestures, choice of words, or syntax in subtle, complex ways.

Recent studies show that even very young children are remarkably sensitive to these details and learn extensively from what people say. This fits with the general idea that talking and reading to children is a good thing. In fact, it's one of the few clear cases where caregivers can consciously decide to do something that really makes a difference. A famous set of studies by Betty Hart and Todd Risley in the 1970s shows that there are striking differences in the sheer amount of conversation and language used by different families, and that these are reflected in the children's language. Middle-class parents simply tend to talk more to their children than less-advantaged parents, and that in turn makes their children talk more, and develop a larger vocabulary, too.

But conscious strategizing about what you say beyond this is not likely to be feasible, and even less likely to make much difference to children. Children are often better at figuring out what you say and what you mean—which may not be the same thing—than you are yourself.

Learning from Testimony

Over the past ten years, a fascinating research program has focused on how children learn from the testimony of others. The basic method is to show children two different people who give conflicting information. For example, you might show the child an unusual gadget from the hardware store. One person says it's a "fep" and the other says it's a "dax." Then you ask the child what it's called. How does the child decide who to believe? Who do they trust? Who will they learn from?

It turns out that toddlers are more likely to take on information from a familiar caregiver, like a parent or a preschool teacher, than from a less familiar person. Even before they are two years old, children will say the gadget is a "fep" if Mom does too, and ignore the stranger.

More unexpectedly, children's specific relationships with their caregivers influence their decisions about who to trust, as well. "Attachment" is the psychologist's name for "love," and attachment researchers study how babies feel about their caregivers— particularly how they feel about love. Psychologists do this by looking at how one-year-old babies act when they're separated from and then reunited with their caregivers.

"Secure" babies are unhappy when their mothers leave and joyful when they return. "Avoidant" babies, in contrast, look away when their mother leaves, and continue to actively avoid looking at her even when she returns. They act as if they simply don't care. But, in one of the saddest findings in all of psychology, it turns out that when you measure the avoidant babies' heart rates, you discover that they are actually terribly upset—they have just learned to hide how they feel. "Anxious" babies, on the other hand, are inconsolable both after the mother leaves and when she returns, the infantile equivalent of the painfully needy lover.

These studies are usually done with mothers, but you get similar results with fathers or grandmoms or other caregivers. In fact, babies can have different kinds of attachments to different caregivers. They may act securely with Dad, but be anxious with Mom. Attachment patterns are the result of complicated interactions between what the baby is like and how the adult reacts to him or her.

These differences in how babies behave are remarkably robust. They even predict what the baby's adult love life will be like, statistically at least (there are always plenty of exceptions). You can probably already think of grown-ups you know who tend to have avoidant or anxious relationships.

Surprisingly, these early relationships also predict how children will learn several years later. Researchers studied a group of babies and determined their "attachment patterns" when they were just a year old. When the same children were four years old, they did the "gadget" experiment. Mom said that the hardware gadget was a "fep" and a stranger said it was a "dax." They also did another experiment. This time, children saw a hybrid animal, a fish-bird that mostly resembled a bird but looked a little like a fish. Mom called it a fish, while the stranger called it a bird. Both answers were possible, but the stranger's was more likely to be right.

The secure children said "fep" in the gadget experiment—they chose to learn from their mother rather than a stranger when either one could be right. But in the fish-bird experiment they said "bird"—they went with the stranger when she was more likely to be right.

But four-year-olds who had been avoidant babies behaved differently: they were equally likely to say "fep" or "dax." They would learn as readily from a stranger as from their mother. Those who had been anxious babies behaved differently still: they chose the mother's word even when she was likely to be wrong, as in the case of the fish-bird.

So children who felt differently about their caregivers also learned differently from them. The parenting model implies that there is a certain way you can talk to children that will shape what they know. But the children themselves are actively interpreting what they hear, and doing so based on very general kinds of information that would be impossible to consciously control. And a stable, secure base of love seems to be more important than the details of what parents say.

Being Sure of Yourself

As children grow older they become sensitive to more subtle aspects of the way people talk to them. Children can tell how confident someone sounds. If two people make competing claims, even three-year-olds go with the one who sounds more sure of herself. If four-year-olds hear someone knowledgeable make a claim, they are more likely to credit that person than someone who is ignorant. And five-year-olds take more specific kinds of knowledge into account—they are more likely to believe what a doctor has to say about medicine, or what an engineer has to say about machines.

Children are also sensitive to consensus, they pay attention to how many people make one claim versus another. When four-year-olds hear three people say that the gadget is a "fep" and one say that it is a "dax," they go with "fep" rather than "dax" themselves. Most of the time this is a good strategy. After all, what more people believe is often more likely to be true. But not always. Enough social pressure can get both adults and children to disbelieve their own eyes.

The developmental psychologist Paul Harris showed three- and four-year-olds three lines and asked them to pick the longest one. Children were very good at doing this. They picked the longest line even when they saw an adult incorrectly pick the middle-length line. But what happened when three grown-ups all incorrectly picked the middle line? About a quarter of the children changed their minds and went with the adult judgment. Disturbing as this may seem, the children were not alone in these errors; adults make them, too. There are many results in social psychology on "conformity effects." At least some adults will also change their minds about what they see, if enough people contradict them.

Who You Gonna Believe?

In the case of the three lines, the children and adults should have trusted their own experience. But it isn't quite so easy. Often we want to use our experience to learn general principles, principles that will let us predict what will happen in the future. As the philosopher Yogi Berra allegedly said about baseball, it's tough to make predictions, especially about the future. As the philosopher David Hume might have added, that's especially true when you have to make predictions about probabilities rather than certainties, and most things in our lives, even those beyond baseball, are uncertain.

In my lab, we've been investigating how children learn to make these kinds of probabilistic predictions. I talked earlier about our blicket detector experiments. Children were remarkably skilled at figuring out which blocks made the machine go, just by observing what happened when you put them on the machine.

Of course if someone simply told them which blocks made the machine go, that would be a big help. We wanted to see how children would combine that sort of linguistic information with the statistical information they got from just watching what the blocks did.

We were especially interested in how children would deal with conflict and uncertainty. In the Marx Brothers' movie *Duck Soup*, Chico asks the incredulous Margaret Dumont, "Who are you gonna believe, me or your own eyes?" We asked children the same question.

Before the children saw what any of the blocks did, one of two researchers came into the room and told them about the blocks. One confidently said, "I know how this machine works. I've played with this box before. The red one almost always makes it go." Alternatively the other researcher said, more tentatively, "I've never played with these blocks and I don't know how they work, but I'll guess that the red one almost always makes it go." Then we watched which block the children would choose themselves.

More often than not, the children believed both people. They chose the red block more often than the blue one even when the researcher was tentative and said she was only guessing. But, in line with the studies I described earlier, they were more likely to believe the confident and knowledgeable person than the naïve one.

So young children are somewhat more credulous than adults, more likely to give speakers the benefit of the doubt. But even the four-year-olds weren't just credulous; they discriminated based on how confident the person seemed to be.

We wanted to extend our study and see what happened when the testimony actually contradicted the child's own experience. To do this, we showed the children that the blue block made the machine go two out of three times and the red one made it go just two out of six times. Then we gave them the blocks and said, "Can you make it go?" In other experiments we've found that, remarkably, even twenty-four-month-old toddlers will choose the block that is more likely to make the machine go. These toddlers, who can't yet consciously add or subtract, nevertheless use the pattern of probabilities to make a rational prediction about the future.

This time, though, the pattern contradicted what the earlier speaker had said. And this time the children seemed to split the difference between the evidence of their own eyes and the speaker's testimony. When the speaker was ignorant and uncertain, they went with the facts as they had seen them. But when she was confident and knowledgeable, the children seemed conflicted, and they chose the "right" block only about half the time. They seemed to give the confident person some of the benefit of the doubt. After all, unlike in the "three lines" experiment, there was some uncertainty about just how effective the blocks were going to be, anyway.

How would this influence a child's decision to trust the person next time? Other experiments show that even four-year-olds pay attention to how reliable someone is. For example, suppose you show the children two people naming a bunch of familiar objects, such as forks and spoons. One person gets the names right and one gets them wrong. He calls the fork a knife and the spoon a fork. Then you show the children a weird gadget and the reliable person says, "That's a fep!" and the unreliable one says, "That's a dax!" Even three-year-olds say the gadget is a "fep." They trust the person who has been right before, just as they trust the confident or knowledgeable or expert person (or simply the person they love most).

To test this, we brought back the original speakers to make pronouncements on two new blocks. After the children had seen that the speakers were wrong, they were less likely to believe the speakers and less likely to pick the block the speakers had endorsed.

But the experiment had one more twist. It makes sense to trust someone who is more confident. But what if someone speaks with great confidence and self-assurance but turns out to be wrong a lot of the time? (We all know such people, especially among academics.) You should actually have less confidence in that person than you should in the more modest fellow who is realistic about his own limitations. Knowing thyself, and whether thyself really knows or not, is just as important as knowing red and blue blocks.

How would the children react to someone who was confident and turned out to be wrong? At the end of the experiment, both people came back and said with equal confidence, "I know about these blocks; the red block is better." Rationally, you might not trust the guy who was confident before but then turned out to be wrong. But the children were no more skeptical of the overconfident fellow than of the modest one. Children seem to be even more vulnerable to blowhards than the rest of us.

The evolutionary explanation for our extended childhood is that children are designed to learn from the previous generation. The new research shows that children are, in fact, remarkably quick to take in information that they hear from other people. They're sponges, as people often say, but they aren't indiscriminate sponges—from a very early age they make judgments about whether other people are credible and reliable. And as they come to understand other people better and better, they learn to calibrate just how credulous or skeptical they ought to be.

Telling Stories

Children learn about the real world through listening to other people. But they also learn about the unreal world—the world of fiction and religion, myth and magic. Stories are ubiquitous in human culture, and telling stories to children is especially common.

Polly Wiessner is an anthropologist who lived with the Ju/'hoansi people in Botswana and Namibia in the 1970s, when they still lived by foraging, much like our ancestors. She recorded their talk.

In what must be the most poetic article to ever appear in the *Proceedings of the National Academy of Sciences*, she analyzed all the Ju/'hoansi conversations she recorded that involved at least five people. She compared how they talked by day with how they talked by night, over the fire.

The daytime talk was remarkably like the conversation in any modern office. The Ju/'hoansi talked about the work they had to do, gossiped, and made rude jokes. Thirty-four percent of the conversations were what Wiessner labeled CCC—criticism, complaint, and conflict—the familiar grumbling and grousing, occasionally erupting into outright hatred, that is apparently the eternal currency of workplace politics.

But when the sun went down and the men and women, both old and young, gathered around the fire, the talk transformed. Eighty-one percent of the time, people told stories—stories about people they knew, about past generations, about relatives in distant villages, about goings-on in the spirit world and even about those bizarre beings called anthropologists.

Some old men and women in particular, no longer so productive by day, became master storytellers by night. Their enthralled listeners, including the children, laughed, wept, sang, and danced along until they drifted off to sleep. At around 2 a.m., some people would wake up again, stir the embers, and talk some more.

This nighttime talk engaged some of our most distinctively human abilities: imagination, culture, spirituality, and "theory of mind." Over the fire, the Ju/'hoansi talked about people and places that were far away in space and time and possibility; they transmitted cultural wisdom and historical knowledge to the next generation; and they explored the mysterious psychological nuances of other minds.

The Ju/'hoansi children were as entranced by the stories as the adults, which suggests that stories have played an important role in children's lives for a very long time—perhaps as long as we've been human. Children are enthralled by stories but they also create stories themselves, and that ability also seems to be both ancient and fundamental. From the time children are eighteen months old, they spontaneously immerse themselves in the fantastic, imaginary worlds of pretend play. Exactly why this ability emerges at this age isn't entirely clear, but it's probably connected to the beginnings of language.

My idea of heaven is to sit on the sofa by the fire with a three-year-old, a mug of cocoa, and a stack of picture books, though a big wicker chair in the garden with lemonade is pretty divine, too. But if, like me, you've spent hours and hours reading picture books to young children, you may wonder how they ever sort out the difference between reality and fantasy at all.

In the course of a single picture-book session, Augie hears about real and familiar things like cats and dogs, real but unfamiliar things like crocodiles and giraffes, and real but historical things like dinosaurs, knights, and coal- and steam-powered trains. And, of course, he hears most of all about wild things who gnash their terrible teeth, giant cooks who bake morning cake in the night kitchen, and rabbits named Peter who wear blue jackets and drink chamomile tea.

When, on a trip to England, I called him on Skype, that nerd's gift to grandmothers, and asked what was new, he gravely informed me that Thomas the Tank Engine was sleeping in the

Telford Shed, in preference to any mundane news about Mom or Dad. At three, he was obsessed with Thomas—an almost-human steam engine from a faraway country in a distant past. What on earth does he make of all this?

For adults, the worlds of fiction and fantasy have what philosophers call a different ontological status—a different way of being—than the world of facts and reality. Peter Rabbit and Thomas the Tank Engine exist in some sense, but not in the same sense that Augie, Dad, and Grandmom do.

In fact, the metaphysics are even more complicated than that. There are worlds that seem to come between fiction and imagination, and fact and reality. When people say that they believe in magic, they think that there is something special about those beliefs. Believing in the supernatural is different from believing mundane true facts, but it is also not just pretending or participating in fiction.

The same is true of religious belief. Most religious believers think that those beliefs have some special status, that they are unlike mundane facts about the world. In fact, this is what gives those beliefs their meaning and significance. If religious facts were just like all the other facts, they wouldn't matter so much to believers.

But children learn about all of this—real, fictional, and supernatural beliefs—through listening to others. How on earth do they sort it all out?

For a long time psychologists believed that children were essentially confused about all these categories, that they were unable to discriminate fact from fantasy or reality from magic. Many parents still believe this; in fact, getting children to differentiate between fact and fantasy is still sometimes presented as a parenting goal.

But recent work shows that even the youngest children are

actually quite good at sensing the subtle cues that make history, fact, and reality fundamentally different from fantasy and fiction.

Jacqueline Woolley and her colleagues have been at the forefront of investigations of children's understanding of fantasy, reality, and magic. Woolley found that, from the time they can pretend themselves, children never seem to confuse pretense and reality, fact and fiction. Children will tell you that a real cat can be touched and seen by many people while a pretend or imagined cat cannot. In an experiment in our lab we asked children to sort story events on cards into a "real" and "just pretend" pile. Even the three-year-olds put events such as talking to a tree into the pretend pile, and events like bumping into the tree into the "real" pile.

Children may seem to be confused because they have such strong emotional reactions to stories, including the stories they make up themselves—it may be hard to believe that the child who is shaking in bed and pointing to the closet monster doesn't really believe that monster exists. But after all, I myself can be scared silly by Hannibal Lecter or fall hard for Mr. Darcy. Natasha Rostova and Elizabeth Bennet played as important a role in my young womanhood as any of my real friends, but I still don't look up Elizabeth Bennet's e-mail or track whether Hannibal is still in jail. Even the youngest children "quarantine" the pretend and fictional worlds from real-life consequences in the same way.

In fact, children even seem to isolate and quarantine different fictional worlds from one another. They say, for example, that Batman, off in his fictional world, can't interact with SpongeBob SquarePants, off in his. Four-year-olds know that none of these characters are real, but they also say that Batman can see and talk to Robin but not to SpongeBob.

The world of fiction and pretense is what philosophers call a counterfactual world. It's a world of possibilities, where potential consequences follow from potential premises rather than from realities. Children seem to understand and respect this difference from the time they are very young. The very fact that Thomas and Peter and the rest so clearly violate the causal laws of our world is a signal to children that their stories are fictions.

In fact, it's interesting that the earliest recorded stories—myths and legends—are wildly fictional. They are very far removed from anything real. The idea of a novel, a fictional construction that nevertheless follows the causal rules of reality, is a relatively recent invention. Children's stories, like myths and legends, are wildly unlike reality too, and that may be one way that children figure out that they are fictional.

There are other signals that stories are not to be taken seriously. Parents unconsciously use a special set of signals when they are pretending with children. They speak in a sort of "pretendese." We say, "Thomas says choo-choo!" in a goofy voice, and waggle our fingers and bare our teeth absurdly as we explicate the ways of the wild things—and so do kids. We help make the imaginary nature of the imaginary world perfectly clear. And children have no trouble getting it. In the real world, real causes have real effects. In the possible world of fiction, possible causes have potential effects. As we'll see in the next chapter, even preschoolers understand this and draw the right conclusions about what will happen in the real world and in the pretend one.

Children also seem to develop an appreciation of the third realm, the realm of the supernatural, magical, and religious. But they do so only after they develop a more fundamental understanding of fact and history, on the one hand, and fantasy and pretend on the other. They may also come to believe, as many adults do, that this third realm can coexist with the realm of fact in a way that the world of mere fiction and fantasy does not.

The trouble with magic is that it's a case where invisible, untouchable entities that violate causal laws, entities that have a lot

in common with fiction, are supposed to have real, causal consequences. In many cultures, children are taught that spirits you can
never see or touch can actually make you sick. It's interesting that
the mythology around two of the best Western candidates for
magic—the Tooth Fairy and Santa Claus—explicitly involves real
consequences. The child awakes in the morning and the tooth
really is gone, and the presents really have appeared.

(My oldest son, Alexei, at five or so, went along happily with
the Santa Claus story one Christmas, though with an unmistak-
able air of condescendingly humoring the adults. His dad, a sophisticated Montreal journalist, poured out a glass of good cognac
for Santa, a more warming treat than the puritan American milk
and cookies, and, of course, polished it off once the children were
in bed. At the sight of the empty glass in the morning Alexei called
out, now in complete astonishment, "So he *is* real after all!")

It appears that children may not sort out how to treat this
sort of magic until they get older. In particular, children gradually
come to appreciate the range of religious and magical cases where
invisible spirits are supposed to have real effects. Moreover, they
also have to distinguish them from apparently similar but un-
magical scientific cases where, for example, mystifying entities
such as invisible germs or gasses also have undeniably real effects.

It takes children quite a while to know how to handle these
cases. But by the time they are ten years old or so, children treat
factual and scientific claims, fictional and pretend claims, and
magical and religious claims differently, even in highly religious
communities. They even do this when the scientific claims involve
entities such as oxygen or *E. coli.*

It's still not entirely clear just what cues children use to discriminate between science and magic, but there are several possibilities. One is that adults explicitly mark the supernatural by using
phrases such as " I believe." No one ever says, "I believe in oranges,"

or "Some people believe in oranges and some don't," or "Some people believe that oranges are orange while others believe that they are blue." But we use just these locutions to describe magical and religious beliefs. Ironically, saying "I believe in magic" may actually make children less likely to think that your belief is true.

Another related possibility is that children are sensitive to consensus, or the lack thereof, among adults. Adults usually agree on both real facts and fictional stories. We saw before that children and adults will sometimes disbelieve their own eyes in the light of a conflicting consensus. But the opposite may also be true. Supernatural and religious beliefs are often variable, and even those who accept them acknowledge that others may not.

By the time they are eight or ten, children who come from communities where magic and religious beliefs are widespread come to have the same sort of "double consciousness" about those beliefs that many adults have. Cristine Legare and Susan Gelman looked at what children in both rural and urban South Africa thought about AIDS. Many adults in South Africa believe both that AIDS is caused by biological factors like viruses and that it is caused by witchcraft.

Both rural and urban children initially preferred biological explanations to those based on witchcraft. Developing the witch-craft ideas seemed to take a while, and adults were actually more likely to believe in witchcraft than children were. By the time the children did endorse witchcraft, though, they also allowed for the coexistence of both kinds of ways of thinking about illness.

Questions and Explanations

The comedian Louis C.K. describes this conversation with his three-year-old daughter: "Papa, why can't we go outside? Because it's raining. Why? Well, because water's coming out of the sky. Why? Because it was in a cloud. Why? Well, clouds form when there's vapor. Why? I DON'T KNOW! I DON'T KNOW ANY MORE THINGS! THAT'S ALL THE THINGS I KNOW!"

Everyone with a three-year-old has experienced this never-ending "why" conversation, the long chain of questions and answers that just seems to go on and on until the dread moment when you hear your own usually reasonable and patient voice say, "Because I said so!"

Are those endless questions really genuine, or are they just a way of prolonging the conversation and getting attention? In fact, the most recent studies show that children really do want answers to their questions, really do look for good explanations, and really do learn from them.

Children absorb a great deal of information from the people around them, but they don't just do this passively. Instead, they make fine discriminations based on the details of how people act. Children control their own learning even more actively; they solicit information as well as soak it up.

The CHILDES database is one of the treasures of developmental psychology. In the seventies, a number of linguists began recording great swaths of children's conversations. The talk was all combined in a single database, and you can roam about there among the charming sayings and unexpected poetry of children who have long since grown up and now have children of their own. Wandering through the database has a certain elegiac quality, like sorting through a cache of old toys and books in the attic.

Researchers have painstakingly searched through these records and analyzed young children's questions. First of all, it turns out that some 70 percent of the children's questions were sensible requests for information rather than conversational gambits or bids for attention. But the most remarkable thing was the sheer scale of their curiosity. Preschoolers averaged nearly seventy-five questions per hour. If you do the math and extrapolate, that amounts to hundreds of thousands of questions just in the first few years. This is remarkable even to parents who are accustomed to thinking of their kids as insatiably curious. When I did this calculation I was just as surprised as you may be. No wonder I sometimes feel as if my name should be Grandma Google.

The CHILDES archives included some working-class children, who also asked many questions, but most of the kids were the children of the linguists who made the recordings. However, researchers have since gotten more representative groups of parents to keep diaries of their children's early questions, and have found the same results. Young children in a poor California immigrant community asked such thoughtful questions as "Why don't fish drown in the water?" and "Why don't earthworms get squished when we step on the ground?"

In fact, in one study researchers gave parents and children a bowl of water and a bunch of objects and asked them to figure out why some things sink and others float. The middle-class highly schooled parents and children treated this like a school activity— they spent more time talking about how the lesson would proceed than they did about sinking and floating. The less advantaged parents, with much less schooling, actually talked more about the actual problem, and their children asked deeper, more conceptual questions.

Almost from the time children can talk at all, they use their own language to try to get more language and information out of their parents. The earliest questions were likely to be factual requests for details of what and where. "What's that?" is one of the very first things that children say. But when the children were still very young, not more than two, they also began to ask for explanations. "Why" and "how" began to show up as well.

Louis C.K.'s kid isn't the only one to produce a never-ending chain of "whys." Children's questions tended to follow on from one another—one question seemed to prompt the next one. In one study researchers looked at more than six thousand early questions, the answers to those questions, and, even more significantly, the children's responses to those answers. They found that children were very sensitive to whether their questions were answered adequately. They responded to an inadequate or empty answer by asking another question or by repeating the question they'd just asked. When they got a more informative answer, they would express their agreement and use the next question to elaborate, differentiate, or ask for more details.

What makes kids ask questions? In another, experimental study the researchers presented four-year-old children with anomalies—things that didn't make sense—such as a picture of a man in a suit with a clown nose, or a nest with two birds and a turtle. Children were especially likely to ask questions about these anomalous events. "Why does he have a clown nose on?" they would ask.

The experimenters systematically varied how they answered those questions. Sometimes they gave an explanation: "Maybe he works as a clown and forgot to take it off." Sometimes they just repeated the facts: "Yes, that's a clown nose!" When the adults gave a reasonable explanation the children moved on or advanced the conversation, asking, for example, "Why do people work as clowns?" When the adults didn't give a good explanation, the children persisted with the original question: "Why does he have a clown nose?"

Why Ask Why?

"Why" questions are particularly common, but they raise an interesting and deep issue—what's the best answer to "why"? It's obvious what counts as a good answer to a factual question. If the gadget actually is a "dax," then that's what you should say when someone asks you, "What's that?" But finding the right answers to "why" questions is a lot more tricky. Parents discover this when they find themselves trying to explain that rain cloud vapor thing, or why there is night and day, or how bicycles work, not to mention trying to respond to the dreaded "But how did the baby get in Mom's tummy?"

What distinguishes a good explanation from a bad one? And what does an explanation do for us, as adults or as children? Why is just restating facts so much less satisfying than explaining why those facts are true? The fact that children are so hungry for explanations makes you think that those explanations must be doing something special. But what could it be?

Tania Lombrozo has argued that "why" questions, and the explanations they lead to, get children to understand the world in a deeper, broader way than they would otherwise. When you explain something, you usually give a causal story about how the events got to be that way. Causal explanations are especially powerful when they explain particular events in a way that will also let you draw conclusions about new events. Explaining that the man has a clown nose because he put a clown nose on this morning applies only to this particular event. Saying that he works as a clown connects this event to many other events—people often don the particular costumes of their professions. In fact, a number of studies show that when children explain things, even just to themselves, that leads them to deeper levels of understanding.

In one study, for example, researchers showed four-year-old children a complicated Rube Goldberg contraption with Lego pieces and gears that went together. Some parts of the machine actually contributed to making it work (a red gear would make contact with a green gear, for instance). Other parts were just decoration—a blue Lego might sit on top of the gear but not do anything.

They either asked the children to explain how the machine worked or just asked them to describe the machine. Then they took the whole thing apart, asked the kids to reconstruct it, and also asked them factual questions about which piece went where. The kids who were asked to give an explanation remembered more about the functional parts of the machine and were much better at reconstructing it.

It wasn't that explaining made the children pay more attention to the machine—the kids who were asked to only describe the machine were actually better at remembering the purely decorative pieces, the pieces that didn't do any work. Instead, explaining made them focus on the information that was relevant to the causal structure of the machine—the information that told them how it worked—even if that meant neglecting less important information.

We found the same pattern in a study with the blicket detector. Most objects work the way they do because of what's inside them—batteries or gears or hearts or brains. We showed four-year-old children blocks with differently shaped and colored outsides, but also different insides: some blocks had little map pins inside them, and some didn't. Then the blocks went on the detector and set it off. When the children had to explain how the detector worked, they were much more likely to talk about the hidden invisible pin than the visible color and shape of the blocks. When they just described what happened, they focused on the superficial external events.

Children don't just want more information about the world;

they want causal information that will let them understand the world in a deeper and broader way—information that will enable future learning. And, remarkably, children recognize when they don't possess this sort of deep, causal information, and they go out of their way to get it.

All children learn from both listening and looking. But it's also plausible that some children, in some cultures and communities, rely more on observation and imitation while others rely more on language. Hearing explanations is one way to get deep, causal knowledge about the world. But as we saw in the previous chapter, you can also make similar inferences by watching people act in a skillful way. The Mayan children whom Rogoff studied could learn a lot more by just watching their elders than Augie can by watching me.

I live in a world of words, after all, and apart from cooking, gardening, and child care, my entire repertory of useful skills consists of pushing those words around. Instead of crafting baskets and hunting deer, I craft sentences and hunt scientific truths. Talking to me, and especially asking those eternal "why" questions, is a much better way for Augie to get the information he needs. It also trains him in the skills of the wordy world he will inherit. But if he needs to learn how to make baskets or hunt deer, or even just make a soufflé or take care of his baby sister, imitation may indeed be a better strategy.

Still, the fact that children ask questions spontaneously from such a young age and across so many cultures also suggests that this way of getting information about the world, like imitation, is biologically very deeply rooted. It's something children need to be allowed to do, not taught to do.

But it's hardly necessary to answer every single question a child asks, and even less so to feel guilty about the occasional Louis C.K.

response. Young children are persistent—they will continue to seek out the information they want and need.

Studies show that children are unconsciously highly sensitive to the status of their own knowledge, as well as to the status of the knowledge they get from others. Just as they may know what you mean better than you do, they may know what they need or want to know better than you do.

The Essential Question

Children can learn from very subtle features of language. The development of what psychologists call essentialism is a particularly fascinating example. Susan Gelman has been studying children's essentialism for thirty years, with fascinating results. All thinking creatures divide up the world into categories. "Essentialism" is the psychologist's term for our tendency to think that those categories are deep, innate, and permanent, that they come from the world rather than from our minds alone.

Where does this essentialist impulse come from? It turns out that what adults say influences how children think about categories. Even quite subtle details of wording can shape how children see the world. In fact, those subtle details may be especially effective in influencing how children think—even more effective than more obvious kinds of teaching.

Children divide up the world into physical categories like TVs and teapots, biological categories like dandelions and ducks, and social categories like boys and girls. But categories can reflect either superficial convenience or deep conviction. I might arbitrarily divide up my closet into black and white clothes, or tops and bottoms, or I might sort my books into big and small, or paperbacks and hardcovers—it wouldn't matter much either way. But for many categories we feel that there is something deeper going on.

Consider the following rather gruesome philosophical thought experiment. (Perhaps because philosophers don't ever have to actually do them, their experiments do tend to be on the violent side.) Suppose I took a cat, cut off its tail, and replaced it with a bigger and bushier one, then painted a big white stripe on it, stitched on stinky scent glands, etc., etc., and so on, until it looked, sounded, and smelled exactly like a skunk. Would it be a skunk or a cat?

Of course, we think, it would still be a cat. But it might be harder to say why. What exactly would make it different from a skunk if it looks and acts exactly like one? The temptation is to say, well, something inside it—its genes or the chemicals in it, or, well, something. You begin to feel a bit like Louis C.K. trying to answer his daughter's questions.

When do kids start thinking about categories this way? The conventional wisdom, from Piaget to Montessori to Freud, was that young children's thinking is restricted to the here and now, to immediate sensation and direct perception. It turns out instead that even the youngest children look below the surface to try to understand the deeper essences of the things around them. In fact, when children make mistakes, it's often because they are looking too hard for essences when there are actually none to be found.

Even two- and three-year-olds seem to share that vague sense that there is some constant, invisible essence underlying natural categories. Deep, essential categories help us make new predictions. If I know that something is a duck, not just superficially but partaking in the deepest essence of duckiness and duckitude, I can predict that it will walk like a duck, and quack like a duck, and swim like a duck—that it will do the same sort of things that other ducks do, even if I'm not sure exactly what those things are. If I find out something brand-new about just a few ducks—say, that they have oil on their feathers that makes them waterproof—I may conclude that all the other ducks have this feature, too.

Preschoolers also seem to think that if one animal of a species has a particular property—even an invisible one—then other members of the species will have that property, too. If you tell them that a duck has an "omentum," they'll say that other ducks have omentums, too. They think that any one duck has the same insides as other ducks, even if they aren't entirely clear what that stuff is. When pressed they might say, for example, that duck eggs have the same insides as adult ducks, since they belong to the same category.

Children (and adults) don't feel that way about all categories. Suppose, for example, I perform surgery on a teapot instead of a cat. I remove the spout and handle, slice off the top, file down the edges, repaint it, and fill it with sugar. We are much more tempted to say the object is no longer a teapot but has been turned into a sugar bowl. Kids respond the same way. Similarly, even if I find out that many teapots are made of porcelain, I won't conclude that all the other teapots are, too.

Along with these rather vague assumptions about common insides, essentialism also implies innateness and permanence. Even toddlers think that ducks are and always have been ducks, even when they were in the egg. They say that if a baby duck were raised entirely surrounded by dogs it would nevertheless walk and talk and swim like a duck.

This kind of essentialist thinking is actually helpful when it comes to understanding the physical and biological world. After all, science tells us that natural categories often do turn out to have unexpected underlying essences. A dolphin looks like a fish and swims like a fish but isn't actually a fish, and penguins and ostriches are birds, though they don't look and act like your typical robin. (Of course, one downside of this kind of thinking is that it may also explain why evolutionary arguments are so hard for people to accept. If we intuitively think about species in an essentialist way, the basic evolutionary premise that species are mutable, variable, and continuous can be particularly hard to understand.)

Children also develop essentialist views of the social world, though, and that's a lot more problematic. When they are still quite young they treat categories such as gender, race, or even language the same way they treat categories such as duck or dog. They think social categories are innate, deep, and unchanging, too.

They even seem to treat arbitrary social groups the same way. If you tell them only that there's a group called Zazes and another called Flurps, they are likely to conclude that the Zazes and Flurps will be different in other ways, and they also, sadly, conclude that Zazes will be more likely to hurt Flurps than fellow Zazes.

In particular, children develop an essentialist view of gender very early. In our culture, essentialist attitudes toward race come later, although you can also see them emerging in children after five or so. But four-year-olds say that girls will always be girls and never become boys.

That sort of essentialism about physical gender traits might seem sensible enough; after all, it's mostly true. But children are often essentialists about psychological gender traits, too, even when you explicitly try to raise them in a nonsexist way. Indeed, they are often more absolute about gender than adults are. They'll tell their very own pantsuited doctor mother that girls wear dresses and women are nurses.

Where does this essentialism come from? Some of it may be an innate or evolved tendency. The anthropologist Scott Atran has argued that in the evolutionary past, foragers needed to identify species of plants and animals, and this led to the essentialist impulse. You can ask foragers who are experts at collecting and using plants to explain their "folk botany." They actually track biological species surprisingly well. They don't just pay attention to superficial features of plants such as their shape or color; instead, their categories are more like the categories in scientific theories.

Essentialism may also come from children's drive to make causal sense of the world around them. If you want to predict what an animal or plant will do, or what you can do with it, it may be better to think in terms of its underlying essence than its superficial features. Knowing that there is an underlying difference between mushrooms and toadstools, despite their superficial similarities, could literally save your life.

Essentialism is also sparked by language. For example, you can describe a particular girl by saying, "Mary eats carrots," or saying, "Mary is a carrot eater." If you tell three-year-olds that she is a "carrot eater" they are much more likely to think that she is *essentially* a carrot eater, that she has always eaten carrots and always will. If you just say that she eats carrots, they are more likely to conclude that her carrot enthusiasm is a passing fad.

But there is a particular kind of language—what linguists call generic language—that is especially likely to lead to essentialist thinking. Consider these sentences: "Birds fly." "A cat will chase a mouse every time." "The zebra has stripes." Now compare them with these sentences: "Some birds fly." "A cat chased a mouse." "The zebra ran away from the tiger."

Although the words are very similar, the meanings are very different. The first group of sentences, the generics, tells you something about a whole group of animals, not just about particular beasts. The second group tells you only about particular birds, cats, and zebras.

Generics allow for exceptions. "Birds fly" is true even though not every bird flies. But they also tell you about the essence of a category, what makes it special. "Birds live at the South Pole" or "The bird is brown" sounds wrong, even though many birds do live at the South Pole and many birds are brown. But those qualities don't define what a bird is.

Now think about these sentences: "Gentlemen prefer blondes." "Boys don't cry." "Girls just want to have fun." "An Englishman's home is his castle." "This year the well-dressed man is wearing spats." These are generics, too, but they define particular social groups—they tell you about the essence of particular people.

In Molière's play *The Would-be Gentleman*, the bourgeois Mr. Jourdain is astonished when his literary tutors tell him that he has been speaking prose all his life. "I never would have suspected it," he says. You may be equally surprised to discover that you have also been using generics.

Children use generics appropriately from the time they are very young. In the CHILDES archives, two-and-a-half-year-old Adam says persuasively, "Adams don't have to take naps." When I took him to see *Star Wars* for his fourth birthday, my own Alexei made an equally impressive deduction: "Four-year-olds don't be frightened—I's four years old—I's not frightened."

Adults also use many generics when they talk to children. And hearing generics from grown-ups leads young children to make new predictions and draw new conclusions. For instance, when children hear "Bants have stripes" and then see a new animal with stripes, they are likely to conclude that the animal is a bant. They don't do this when they hear "This bant has stripes."

Even twenty-four-month-old toddlers seem to move from generic sentences to essentialist categories. In one study, the experimenter showed children two little toy animals, one orange and one blue, and a little toy cup of milk. Then she made one of those little animals drink, and either said, "Blicks drink milk!" or "This blick drinks milk!" Afterward, she gave the children both toys and said, "Can you show me?"

When these little toddlers heard the generic sentence "Blicks drink milk," they concluded that all the animals drank milk and they made both blicks drink. When they heard the nongeneric "This blick drinks milk," they only made the orange blick drink—they concluded that just this particular animal drank milk.

Would generics have the same effect for social categories, for gentlemen and blondes as well as bants and blicks? Gelman and her colleagues looked at conversations about gender between children and their mothers. They gave the children a picture book that alternated between pictures that were stereotyped, such as a girl sewing, and those that went against the stereotype, like a girl driving a truck.

They discovered that even mothers who were completely committed to sexual equality used generics most of the time they talked about gender (for example, "Boys drive trucks," or for that matter, "Girls can drive trucks"). The youngest children they tested didn't use gender generics much themselves, although their mothers did. By the time they were six or so, though, the children were actually using the generics to talk about gender more than their mothers were. And there was a strong correlation between how often the moms used generics and how often the children did.

In one of those bitter, teeth-gritting ironies, it turned out that moms used generics even when they were trying to combat sexism.

Saying "Girls can drive trucks" still implies that girls all belong in the same category with the same deep, underlying essence.

Could using generics actually cause children to be more essentialist about social categories? In another study, the researchers showed four-year-olds a diverse group of people, including different sexes, races, and so on. Then they talked about some fairly bizarre feature of these people. They described them either with a generic phrase, "A Zarpie is afraid of ladybugs," or a non-generic one, "This Zarpie is afraid of ladybugs."

Then they asked whether other Zarpies were afraid of ladybugs, whether Zarpies always had been and always would be afraid of ladybugs, and so on. The children were much more likely to give essentialist answers when they heard generic descriptions.

Conversely, the experimenters told adults either that being scared of ladybugs was an essential part of Zarpieness or that it was just an occasional quirk. Then they got the adults to tell children about Zarpies. The adults used many more generics when they thought Zarpies were an essential category.

Subtle aspects of how the adults talked influenced how the children thought about the Zarpies. But they also influenced how children talked about real ducks and squirrels—and real boys and girls. It doesn't take much extrapolation to see that children might interpret generics the same way when they are applied to other social groups: Mexican and American, black and white, Hutu and Tutsi, Serb and Croat.

Letting the Dude Figure It Out

What does this all mean for parents? In another of his routines, Louis C.K. describes his parenting technique by modifying an old proverb. Give a man a fish and he'll have fish for a day. Teach a man to fish and he'll have fish for a lifetime. Or you can leave the dude alone and he'll figure it out.

Parents matter. Children learn from their parents and other caregivers, whether they are learning by observation or learning through testimony. They look carefully at what parents do and listen just as carefully to what they say. Talking and listening to children, asking and answering "why," helps them thrive.

The studies I've described in this chapter and the previous one beautifully illustrate the paradox of tradition and innovation. Learning by looking and learning by listening are both extremely important vehicles for the transmission of accumulated cultural knowledge. But children don't simply mindlessly reproduce what they see other people do or what they hear them say. Instead they take in that information in an intelligent and thoughtful way. They actively combine what they learn through observation with many other kinds of information. And they use it to create new tools, new techniques, new stories, new explanations.

The role parents play is quite different from the role that the parenting model suggests. Parents and other caregivers don't have to teach young children so much as they just have to let them learn. Young children learn from others with alacrity and ease, and they are remarkably skilled at getting the information they need and interpreting that information. Parents don't have to consciously manipulate what they say to give children the information they need.

In fact, given how sensitive and subtle children's learning is, conscious manipulation probably wouldn't work. Even if I wanted to, it's unlikely that I could keep track of whether I am using generics or speaking in "pretendese." It's even less likely that I could consciously control those things. And there's no reason at all to think that I should.

The alternative gardener's picture, that being a parent is fundamentally a relationship, a form of love, gives you a different take on how children learn from adults. And it actually fits better with the research.

Being a caregiver who is a stable and reliable resource for learning is more valuable than being a caregiver who explicitly teaches. In the attachment studies, we saw that children recruit information and learn differently depending on who the person is and how they feel about them. Fundamental relationships of trust are more important than teaching strategies.

If imitation is like a pas de deux, conversation is like a duet. The CHILDES studies show the fine-grained play, the back and forth, the call and response, of even simple conversations over picture books. It is true, of course, that sometimes we use language to purposefully convey particular information, both to children and to adults. But more often, both for adults and children, conversation is a way of establishing a relationship, a way of being with another person. There is no surer sign of love than the back-and-forth of teasing and banter, diminutives and endearments, soul-searching and chitchat. There is no signal of a failed intimacy more devastating than refusing to talk to the other person. Children learn by being part of that kind of intimate, open-ended, dynamic conversation.

Just as children can learn from observing and imitating many different kinds of people with different skills, so children learn about the world around them by listening to many different kinds of people talking about many different kinds of things in different kinds of ways. Paradoxically, even hearing inaccurate or misleading information can help children learn. They learn not only what someone has said but how reliable they are, and how much to trust them in the future.

Giving children the chance to intimately observe what many different people do is the best way to help them learn by looking. Giving children the chance to talk with many different people is the best way to help them learn by listening.

6. The Work of Play

n Dickens's *Great Expectations* there is a moment, both comic and chilling, when the mad Miss Havisham, sitting in her crumbling mansion, tells Pip, the impoverished child hero, to play.

> "I am tired," said Miss Havisham. "I want diversion, and I have done with men and women. Play."
>
> I think it will be conceded by my most disputatious reader, that she could hardly have directed an unfortunate boy to do anything in the wide world more difficult to be done under the circumstances.
>
> "There, there!" with an impatient movement of the fingers of her right hand; "play, play, play!"

Miss Havisham may be an extreme case, but Dickens's chilling comedy reflects some deep riddles about play.

Children play. Childhood and play just go together. And most parents and teachers have a vague sense that play is a Good Thing.

We might even think that encouraging play is a good parenting technique.

But if you think about it, there is something paradoxical about play as a goal of parenting. After all, by definition play is what you do when you're not trying to do anything. It's an activity whose goal is not to have a goal. If it's shaped by what a grown-up wants, should it even count as play at all? Even if you're not Miss Havisham, can you tell children to play?

There is also something scientifically paradoxical about play. The idea that play is good for learning has an intuitive appeal. But if play really makes you smarter, more focused, or better at understanding other people, why not just aim to be smarter or more focused or more empathic directly? Why go through the elaborate detour of play?

The paradox is echoed in the actual scientific evidence up to now. Until quite recently, there was surprisingly little research that confirmed our intuition that play helps children learn.

Part of the problem is that there are so many different ways of both playing and learning. Are we talking about exploratory play, rough-and-tumble play, pretend play, or game play? Do we mean learning language, developing motor skills, understanding other minds, improving executive function, or perfecting everyday theories? Each type of play might be related to a different kind of learning and there is no reason to believe that all sorts of play will be related to all sorts of learning.

In this chapter I'll outline some of the different kinds of play and what we know about how they help children learn. But first let's consider an evolutionary question: Why do animals play?

Young human beings play, but so do young wolves and dolphins, rats and crows. Even octopuses seem to play with plastic bottles. Wolf pups play at hunting, fledgling crows play with sticks, young rats play-fight with their brothers, kittens play with balls of string.

Play is especially common in social animals with relatively long childhoods, lots of parental investment, and large brains—animals like us. Almost any animal with a long childhood spends a lot of that childhood playing.

But what do we mean by play? What do playacting and play-fighting, playing hockey and playing house, all have in common? What's the underlying link that connects the rat and his brothers, the crow and her digging stick, and the kitten and his ball of string?

Biologists who try to define play point to five characteristics that all kinds of play share. First of all, play is not work. It may look like fighting or hunting, digging or sweeping, but it doesn't actually accomplish anything. The kitten doesn't really eat the string, the fledgling doesn't dig out any insects, and the wrestling rat doesn't actually hurt his brother, just as playing house doesn't put more food in the fridge or leave the living room any neater—quite the opposite, in fact.

But play isn't just incompetent work; it has special character-istics that let you distinguish it from the real thing. When rats play-fight they nuzzle each other's necks; when it's for real they bite each other's flanks. When children pretend to pour tea they exaggerate, making big movements that would normally lead more to sloshing than pouring. And, of course, very young ani-mals who pretend to hunt or play at sex aren't going to bring home the bacon—or the babies.

Play is fun. Nine-month-olds giggle when they play peek-a-boo. Even among animals, play leads to joy, delight, and the equivalent of smiles and laughter. For example, rats laugh when they play-fight, making a distinctive ultrasonic chirp that is too high for humans to hear.

Play, *pace* Miss Havisham, is voluntary. It's something that animals do for its own sake, not because they are instructed to do it or rewarded for doing it. In fact, young rats will actually work in order to get to play—they will learn to press a bar that lets them play. If they're deprived of play, the desire builds up like a drive, so that the instant they get the chance they are on it. Children are the same way—think of the cheerful, exultant cry of schoolchildren who are finally released to recess.

But play is not like other basic drives, the drives for food or water or warmth. Animals play only when all those other basic needs are satisfied. When an animal is starved or stressed, play diminishes. Play, like childhood in general, depends on safety and security.

Play has a special structure, a pattern of repetition and variation. When the rats play-fight they try different patterns of offense and defense against each other. When a six-month-old plays with a rattle she tries shaking it louder or softer, banging it against the table with more or less vigor. The octopus moves the bottle in and out of the water. The dolphin puts a hoop first over her nose and then her fin. This kind of theme and variation is the opposite of the sort of repetition—the pacing or rocking—that we see in captive and stressed animals, and even sometimes in humans.

If play is so biologically ubiquitous, what does it do for animal lives and animal brains?

Rough-and-Tumble Rats

Rough-and-tumble play is the rolling and wrestling, nipping and pinning, and general roughhousing that we see especially clearly in some human boys (though girls do it, too). As the mother of three large sons, I found it to be the source of some of my most frustrating parenting dilemmas. What should a pacifist with strong, nonviolent values do when she sees her beloved, sweet boys apparently beating the hell out of one another, not to mention their friends? And how should she react when those adorable children patiently explain that she just doesn't get it? With only a little eye-rolling, they would assure me that in the community of little boys, rough-and-tumble is the most definitive sign of friendship.

The science suggests that my boys were right. In human children, early rough-and-tumble play is associated with better social competence later on. Of course, this correlation could mean many things. Maybe it's just that social competence gives children more opportunities to play with other kids.

But human children aren't the only ones who roughhouse. Young rats do, too. Scientists know much more about how rat brains develop, and with rats, they can systematically explore how play influences that development.

Scientists start by carefully watching just what rat play-fighting looks like, and recording how it differs from real fighting. Some differences, like those between nuzzling and biting, are obvious. But there are also more subtle differences. In play-fighting, the young rats try a greater variety of attacks and defenses, and they give each other the chance to swap and take turns. They almost get out of control in much the same way that two separate little boys can turn into a blurred, roiling tangle of arms and legs.

Scientists can also compare rats that grow up playing with fellow juveniles to rats that don't. We know that rats who are isolated when they are young have trouble interacting when they grow up. But is that just because they don't get any social contact? Or is it specifically because they don't have a chance to play?

Grown-up rats, like some grown-up humans, forget how to play. Or maybe they're just too busy and worn out from the grown-up rat race—all that running through mazes for unfulfilling rewards. So young rats who live only with adults don't get much chance to roughhouse either, although they do get lots of other social contact. Scientists can compare these rats to rats who were raised in an identical way but also played with other pups.

As adults, the play-deprived rats have difficulty dealing with other rats, and their difficulties are instructive. They can do the same kinds of things as the rats who played. They know how to attack and defend, how to make overtures to others, and how to retreat. But they don't know when to do what. Whether they are fighting or courting, they can't react to the other rats in the swift, flexible, and fluid fashion of the roughhousing rats. They may sting like a bee, but they sure don't dance like a butterfly. That ability to dance, to take in a complex social context at a glance and know how to respond to it intuitively, is what makes a rat, or a human being, so smart and sociable.

We can even figure out some of the brain mechanisms that underpin these abilities. In rats, and in people, too, particular parts of the frontal cortex play an especially important role in social coordination. If those areas are damaged, the affected rats look a lot like the play-deprived ones. They can master the actions of courting or fighting, but they can't respond to other rats in a flexible and fluid way. They get the words right but not the melody; they know the steps, but they can't master the dance.

Rats that play develop somewhat different brains than rats that don't. Some areas become more complex and others become more streamlined. Both kinds of change contribute in different ways to social competence in adults. Rats who play also produce certain chemicals, particularly a variety called cholinergic transmitters, in the more social parts of the frontal cortex. Those chemicals make their brains more plastic, as neuroscientists say.

For neuroscience, a plastic brain is a brain that changes more easily. A more plastic young brain will quickly make many new neural connections after a particular experience, while an older brain is more likely to stay the same. Early play not only produces these chemicals, it also helps to preserve plasticity by making the brain more sensitive to these chemicals later on.

To demonstrate this the researchers administered nicotine to adult rats who had or had not played when they were young. Chemicals such as nicotine mimic the natural cholinergic chemicals that make brains better at learning—that's why smokers feel more alert and focused when they've had a cigarette. A drug such as nicotine makes your brain more like its younger, more plastic self, but just how much more plastic that brain becomes can vary. Nicotine had a much bigger effect on adult rats who had roughhoused when they were young than on their more staid siblings—an early history of play maintained the potential for plasticity even in adults.

All the rats' brains became less flexible as they grew older. But the rats who had played when they were young still maintained the ability to change even once they had grown up—their brains were more plastic. Play didn't help the rats to do any one thing, in particular. Instead, it helped them to learn to do many things in a more flexible, varied way.

Getting Into Everything

Rough-and-tumble play is inherently social—it takes two to tangle. But animals, and children, also play with things. When you give even tiny babies a new toy, they will mouth it, shake it, drop it, and turn it over. (In fact, they do the same thing with objects you definitely don't want to give them, like a carpet-fuzz-covered crust of biscuit.)

A fascinating set of experiments, dating back to the 1960s, compared rats who are well-fed and cared for, but who grow up in the usual sterile cages, with rats who are raised in "enriched" environments, with many things to play with. In fact, the "enriched" environments were more like the natural environment for most rats—think about the quintessential New York City rat surrounded by fascinating empty soda cups and discarded pizza boxes.

Over every age range and across just about every measure of brain development, the rats who had things to play with developed better. Their brains grew bigger than the other rats, with more connections and larger frontal areas. And like the rough-and-tumble rats, they produced more of the learning chemicals than rats who grow up in plain cages. Playing with toys, as well as other rats, also seemed to help make for a more plastic brain. This is also true for other animals, such as monkeys.

But are young animals actually playing with the toys? Baby crows do, for sure. Crows, rooks, and ravens are incredibly intelligent animals. They're as smart as monkeys, maybe even chimps. I talked before about the especially intelligent kind of crow that is found only in New Caledonia, a remote Pacific island.

New Caledonian crows, like monkeys and apes, can use tools. But they can also use one tool to make another, and can pass innovations in tool design on to the next generation, rare abilities among animals.

It's no coincidence that these animals also have an exceptionally long childhood. New Caledonian crows can stay fledglings for as long as two years—a very long time indeed in the life of a bird. What do they do with that long childhood? Like human children, they play. But instead of playing with Lego and dolls, they play with sticks and palm leaves.

As I described earlier, in the wild, the grown-up New Caledonian crows use their high IQ to make digging tools from palm leaves. They do much the same thing with thorny sticks, and in the lab they can make similar hook tools out of wire.

How about the babies? The babies play with the pandanus palm leaves, too. But as you'd expect from babies, they are thoroughly incompetent. They pick up the leaves by the pointy end instead of the straight one, put the stems in with the barbed side up instead of down so that it can't grab the grubs, and generally muck about ineffectively.

Through all this, the parent crows patiently provide the kids with grubs themselves. And they let the babies come and take sticks and leaves from them—something they would never allow another adult to do. (Other, less bright species of crows are less tolerant of their babies, too.) In effect, the New Caledonian parents give the babies toys to play with.

The fledglings' actions look as if they make no sense—and they certainly aren't effective. But the young crows are able to try out all the various possibilities of the leaves and sticks, successful and unsuccessful, smart and dumb. And this allows them to develop the intelligence that is so striking in adult behavior, at least where sticks are concerned.

There are other birds who can produce amazingly complex behaviors. But many of these birds seem to have that complexity in place at birth, fixed there by natural selection. Newborn chicks, for example, have strikingly sophisticated and specific kinds of knowledge and skill as soon as they hatch. Those skills make adult chickens enormously effective at pecking grain. But when it comes to doing just about anything else, the chickens are stymied. The distinctive thing about the crows is that they are so flexible. In the lab they can figure out how to make a hook out of a bit of wire, even though there are no wires in their natural environment.

The philosopher Isaiah Berlin once divided philosophical thinkers into foxes and hedgehogs, based on a saying by the ancient Greek poet Archilochus, "The fox knows many things but the hedgehog knows one big thing." Chicks, like hedgehogs, know one or two big things, and they know them very well, very early. Crows, like foxes, can learn many new things.

Why are foxes and hedgehogs so different? Berlin, like most philosophers, didn't think much about childhood. But biology suggests that the difference may be due to how much those animals play when they're young.

Hedgehogs have a much shorter childhood than foxes. Hedgehogs are independent when they are six weeks old; foxes need their mom and dad until they've reached six months. Fox couples stay together and the fathers help bring food to the babies. Hedgehog fathers mate and then disappear.

Baby foxes also play much more than hedgehogs, though in a slightly creepy way. Mother foxes start out by feeding the babies their own regurgitated food. But then they actually bring the babies live prey, like mice, when they are still in the den, and the babies play at hunting them.

Berlin doesn't have much to say about whether Plato the hedgehog and Aristotle the fox had devoted or deadbeat dads, or if they had much playtime as philosopher pups, although the young cubs' game of chasing and eating live prey in a protected setting, surrounded by their approving elders, will seem familiar to those who have attended philosophy graduate seminars.

But in fact, a much earlier, anonymous philosopher understood the links between intelligence, parental investment, and play, even if Berlin didn't. The splendid song "The Fox," beloved by every four-year-old, was first written down on the blank flyleaf of a fifteenth-century copy of *Sayings of the Philosophers*. Here's the familiar modern version: the clever fox runs into town, outwits the farmer, and escapes with the gray goose on his back.

He ran till he came to his cozy den;
there were the little ones eight, nine, ten.
They said, "Daddy, better go back again,
'cause it must be a mighty fine town-o, town-o, town-o!"
Then the fox and his wife without any strife
cut up the goose with a fork and knife.
They never had such a supper in their life
and the little ones chewed on the bones-o, bones-o,
    bones-o.

The anonymous philosophy student not only described the clever, sociable carnivore who outwits even *Homo sapiens*, but he (or perhaps she? Anonymous is often a woman) also noted that the fox is the kind of creature who brings back the prey to the little ones in his cozy den. That gray goose was a source of cognitive practice and skill formation, as well as tasty bones-o.

Among animals, we humans are, of course, even foxier than the foxes.

Pop-Beads and Popper

Recently, Laura Schulz and her students at MIT have done some fascinating studies that examine how young humans master our equivalent of pandanus palms—namely, the many technological gadgets that surround us. When you leave a preschooler alone with an interesting new gadget, it's no surprise that they play with it. What may be surprising, however, is that they play in a way that's structured to give them just the information they need to figure out how that gadget works. For these children, play is, literally, experimentation.

In one study, for example, the experimenters gave four-year-olds one of our blicket detectors—that box that lights up and plays music when you put certain things on top of it. Instead of putting blocks on the machine, though, they used Pop-Beads, the kind of toy plastic beads that you can stick together or pull apart.

First, the experimenter showed the children that only some separate, individual beads made the toy go and not others. Then she gave them a new set of beads that were stuck together, and left them alone to play. The children carefully pulled the beads apart and tested them individually on the machine. When the experimenter sneakily glued the beads together, the children ingeniously tipped one end of the glued pair on the machine and then flipped it to try the other end, so that they could discover the effect of each bead separately.

In another version of the study, all the beads made the machine go. Now when the experimenter gave the children the stuck-together beads and let them play, they were much less likely to pull the beads apart. Instead, they just put the attached beads on the machine together. They seemed to realize that, in this case, pulling the beads apart wouldn't tell you anything new.

In another experiment, the researchers gave slightly older children a balance beam to explore. It was the kind of seesaw scale that balances on a fulcrum, and you can add a heavy weight to one end or the other. It turns out that six-year-olds have an inaccurate but intelligent theory of how balance beams work. They think that if the fulcrum is at the center of the beam, it will balance, no matter how heavy the weights are at each end.

By around seven or eight, the children start to develop a more accurate theory of mass. They recognize that the balance point depends on how heavy the ends of the beam are. If you add a heavy block to one end, you will have to move the fulcrum toward that end to get the beam to balance.

The researchers used a magnet to design trick beams that balanced at the center when the weights were uneven, or balanced to one side even when they were not. They checked to see whether children were center or mass theorists, and then left the kids alone with the trick balance beam and a new toy.

The "center theory" children played more with the beam when the balance was off-center—in other words, when the data contradicted their theory. When it balanced in the middle, as they expected, they weren't as interested and played more with the new toy. The "mass theory" children, on the other hand, behaved in just the opposite way. They played more when the balance looked centered but the weights were uneven. And both groups were more likely to discover the trick magnet when they played with the beam than when they didn't.

So the children played in a way that helped them learn about the beam. But the way they played, in turn, depended on what they already thought about how balance beams work. The great philosopher of science Karl Popper pointed out that good scientists should be more interested in evidence that contradicts their theories than evidence that confirms them. These young children followed Popper's advice. When they saw evidence that contradicted their theories they were driven to experiment—only they did it by playing.

A very recent study showed that this was true even for very young babies. Aimee Stahl and Lisa Feigenson showed systematically that eleven-month-old babies, like scientists, pay special attention when their predictions are violated, learn especially well as a result, and even do experiments to figure out just what happened.

They took off from some classic research that shows that babies will look longer when they see something unexpected. The babies either saw impossible events, such as a ball apparently passing through a solid brick wall, or straightforward events, such as the same ball simply moving through an empty space. Then they heard the ball make a squeaky noise. The babies were more likely to learn that the ball made the noise when it had behaved unexpectedly than when it had behaved predictably.

In a second experiment some babies again saw the mysterious dissolving ball or the straightforward solid one. But other babies also saw the ball either rolling along a ledge or rolling off the end of the ledge and apparently remaining suspended in thin air. Then the experimenters simply gave the babies the balls to play with. The babies explored objects more when they behaved unexpectedly. And they explored them differently: they banged the ball when it had mysteriously vanished through the wall, but they dropped it when it had hovered in thin air. It was as if they were testing to see if the ball really was solid or really did defy gravity.

In fact, these experiments suggest that babies may often be even better scientists than grown-ups are. Adults often suffer from "confirmation bias"—we pay attention to the things that fit what we already know and ignore the things that might shake up our preconceptions. Darwin famously kept a special list of all the facts that were at odds with his theory, because he knew he'd be tempted to ignore or forget them otherwise.

The babies, on the other hand, have a positive hunger for the unexpected. Like Karl Popper's ideal scientists, they're always on the lookout for a fact that falsifies their theories. And they play and explore to discover those facts.

Making Believe

Rats and foxes and kids play rough-and-tumble, and crows and dolphins and kids play with things. But human children also play in a way that is more unusual—indeed, quite possibly uniquely human. They pretend.

Children start to pretend when they are just a year old, and pretending reaches its zenith around three or four. Since Augie began to visit my garden, it has become the home of a tiger who lives in the avocado tree, a friendly *Monsters, Inc.* kind of monster hiding among the cacti, and three fairies who inhabit the solar lanterns and dance to the wind chimes. You can venture out at night to watch them, as long as you hold tight to Grandmom's hand.

The content of pretend play varies across cultures, ranging from wilder fantasies to more practical games of house and hunting. In some communities, even including some in the United States, parents actively discourage children from pretending. But in all cultures, children pretend anyway, at least some of the time. It seems that they always have. Archaeologists have recovered four-thousand-year-old dolls and miniature kitchen utensils in Bronze Age children's quarters.

But why pretend? You can see the possible advantages of rough-and-tumble or exploratory play. The young animals have a chance to exercise the skills they'll need as adults, or to discover something new about sticks or blicket machines. But why practice thinking things that not only aren't true but never could be true?

In the past, psychologists such as Piaget thought that children pretended because they couldn't distinguish between reality and fantasy. But, as we've seen, even very young children are adept at distinguishing between the two. At some level, they know that even the most beloved imaginary friends and feared imaginary enemies aren't real.

So if children don't pretend because they're confused, why do they pretend? Pretending is closely related to another distinctively human ability, hypothetical or counterfactual thinking—that is, the ability to consider alternative ways that the world might be. And that, in turn, is central to our powerful human learning abilities.

Bayesian Babies

Bayesianism is one of the most influential recent accounts of human learning. It's named after the Reverend Thomas Bayes, an eighteenth-century theologian and pioneer of probability theory. Bayesians think that learning is much like scientific progress. We consider a range of different hypotheses, different pictures of how the world might work. Some of the hypotheses may be more likely than others, but none of them are absolutely sure to be true. When we say that we believe a hypothesis is true, what we really mean is that, right now, it's the best guess we've got.

Now suppose we do a new experiment or make a new observation. The new evidence might make us reconsider that best guess. Maybe there's a different hypothesis that actually does a better job of explaining the new data. What would happen if that other hypothesis was true?

If the new hypothesis does a better job of explaining all the data, old and new, we might decide that it's actually more likely to be true. It would replace our former idea as the still-tentative and temporary truth.

Children do experiments and make observations, although we call it "getting into everything." When the children in Schulz's lab pull apart the Pop-Beads or test one and then the other on the blicket machine, they are gathering new data about how the machine works. And in the balance beam experiments, they're especially intrigued by new data that contradict what they currently think about how the world works.

In much the same way, Saul Perlmutter and his fellow experimental physicists fiddled around with radio telescopes and discovered that the universe was expanding more rapidly than we thought. (The toys they used were considerably more expensive, but then again, those toys won them a Nobel Prize.)

The first step toward a new discovery is discovering that your current hypothesis is wrong. But there is another stage of the process—thinking up other hypotheses. Perlmutter's discoveries sent theoretical physicists scurrying for alternative explanations. Think for a minute about what this requires. You have to take a hypothesis and consider just what would happen if it was true. What data pattern would we expect, for example, if there really was a multiverse? Or a cosmological constant? Would it look like Perlmutter's unexpected data?

The process is a lot like pretending. You start out with a premise that you currently think is false. There probably aren't any tigers in the avocado trees of Berkeley backyards. But then you figure out what the consequences of that false premise would be anyway. If there *was* a tiger, you would do well to approach it gingerly. If the tiger was asleep, you and Grandmom might want to tiptoe by, rather than risk waking him.

Of course, there's a difference between Augie's tiger and theories of dark energy. The physicist is looking for theories that he currently doesn't believe but that could turn out to be true, and Augie doesn't seem to care whether the tiger is truly there or not. But that's a lot like other kinds of play. In fact, according to the biologists' definition, play is what happens when young animals exercise a useful skill even though it doesn't immediately lead to a useful result.

Thinking counterfactually in this way is a tremendously useful skill for adult human beings. It's what we mean when we talk about the power of imagination and creativity. Counterfactual thinking is crucial for learning about the world. In order to learn we need to believe that what we think now could be wrong, and to imagine how the world might be different.

But counterfactual thinking is also crucial if we want to change the world. In order to change the world, we need to imagine that the world could be different, and then actually set about making it that way. In fact, just about everything in the room I'm sitting in—the woven fabrics, the carpentered chairs, not to mention the electric lights and computers—is wildly fictional from the perspective of a Pleistocene forager. Our world started out as a counterfactual imaginary vision in an ancestor's mind.

One way of thinking about pretend play is that it gives children a safe space to practice higher-order mental skills, just as rough-and-tumble gives baby rats a safe space to practice fighting and hunting, and exploratory play gives baby crows a safe space to practice using sticks.

But could you show that this is actually true? Play isn't easy to study in the lab, precisely because of the Miss Havisham principle: You can't tell kids to play in a particular way without defeating the whole point of the exercise. But my graduate student Daphna Buchsbaum thought up a clever way to get kids to pretend spontaneously.

First, she introduced a toy monkey and told the kids that it was Monkey's birthday. She had a special machine that would play "Happy Birthday" so that they could sing to Monkey. It was a disguised version of our old friend the blicket detector. Some blocks, called zandos, made it go. The children quickly learned how the machine worked, and became adept at using zandos. They discovered, for example, that a green block was a zando and a red one wasn't.

Then we asked a hypothetical question about the machine. What would happen if the green block *wasn't* a zando? And how about if the red block *was* a zando? To answer the question, the kids, like the theoretical physicists, had to consider what would happen if a true premise was false.

Surprisingly, most three- and four-year-olds were able to do this. But not all of them did. About a third of the children were stern and earnest literalists. They answered by reporting what would really happen, rather than what could happen if things were different.

Now the clever part of the experiment started. There was a knock at the door, and a harried and peremptory stooge entered and demanded the birthday machine. Daphna acted dismayed, of course, but the stooge insisted on taking the machine away. Crestfallen, Daphna turned to the equally dismayed children and said, "Oh no, we can't play music for Monkey. What shall we do?" Suddenly, she had a bright idea. "I know, we'll pretend." She picked up a plain cardboard box and a couple of blocks that happened to be lying around. "Let's pretend this box is the machine and this block is a zando." The children were enthusiastic about this clever solution to the problem. (The story was a bit like the implausible plot point in *As You Like It*: Orlando loves Rosalind, but when they meet in the forest she is disguised as a boy. So she suggests to Orlando that he should pretend that she is a girl; in fact, she suggests that he should pretend she is Rosalind. But the children bought it as easily as Orlando does.)

Having solved the Miss Havisham problem, Daphna proceeded to ask the children to pretend. More specifically, she asked them to pretend that the block was a zando. The children happily put the block on the box, and then pretended that the box was playing music. They even hummed and sang along.

Then she asked them to pretend that the block was not a zando. Now if you put the block on the machine, it should lead only to pretend silence. The children pretended that, too. (This last one is a bit of a mind-boggler if you think about it—the children had to pretend that a machine that really wasn't playing music, wasn't playing music, like Orlando pretending that Rosalind, who really was Rosalind, was Rosalind.)

Most of the children not only pretended, they also spontaneously elaborated on the pretend premise. Like Augie in the garden, they were delighted to go even further than the grown-ups. They pretended that the machine was playing different songs, and they presented Monkey with elaborately wrapped invisible pretend presents. And they spontaneously "experimented," trying different pretend blocks on the machine and noting the pretend results.

Once again, though, about a third of the children were sternly literal. They simply told the experimenter the truth—there was never any music playing.

The interesting thing was that these were the same children who answered the serious counterfactual question literally, too. Playful pretending was strongly associated with the ability to think about possibilities.

But was it just that the pretenders were brighter than the other children, or were better at resisting the impulse to answer the question literally? In a second experiment, we also tested each child's general cognitive ability and executive function. There was no relationship between these abilities and the ability to pretend or think counterfactually. Pretending and thinking about possibilities were very specifically linked. And in experiments we've done since, we've found that actually getting children to pretend first makes them better at these counterfactual inferences later on. We don't know for sure why some children pretended more than others, but we are currently exploring whether this depends on how much pretending they see other people do.

Kinds of Minds

If pretending helps you practice the kinds of counterfactual thinking that are so important for learning, you might expect that children who pretend more would also learn more. And, in fact, there is some evidence that they do. There is not much evidence that pretending improves the kinds of academic skills we cultivate in schools. But that kind of academic learning is far from being the most important or challenging kind of learning for young children (or for the rest of us).

By far the most important and interesting problem for young children is figuring out what's going on in other people's minds. Theory of mind, as it's called, is the ability to figure out the desires, perceptions, emotions, and beliefs of other people. It's quite possibly *the* most important kind of learning people ever do.

You can see how important it is when you look at people with autism. Autism Spectrum Disorder (ASD) is a complicated syndrome, of course, but one of the central problems seems to be that ASD children have a very hard time understanding what is going on in the minds of others. That leads to the painful social difficulties that are characteristic of the disorder.

Even very young babies understand some important things about how other people's minds, and their own, work. And even twenty-year-olds (and thirty- and forty- and fifty-year-olds) are still learning. But the period from eighteen months to five years is the great watershed for developing theory of mind. Children learn fundamental facts about how people's desires, emotions, and beliefs work. They learn that different people may want and believe different things. And they learn that those differences may lead people to act in very different, and very confusing, ways.

Children pretend about the physical world, but most of their spontaneous make-believe concerns what people (or such people-like beings as tigers, monsters, and fairies) do. When Augie and I tiptoe through the moonlit garden, we are predicting the actions of those unaccountable creatures Titania, Ariel, and Tinkerbell.

Imaginary companions are a particularly vivid example of this kind of pretending. Imaginary friends are both fascinating and sort of creepy, and people often assume that they are symptoms of genius, craziness, or both. But they are actually very common: the psychologist Marjorie Taylor found that some 66 percent of preschoolers have some kind of imaginary companion, often friendly but sometimes threatening, and generally a little weird—a dinosaur with a large spotted tail, or a girl with floor-length pigtails who lives in Antarctica.

The kids with imaginary friends weren't any smarter or crazier than the others. But Taylor found a very clear and robust relationship between pretending about people and theory of mind. She gave the children problems to solve that required them to understand the minds of other people. One very well known task, for example, is called the false-belief test. You can show children a Band-Aid box that turns out to be full of paper clips instead of Band-Aids. Then you can ask them what they thought was in the box, and what someone else will think is in it. Younger children say that they always thought there were clips in the box and so will everyone else. By five most kids can understand their own past false beliefs and the false beliefs of others. Children with autism, though, have special difficulty solving this kind of problem.

Children who pretend more have a distinct advantage in understanding other people; they do much better on these "false-belief" tests. And that advantage is particularly clear for children who have imaginary companions.

Pretending even seems to make grown-ups into better psychologists. For adults, fiction and drama are the equivalent of pretend play and imaginary companions. And studies show that reading fiction can have the same advantages as pretending. People who read a great deal of fiction are consistently more empathetic and better at understanding other people. They do better on adult versions of theory of mind tests than people who read an equal amount of nonfiction.

Cause or just correlation? In one study, researchers got people to read passages of literary fiction, popular fiction, or nonfiction. Then they asked them to figure out what someone was thinking about based on his actions, or what someone was feeling based on her facial expressions. Literary fiction led to an immediate boost in solving theory of mind problems. Popular fiction and nonfiction didn't have the same effect. (So, perhaps, if you're really interested in improving your understanding of psychology, you should drop this book immediately and go read George Eliot's *Middlemarch* instead.)

Dancing Robots

So rough-and-tumble play seems to help animals and children to interact with others. Exploratory play helps animals and children learn how things work. And pretend play helps children think about possibilities and understand other people's minds.

But we still haven't really answered the question about *why* play helps. An answer may come from engineering instead of psychology. Mother Nature may sometimes use the same techniques as the nerds who also create new creatures.

Suppose you're trying to make a robot. You don't just want the kind of big industrial robot that does the same thing over and over. Instead, you want a robot that will be able to adjust to an ever-changing world, the way that animals and people do. What should you do?

Designing a robot that does one thing is relatively easy. It's much harder to design a robot that can deal with changing circumstances. You can design a robot that will walk, but what happens if you turn it on its side, or it bumps into a wall, or it sprains a knee, or even loses a limb? Living things can fluidly adjust to changes like these. Think about how a wounded soldier can make drastic adjustments to her normal gait, and learn to walk and even run on an artificial leg. But robots, on the other hand, are usually rendered helpless.

The computer scientist Hod Lipson has found that one strategy is to allow the robot to develop an internal picture of how its own body works. Then the robot can predict what will happen if something changes inside its body, or outside in the world. It's a lot like the Bayesian children working out what would happen if the block was a zando. And the best way to do that turned out to be giving the robot a chance to play—to randomly try out different movements and work out the consequences.

A Lipson robot would start out by dancing around in a silly, random way—like a drunken cousin at a wedding—before it tried to do anything useful. But, afterward, it could use the information it collected in the playful dancing phase to decide how to act when unexpected things happened. It could still walk even when the engineers removed one of its robotic limbs. That first apparently useless dance would make the robot more robust later on.

The robot may give us a clue about the advantages of play for children, too. Play lets children randomly and variably try out a range of actions and ideas, and then work out the consequences. It might be Lipson's robot testing the movements of its own body, the young rat trying different modes of attack and defense, the baby crow turning the stick upside down and right side up, or the child fiddling with the balance beam.

Or in pretend play, the experimentation might be more internal. The children, or the grown-up fiction readers, are considering what would happen if the world were different, and working out the consequences. How about if it was Monkey's birthday? Or Natasha's first ball? Or Pierre's first battle?

The very silliness of play, the apparently random weirdness of it all, is what makes it so effective. Lipson could have tried to anticipate what his robot offspring should do in every situation, as we are tempted to do with children. But that would only give them information about what to do when the expected happens. The gift of play is the way it teaches us how to deal with the unexpected.

That may also help explain another puzzling fact about play. Why is play fun? Why do we take special pleasure in playful actions? It's easy to learn that a goal-directed action is worth doing—after all, we reach the goal and get rewarded. But how do you ensure that an animal or a child will be able to deal with a situation that evolution hasn't anticipated beforehand? We all perpetually face the unexpected, whether it's a busted knee, a new wrestling (or flirting) move, or any of the psychological surprises our fellow humans throw at us. The engineering work suggests that letting a robot or an animal or a child have a chance to play—a chance to explore widely, act randomly, be silly, and do things for no reason at all—is the solution.

But to do that you need to make exploration enjoyable for its own sake, independent of any particular outcomes. It's a bit like what happens with sex. From our internal perspective we pursue sex in search of pleasure, and babies are just a side effect. But from an evolutionary perspective it's the other way round—reproduction is the final end and our pleasure in sex is just an incentive to get us there.

And so, we don't play because we think that eventually it will give us robust cognitive functions—although that may be the evolutionary motivation for play. We play because it is just so much fun.

Beyond Miss Havisham

Although there's much more research to do, playing and learning go together, just as much for rats as for readers of Alice Munro. Clearly, letting children play is important. But is there any more to say about the role of caregivers? Can parents somehow help children play better?

A depressing, Miss Havishamesque finding is that grown-ups can actually get in the way of play. Elizabeth Bonawitz and her colleagues contrasted the playful, exploratory learning in the Pop-Bead experiments with the direct instruction you get in school. They gave preschoolers a toy with many plastic tubes that did different things. If you pushed on one tube, a beeper squeaked, another held a hidden mirror, a third lit up, a fourth played music.

For half of the children, the experimenter brought in the toy and said, "Oh, look at this neat toy! Oops!" Then she "accidentally" bumped into the tube so that the beeper squeaked. For the other half, the experimenter acted like a teacher. She said,

"Oh, look at my neat toy! Let me show you how it works," and deliberately pushed the tube that squeaked the beeper. Then she left the children alone to play with the toy.

Both groups of children immediately made the beeper squeak—they'd learned how the beeper worked. The question was whether they would also learn about all the other things the toy could do. When the experimenter activated the toy accidentally, the children were fascinated and they played. Just by randomly trying different actions they discovered all the things that the toy could do. But when the experimenter acted like a teacher, the children would squeak the beeper, and then squeak it again and again, ad nauseam, instead of trying something new.

The children played with the toy longer, tried more different actions, and discovered more of the "hidden" features when the experimenter squeaked the beeper accidentally than they did when she deliberately tried to teach them.

So teaching is a double-edged sword. The children were re-markably sensitive to the fact that they were being taught, just as we saw in previous chapters. But teaching seemed to discourage the children from discovering all the possibilities the toy had to offer. The children were more eager to imitate the teacher than to discover things themselves. (College teachers like me will recog-nize that this syndrome continues into adulthood.)

And remember the three-action experiment I described in the chapter on imitation? In that experiment, four-year-olds saw an adult act on a toy in a complicated sequence, shaking it, squeez-ing it, and then pulling a ring; or tapping it, pushing a button, and then turning it over. Sometimes the toy played music and some-times it didn't. The pattern of events indicated that there might be a much simpler way to make the machine go. For example, all you really had to do was just pull the ring.

When the adult said that she had no idea how the toy worked, the children discovered the more intelligent strategy. But when she acted like a teacher and said that she was showing the child how the toy worked, the children imitated everything the teacher did instead.

So do grown-up teachers always screw things up? Not necessarily. By its very nature spontaneous play is undirected and variable. But how about if you want to teach children something in particular, as we often do in school?

In one study, the researchers tried to teach preschool children a challenging geometry concept, the concept of shape. Preschoolers don't yet know some basic principles about shape that are important for geometry. They don't initially get that a triangle is a shape with three sides, no matter how long or short, acute or obtuse.

The researchers gave four-year-old children a set of cards with different kinds of shapes on them—both more typical shapes, like an equilateral triangle or a square, and more unusual ones like a parallelogram. One group just got to play with the cards.

For a second group, the experimenters joined in. They donned detective hats and explained that they were going to discover the secrets of the shapes. Then they pointed to a group of geometrically defined triangles or pentagons and asked the children to figure out their common secret. When the children responded, the grown-ups elaborated on what they said and asked them questions as part of the game. I elaborate on Augie's tigers and fairies in much the same way—he probably wouldn't have come up with the names Titania and Ariel on his own.

For a third group of children, the experimenters acted like teachers. They said all the same things as the experimenters in the second group. However, rather than encouraging the children to generate the secret themselves, they simply told them what it was.

A week later the researchers asked the children to sort out a new group of shapes into "real" shapes that obeyed the geometrical rules and "fake" ones that didn't. The children in the second, "guided play" condition did a much better job than either of the other two groups. They had learned the nature of the shapes more deeply, and understood the principles more completely.

This kind of guided play can serve as a model for teachers and educators. Scientists use the word "scaffolding" to describe this kind of interaction. It's not that the grown-up builds knowledge for the child. Instead, the grown-up builds a scaffold, and the scaffold helps the child to build knowledge herself. This work on guided play parallels the work on children's learning and listening I described earlier.

There are many ways that caregivers can contribute to play without telling children to play or trying to control how they play. First, there is an important lesson from the animal studies. Play is such a fundamental part of human childhood that it emerges even in awful circumstances. Children played even among the horrors of Nazi concentration camps. But clearly, play flourishes in a stable, safe environment. Caregivers have a more important role than anyone else in finding the resources to create that environment. It's not easy or particularly fun, and none of us do it perfectly, but it's a gift that lets children play.

Second, caregivers can contribute to the richness of a child's world. Children play differently in different cultures partly because they are surrounded by different things to play with, from sticks, rocks, and corncobs to iPads. Grown-ups can provide those playthings. They can give children a chance to master the tools of their particular culture, like the adult crows that let the babies play with their sticks and leaves.

A *Wired* magazine contest awarded sticks the prize of the all-time best toy. But they can be joined by pots and pans, watering cans and flowerpots, goldfish and caterpillars, and even iPhones and tablets.

And grown-ups can sometimes join in the play themselves. If children are exploring the minds of others, then the actual minds of actual others are the best toys of all. "Guided play" is a nice example. The grown-ups allow the children to lead the way, but they are also there to suggest or elaborate (and wear those silly detective hats).

But there is a more important reason to play with children. Play is really fun for grown-ups, too. It's a little compensation for the not-so-fun work of gathering enough resources for children to thrive. The plain truth is that I enjoy the fairies in the garden quite as much as Augie does, and it's extremely unlikely that I would engage in so spectacularly twee a game if it weren't for him. Nor would I race Lightning McQueen cars on the carpet, fill an old pot with blocks to make pretend soup, or jump on the bed like those five notoriously accident-prone little monkeys. Peek-a-boo and itsy-bitsy spider with baby sister Georgiana are pretty fun, too, especially with her contagious giggle.

Ironically, contemporary middle-class parents may allow themselves license to play only if they are convinced that it is part of the work of parenting. There is a famously puritan streak in America. We have a knack for taking what are simple pleasures in other cultures, from food to walks to sex, and turning them into strenuous work projects. We follow a Mediterranean diet instead of just eating spaghetti and tomatoes, take aerobic hikes instead of after-dinner promenades, and practice *The Joy of Sex* instead of, well, the joy of sex.

There is good reason to think that letting children play—

spontaneously, randomly, and by themselves—helps allow them to learn. But another part of the evolutionary story is that play is a satisfying good in itself—a source of joy, laughter, and fun for parents as well as children. If it had no other rationale, the sheer pleasure of play would be justification enough.

7. Growing Up

So far, I've been talking mostly about very young children, up to around six years old. Young children are especially variable, creative, and downright messy, and taking care of them is especially demanding. But what happens when children get older?

For our children, of course, what happens is school. Schools become the caregivers of older children. In fact, psychology textbooks divide children up into preschool and school age as if school defined an essential biological difference. But "schooling" is actually only a little older than "parenting." Schools have really only been around for a couple of hundred years, an eye-blink in human history.

There is a parallel between the contemporary dilemmas of parenting and the equally ferocious dilemmas of schooling. Like parents, educators often have a scientifically inaccurate picture of learning and development. In fact, they share the same inaccurate picture. The misleading idea is that education is supposed to shape a child into a particular kind of adult. The remarkable spread of standardized testing is a particularly good example of this. A school's job becomes creating children who will score well on standardized tests.

At least the parenting project has sensible goals, such as turning your child into a happy, successful adult, even if there's actually no clear prescription about how to accomplish those goals. But in practice, if not in principle, schooling ends up being aimed at arbitrary goals like the high test score, the A grade, and admission to the next school.

The parenting misconception not only parallels the schooling misconception, it interacts with it. In a world where schooling is the key to many kinds of success, parenting inevitably becomes focused on trying to ensure that your children succeed in school.

If schools give the wrong picture of older children, what's the right picture? From a scientific perspective, learning isn't about test scores at all—it's about tracking the reality of the world around you. All children are naturally driven to create an accurate picture of the world, and to use that picture to make predictions, formulate explanations, imagine alternatives, and design plans. They all want, even need, to understand the world.

But it is true that six-year-olds learn in very different ways from younger children, and they always have. The period between about six and adolescence is just as distinctive as the earlier periods of infancy and early childhood. There is a real and striking change from the wild, crazy, poetic preschoolers to the sane and sober seven- and eight-year-olds. Indeed, there may be no saner and more sober creature on earth than your average eight-year-old.

The preschoolers' evolutionary task is to explore as many possibilities as widely as possible. This kind of exploration lets children discover foundational principles about how the world works, principles that will underpin competence in adulthood.

The job for school-age children is to start actually becoming competent adults themselves. Their evolutionary agenda is to practice and master the particular skills of their own culture, especially social skills, while they're still within the safe cocoon of adult caregiving.

This transition to a new kind of learning may be intensified by the transition to school. But in historical periods before school was invented, and in other cultures where schooling is much less common, people have also recognized that something changes at around six or seven. Historically, this was the time when children began to become informal apprentices, learning to become hunters or knights or chefs. Back when children actually worked, this was when their work life began. And rituals such as First Communion—the dawning of the traditional Catholic "age of reason"—also mark a new phase of life. With adult teeth, apparently, come new adult-like responsibilities.

Some of the same kinds of learning that we see in younger children continue to be important in older ones. Older children, as well as younger ones, create and revise intuitive theories of how the world works. They spontaneously develop new concepts of physics, biology, and psychology. For example, at around ten, children begin to develop concepts of density and to differentiate density from weight. Six- and seven-year-olds start to understand biology in a new way. Four-year-olds think that when you die you simply move to a different location, while older children develop the tragic understanding that death is an irreversible process, especially if they have pet fish or live on a farm. And older children begin to grasp subtle psychological concepts like sarcasm and ambivalence; they know that you can say one thing and mean something quite different, or feel sadness and happiness simultaneously.

Seven- and eight-year-olds also engage in the exploration and discovery that we see at such a fever pitch among babies and preschoolers. Older children are also adept at intelligent imitation and observational learning. They make sense of the varied testimony of others—the many, often conflicting, kinds of information they hear from the adults around them. And variability, messiness, and play continue to help children learn in robust, flexible, and creative ways.

But school-age children also engage in what I'll call mastery learning, rather than discovery learning. In mastery learning, you aren't learning something new so much as taking what you've already learned and making it second nature. You get to know the solution to an old problem so well you don't even have to think about it, and that lets you perform skills effortlessly, quickly, and efficiently. Mastery learning is about exploiting, not exploring.

There may be a trade-off between the two types of learning. Children sometimes learn new things more easily than adults, and in the same way, preschoolers are better at certain kinds of learning than school-age children. Especially through the school-age years, children's knowledge becomes more and more ingrained and automatic, and they act on it more efficiently. But for that very reason, it also becomes harder to change.

In a sense, mastery learning is less about getting smarter than about getting stupider. We can turn some of what we've learned into automatic and even mindless procedures. This frees up our attention and thought for new discoveries.

The activities that promote mastery are different from the activities that promote discovery. What makes knowledge automatic is what gets you to Carnegie Hall: practice, practice, practice. By using a particular piece of information or performing a particular skill over and over, human beings eventually get to the point where they don't even need to think. In some settings, like the Guatemalan villages that Barbara Rogoff studies, this sort of practice happens naturally; make tortillas every day for a year, and you'll get to be pretty good at it. In our culture the same is true for children, rich and poor, who become astonishingly skilled at the video games they play for hours on end.

The two kinds of learning seem to involve different underlying mechanisms and even different brain regions. Children develop mastery learning later than discovery learning. Babies are as good at discovery learning as the smartest adults, or even better. But humans seem to get better at mastery learning as they get older.

In particular, as we saw earlier, as children grow older, the prefrontal area of the brain—the brain's executive office—exercises increasingly greater control over the rest of the brain. Babies and young children pay attention to anything that's interesting and informative, and they learn as a result. But as we get older more and more of our learning is directed toward particular goals. Mastery learning requires a kind of controlled focus that is just not possible for younger children.

Other changes also contribute to the rise of mastery learning. Neural connections are extensively "pruned"; many connections disappear. The neural connections that remain, especially the connections that are used often, become increasingly covered with a substance called myelin, which makes them more efficient conductors. At the same time the brain becomes more specialized. Younger children typically use more brain areas to solve a task than older children or adults do.

All these changes contribute to transform the young brain. The preschool brain is enormously flexible and changes easily, but it is also noisy. The school-age brain is much more efficient and effective, but it is also more rigid.

Mastery learning may become possible partly because of these changes, but the experiences of practice and control that lead to mastering a skill also themselves change the brain. When you make the same neural connections over and over again, when you play scales on the piano over and over, for example, those connections become stronger and more efficient, just as throwing a baseball over and over strengthens your shoulder muscles. But they also become more difficult to change. Most likely the two kinds of changes interact. Brain changes make new kinds of experiences more likely, and in turn those experiences reshape the brain.

Apprenticeship

How does mastery happen? For most of human history, learning in middle childhood meant apprenticeship, not school. Children learned to master skills informally inside the family, or outside the family, more formally and later. Most people were foragers or farmers, and foraging and farming children learned by helping out—they still do. Children also learned more-specialized skills by becoming apprentices to master tradesmen and artisans.

Preschoolers show some of the beginnings of apprenticeship when they imitate the people around them. Anthropologists and cultural psychologists, not to mention parents, see how even very young toddlers are drawn to imitate everything that they see their elders do, from machete handling to pancake making. But while preschoolers are essentially playing at those adult skills, school-age children begin to genuinely master them. It is more work to make pancakes with a two-year-old than to just do it yourself, but by eight or nine, children can honestly contribute to a family's economy. Apprenticeship is a kind of work as much as it is a kind of play.

School-age children observe and imitate like younger children. But they learn especially well when they interact with particularly skilled adults in a distinctive cycle of trial and error. The appren-

tice watches the master attentively, and then tries out a simplified part of the skill. It might be stirring the stockpot, cutting
out a pattern, or roughing a carpentry frame. The master, in turn,
comments (often quite critically) on what the apprentice has done
and gets her to do it again. With each round of imitation, practice, and critique, the learner becomes more and more skilled, and
tackles more and more demanding parts of the process (the bé-
chamel sauce, the darts in a bodice, the mortise-and-tenon
joint).

Apprenticeship can require grueling practice. A Japanese Zen
story tells of a student, Matajuro, who was desperate to be instructed by Banzo, the great teacher of swordsmanship. Banzo
sent him to the kitchen to prepare vegetables instead. On the first
day, as Matajuro was slicing radishes, Banzo suddenly appeared
without warning and smacked him with a large wooden sword,
offering no explanation. This went on for months, and each time
Banzo would appear more unexpectedly. By the end of three years
in the kitchen Matajuro was perpetually alert, on the balls of his
feet, preparing to duck at any moment. Then and only then did
Banzo announce that Matajuro could begin training. Matajuro
became, of course, the greatest swordsman in all of Japan.

A journalist I know tells a similar tale of learning to write
radio news. He started as the youngest and lowest of copywriters
in a desolate overnight newsroom. The grizzled, half-drunk, and
extremely cranky old editor would tear off a piece of copy from
the Teletype machine (this was a very long time ago) and tell the
novice to write it up into a radio script. He would type a script up
frantically, and return his finished piece to the editor. Four out
of five times the editor would grunt, "This is crap," and throw it in
the wastebasket. But occasionally, he would grunt and throw it
into his in-box instead. Gradually the editor would accept a few
more stories and reject a few less. At last, more than half made it

into the in-box. Like the swordsman apprentice, the journalist discovered that he had somehow learned how to write a radio news story.

This is not exactly how we would ideally want schools to unfold, of course. But these stories are instructive parables of how apprenticeship can lead to mastery. Many of the most effective teachers, even in modern schools, use elements of apprenticeship. Ironically, though, these teachers are more likely to be found in the "extracurricular" classes than in the required ones. The stern but beloved baseball coach or the demanding but passionate music teacher let children learn this way.

Poor, inner-city children have a tendency to focus on sports and music, even though these skills are far less likely than math or science to help them to actually make a living. Perhaps this reflects unrealistic cultural expectations. But I think it also reflects the fact that sports and music are much more likely to be taught through apprenticeship than math or science or literature.

There is no particularly good reason why ballet or basketball should be taught through apprenticeship while science and math are not. As any scientist will tell you, our profession is as much a matter of hard-won skill as piano or tennis. In graduate school, where we really teach science, we use the same methods as a chef or a tailor. My students begin by writing up the easy part of a paper, or designing a substudy of a big grant, and slowly graduate to doing a completely original experiment themselves. And though I don't exactly wield a wooden sword—or even a wastebasket— I'm told that my "track changes" comments on a student manuscript can be pretty ferocious.

Writing, my other profession, is the same way. You learn to write by writing, over and over again, especially with a good editor. (John Kenneth Galbraith said that the note of spontaneity his critics liked so much generally came in around the ninth draft.)

But how many schoolchildren get to actually practice science or mathematics or even essay-writing, or get to watch scientists or mathematicians or writers at work? How many public school teachers are as good at science or mathematics or writing as the average coach is good at baseball? And even when teachers *are* experts, how many children ever actually watch a teacher work through writing an essay or designing a new scientific experiment or solving an unfamiliar mathematics problem?

Imagine if we taught baseball the way we teach science. Until they were twelve, children would read about baseball technique and history, and occasionally hear inspirational stories of the great baseball players. They would fill out quizzes about baseball rules. College undergraduates might be allowed, under strict supervision, to reproduce famous historic baseball plays. But only in the second or third year of graduate school, would they, at last, actually get to play a game. If we taught baseball this way, we might expect about the same degree of success in the Little League World Series that we currently see in our children's science scores.

Matajuro and the copywriter didn't learn in order to pass the swordsmanship SAT or the copywriting final exam. The process and the outcome of their learning were indistinguishable. Learning to play baseball doesn't prepare you to be a baseball player—it makes you a baseball player.

Scholastic Skills

Schools have largely replaced apprenticeship. Public and universal schooling was invented quite recently, in concert with the industrial revolution. It was designed to give people a new set of skills that were essential for success in an industrial world. School was invented to allow children to master the technical details of reading, writing, and arithmetic calculation. And not incidentally, it came to give children a protected haven while their caregivers were, for the first time in human history, far away at work.

These scholastic skills may be tremendously important in the long run, but they are meaningless in themselves. There is no intrinsic discovery involved in learning a particular artificial mapping between letters and sounds, or a set of multiplication algorithms such as the times tables. In the natural environment no one would ever think of looking for that sort of mapping, or engaging in those kinds of procedures.

Nonetheless, mastering these skills or others like them, and mastering them in a way that makes them automatic, effortless, and transparent, was, is, and will continue to be absolutely necessary. (Though in an age of computers, arithmetic calculation skills arguably should be replaced by coding and programming skills, just as keyboarding has already replaced handwriting.) These skills are necessary because they allow us to exercise our learning abilities in a far wider world. Reading lets us learn from all the human experts who have ever lived, not just the ones who live nearby. Mastering the meaningless skills of mapping words onto sounds or memorizing a multiplication table in turn lets you master the far from meaningless skills of writing an essay, testing a scientific hypothesis, or analyzing a statistical pattern.

The problem is how to leverage children's natural learning capacities to allow them to master these unnatural skills. This is an important and difficult challenge, and psychologists have been working on it for decades. For example, we have come to understand that difficulties in reading, such as dyslexia, are usually connected to difficulties in analyzing the sounds of language. You don't need to analyze sound in a fine-grained way in order to talk, but you do if you want to map sounds onto letters. In much the same way, psychologists have begun to find continuities between the intuitive understanding of numbers we see in very young children and the explicit skills of mathematical calculation.

For many children in elementary school the problem may not be that they're not smart enough, but that they're not yet stupid enough. They haven't yet been able to master skills such as reading, writing, and calculating in a way that makes them transparent and automatic. This may be particularly true for children who don't have natural opportunities to practice reading and writing. In middle-class households, reading and writing may be as ubiquitous as tortilla-making is in the Guatemalan village. Augie would spontaneously take a book with him to the potty even before he was two. But the scene is often very different in poor households. In fact, there is good evidence that the best predictors of reading performance in school are how much children hear language at home and how many books they encounter.

But the mastery of scholastic skills such as reading, writing, and arithmetic isn't an end in itself. It's a means to make new discoveries.

Of course, almost from the time that people began to think seriously about education, they've noticed the mismatch between the natural discovery and curiosity that is such a feature of childhood and the kinds of learning that happen in school. That observation underlies the many "progressive" and alternative forms of education that are based on "inquiry learning." Many schoolteachers intuitively appreciated discovery learning even though we've only really just begun to understand it scientifically, just as preschool teachers intuitively appreciated pretend play before we scientists did.

But it's worth pointing out that in most schools, outside of the gym children not only have limited opportunities for discovery, they also don't get a chance to attain real mastery. Schools aren't institutions that promote discovery, and they aren't centers of apprenticeship, either.

Instead, what schools do best is teach children how to go to school. School-age children are fascinated by adult skills and inclined toward apprenticeship. It's natural for them to imitate and practice the activities that are most important to the adults around them. In school, intentionally or not, that means paying attention, taking tests, and getting grades.

In the worst case, those skills are simply alien or impossible for many children. But even in the best case, among the high-achieving children, we might wonder whether sending children to school just to learn how to go to school is really such a great idea.

By the time they arrive in our classes, many Berkeley undergraduates are absolute Matajuros of test-taking. It's no wonder we're gravely disappointed—and they're resentfully surprised—when we ask them to actually be apprentice scientists or scholars instead. Skilled adults continue to face difficult challenges, of course, but passing exams isn't one of them. Being the best test-taker in the world isn't much help for discovering either new truths about that world or new ways of thriving in it.

Thinking Differently

This is another respect in which schooling and learning don't go together well. Individual human children try out all sorts of new and different ideas and actions. But they are also very different from one another. From birth, children have a wide range of temperaments and interests, strengths and weaknesses, even in the same family. As we saw earlier, from an evolutionary point of view this variability is a route to flexibility and robustness. It ensures that a community, a village, or a country can deal with shifting circumstances. It's a recipe for cultural evolvability.

But the goal-directed "schooling" perspective makes that same variability into a disadvantage. If you think of schools as institutions that are designed to produce children with particular characteristics, variability is a drawback, not a strength. In fact, in the worst cases, variability goes beyond just being a problem—it becomes a disease. Children who don't fit the demands of school are treated as if they were ill or defective or disabled. And this "disease" model is especially prevalent because many of the skills that are most important for school are far removed from the natural abilities and inclinations of most children.

In particular, schooling requires the ability to focus attention narrowly. In a classroom, focusing attention on what the teacher says, and just what the teacher says, is essential. We're so used to scholastic learning that this kind of focused attention might seem like an obvious prerequisite for any kind of learning.

But in the Guatemalan villages that Barbara Rogoff studied, adults actually encourage children to divide their attention. If a child is paying attention to just one toy, his mother will place another toy in his other hand. Children in these cultures become adept at learning even when no one is actively teaching them; they are alert to anything around them that might be instructive or informative. Remember the origami experiment: indigenous children learned by just watching the teacher demonstrate the skill to another child, while Western children learned only when the teacher explicitly taught them.

During the transition from early to middle childhood, children naturally shift from a wider form of attention to a more narrow one. The same brain changes that move children away from pure discovery learning and toward mastery learning also change the way that children pay attention. As the executive prefrontal regions exert more and more control over other parts of the brain, attention and even consciousness itself narrows. Attention becomes like a bright spotlight, illuminating some parts of the world and leaving adjacent parts in darkness.

For younger children consciousness seems to be more like a lantern, illuminating everything at once. When we say that preschoolers are bad at paying attention, what we really mean is that they're bad at *not* paying attention—they have difficulty keeping themselves from being drawn to distractions.

In fact, recent studies show that young babies' attention is consistently drawn to precisely the events in their environment that they are most likely to learn from. In these studies, the researchers showed one-year-olds carefully calibrated videos of objects moving against a background. They calculated how much new information there was in a particular video and then recorded how long the babies looked at each image. One-year-olds paid the most attention to scenes that were within an informational "sweet spot"—complex enough to learn but not so dizzying as to be incomprehensible. In fact, the babies' attention and eye movements finely tracked how much information was in the scene.

But this kind of attention is very different from the kind of attention that comes when, in school, we must simply attend to a lesson, no matter how informative it actually is.

In fact, a fascinating recent set of studies has found parallels between the brain activity of people on psychedelic drugs such as psilocybin and the brain activity of very young children. Compared with typical brains, your brain on these drugs is less coordinated: the different brain areas are more independent, and the executive frontal areas exert much less control. It's as if the drugs somehow lead your brain to regress to a state that resembles the preschool brain.

Obviously, these drugs are not exactly a recipe for effective, well-coordinated, and goal-directed action. But when the drugs are taken in a controlled way, in a safe, caring, and protective environment, they do seem to allow a kind of flexibility, exploration, and learning that might not be available in more sober conditions, and these are just the strengths of young children.

The phenomenology, the very experience that results from taking these drugs, includes a wide-ranging attention that is very reminiscent of babies and young children. Habit makes much of the world invisible. Psychedelics and other forms of "expanded consciousness" make us sensitive to those parts of the world again. The ability to be entirely captivated by a branch, a dandelion, a crack in the pavement, or a piece of music is part of the distinctive texture of these experiences. It may also give us a hint about what the world feels like for Augie and Georgie.

There is a familiar trade-off here. Wide-ranging, preschool attention goes with wide-ranging and flexible learning, while the more focused and controlled attention of the school-age child enables swift, skilled execution.

Attention Deficit Disorder

School requires even more extreme forms of focused attention than ordinary adult life. Many children are able to develop that kind of attention as they get older. But many more continue to have difficulty focusing even well into the school-age years.

In particular, there is a close connection between the rise of schools and the development of attention deficit disorder. In the past two decades, the number of children who are diagnosed with attention deficit hyperactivity disorder has nearly doubled. One in five American boys receives a diagnosis by age seventeen.

More than 70 percent of those who are diagnosed—millions of children—get drugs.

Many people have suspected that there is a relationship between the ADHD explosion and the increasing emphasis on school performance. In the same two decades that saw a precipitous rise in diagnoses, more states began to evaluate schools and teachers based on test scores.

But how could you prove such a link? It could just be a coincidence that ADHD diagnoses and high-stakes testing have both increased so dramatically. Steve Hinshaw and Richard Scheffler used a kind of "natural experiment" to test this. Different parts of the country introduced new education policies at different times. The researchers looked at the relationship between when a state introduced new policies that included high-stakes testing and the rate of ADHD diagnoses. Immediately after the policies were introduced, the diagnoses increased dramatically. Moreover, the diagnoses rose particularly sharply for poor children in public schools.

When schools are under pressure to produce high test scores, they become motivated, consciously or unconsciously, to encourage ADHD diagnoses—either because the drugs allow low-performing children to score better or because ADHD diagnoses can be used to exclude children from testing. Notably, the researchers didn't see comparable increases in places where the law expressly prevented school personnel from recommending ADHD medication to parents.

These results have wide-reaching implications for how we think about ADHD. We think we know the difference between a disease and a social problem. Diseases such as smallpox, pneumonia, and kidney stones occur when a body breaks or is invaded by viruses or bacteria. You give the person the right medical treatment, and they're cured. Social problems such as poverty, illiteracy, and crime occur when institutions fail—when instead of helping people to thrive, they make them miserable.

Much of the debate over ADHD has focused on whether it is a biological disease or a social problem. But the research suggests that these categories are themselves misguided.

Rather than thinking of ADHD as a disease like smallpox we should think of it as a particular point on a continuum of attentional style. Some children have no trouble achieving even "unnatural" levels of highly focused attention; others find it practically impossible to focus attention at all; and most are in between.

That variation didn't matter much for hunters, foragers, or farmers—in fact, broader attention might actually be an advantage for hunters. But in our society, it matters terrifically. School is more and more essential for success, and highly focused attention is more and more essential for school. Stimulant drugs don't "cure" ADHD the way that antibiotics cure pneumonia. Instead, they appear to shift attentional abilities along that continuum. They make everybody focus better, though sometimes with serious costs in the form of addiction and side effects.

For children who are at the far end of the continuum, the drugs may help make the difference between success and failure. There is some evidence that the drugs do, in fact, make children do better at school at the time, and in a school-crazy world that may be important. But though the drugs do change some children's behavior in the short term, for many more children the drugs don't help and may do harm. There are behavioral therapies that are just as effective and far less dangerous. And there is almost no evidence that the drugs make a difference in the long term.

The fact that younger and younger children, including preschoolers, are not only being diagnosed with ADHD but are also receiving drugs is particularly disturbing. Narrowing attention may be part of growing up, but wide attention is part of being young. It's not something we need to fix.

One of the other disadvantages of the goal-directed view of parenting and schooling is that it treats childhood itself as little more than a way station toward adulthood. Drugging three-year-olds so that they will be more like an exaggerated form of focused adults is an especially dramatic expression of this attitude.

ADHD is both biological and social, and altering institutions could help children thrive. Instead of drugging children's brains to get them to fit our schools, we could change our schools to accommodate a wider range of children's brains.

Schooling and Learning

The ADHD problem is just the most dramatic example of a general challenge for schools. Schools should be places where children can genuinely exercise their continuing capacities for discovery. They should be places where children can master real-world skills. And they should be places where children can master scholastic skills such as reading, writing, and calculating. The problem is how to adapt children's prodigiously varied natural learning abilities to meet these different agendas.

But rather than respecting variability more, schools increasingly respect it less. Consider standardized testing. It's become a truism that assessment and accountability—extremely worthy goals—require standardized tests. A standardized test score is the apotheosis of the goal-directed, child-shaping, carpentry picture of schooling—the idea that schools should be designed to turn all children into creatures with particular characteristics.

When we do recognize variability, we do it through a medical model, as in ADHD. From a medical standpoint, there is a sub-set of children who suffer from learning disabilities, or dyslexia, or ADHD, and who therefore should be treated differently from "normal" children. Diagnosing those children becomes a cottage industry. Through these diagnoses we reduce variability to one group of normal children, and another of disabled or ill children. In fact, there are ranges and continua of abilities, and designing a way of recognizing and responding to that variability would help all children, diagnosed or not.

The curious thing is that assessment and accountability intrin-sically have very little to do with standardized test scores. Suppose we thought of schools as environments that were designed to make children thrive, in the same way that we might think of parenting as a way of designing a safe, stable, structured, rich en-vironment in which variation, innovation, and novelty can blos-som. In either case, this doesn't mean abnegating judgment and responsibility. Just as parents matter, schools can matter, too. And just as we can evaluate whether a caregiver cares, we can do the same thing for schools.

Assessing schools and teachers in this way would be entirely different from our typical assessments. We should be judging schools on how well they educate children in general, not how well each child does on a test. We could visit classrooms and score the quality of teaching and learning that goes on there, including, for example, whether the teacher responds differently to different kinds of students, rather than relying on a single test score.

The People in the Playground

Do you know what an Indian burn (or an Indian rub, or a Chinese sunburn) is? Complete the following phrase: "John and Mary sitting in a tree . . ." Why should you avoid stepping on cracks? Every year I ask the students in my Berkeley developmental psychology class these questions. And remarkably, year after year, these undergraduates, who come from every race and religion, and every corner of the United States, converge somewhat shamefacedly on the same answers: (a) an Indian burn is when you twist someone's arm until it turns red, (b) K-I-S-S-I-N-G, (c) you really don't want to break your mother's back.

Some of the most important kinds of middle childhood learning don't happen in the classroom at all—they happen at lunch and during recess, in the hall and riding the bus. The greatest and most challenging transition in the school-age period is the transition from a life that is centered on our caregivers to one that is instead centered on our peers—the friends and enemies, leaders and followers, and lovers and rivals who will dominate our lives as adults.

Ironically, the typical schooling agenda treats this kind of outside-the-classroom learning as a distraction or problem, even though from a developmental point of view it is more central than any other. I once had a conversation with a teacher who was lamenting the fact that the children in her middle school classrooms no longer seemed to show any of the curiosity and motivation for learning they had when they were younger. "Are they curious and motivated about finding out who likes who?" I asked. "Oh, of course," she said, "they spend all their time talking about that—it's a big problem."

A three-year-old's relationship with her parents is the white-hot center of her emotional life. Freud's theories have been pretty thoroughly discredited in modern developmental psychology, but the basic Freudian insight of the "family romance" is remarkably robust. The Oedipal dramas that come from the passionate attachments between children and mothers and fathers are still a startling part of every preschooler's life. From an evolutionary point of view this makes perfect sense, of course. The distinctive feature of preschool children's lives is their profound dependence. The relationship to their caregivers is, for them, literally a matter of life and death.

Yet somehow, in a few short years, human children must transform their intense family attachments into the very different relationships they have with their peers.

Our distinctively human knack for cooperation and coordination is one of our most important evolutionary features. Managing wide-ranging networks of friendships and alliances, divisions of labor, negotiations, compromises, and interests is among our most significant human challenges. When school-age children play with their friends, they are developing these abilities.

Preschoolers' play explores the possibilities of other people's minds, in their imaginary companions and endless pretense. School-age children instead focus on the ways that a social group can be organized. Kids move from solitary pretending to playing games with rules in groups.

We're used to the organized games such as baseball or soccer that dominate children's after-school lives. But the games that children organize themselves—all the many variants of four square and wall ball, hopscotch and jump rope—are more interesting and profound. And consider, too, all the kinds of fort building, tree house construction, and club formation. These games tap into the negotiation and cooperation that are integral to adult life. Deciding on rules for wall ball is a prelude to legislation; building a tree house is building a city in miniature.

Children's pretend games are transformed, too. While younger children use imaginary friends to explore psychological possibilities, school-age children explore cultural and social possibilities by creating "paracosms"—imaginary worlds complete with alliances and battles, leaders and rebels. And even children who don't directly create their own worlds avidly adapt the complex alternative societies created by others—from J.R.R. Tolkien's Middle-Earth to J. K. Rowling's Hogwarts.

The lore of childhood—Chinese sunburns and stepping on cracks and John and Mary—also plays a crucial part in establishing peer groups. The greatest investigators of the world of school-children weren't developmental psychologists but folklorists. Peter and Iona Opie were part of the great folklorist tradition of the early twentieth century, like the scholars who traveled to the Balkans to record native ballads or to Mississippi to record the blues. But the Opies found an equally exotic and unexplored country much closer to home—the country of the schoolyard and the playground. They set out to record the lore and language of schoolchildren.

The Opies' great discovery was that there was a schoolyard culture. School-age children created their own culture, and they used that culture to explore the social world in much the same way that younger children explored the psychological world.

The games, rhymes, routines, and mythologies the Opies recorded came from a remarkably wide range of sources. Fragments of seventeenth-century political satire were preserved from generation to generation in rhymes like "Little Jack Horner." The "Nazi submarine" of my mother's World War II skipping rhyme became the "nosy submarine" of my 1960s version. When my children were growing up they heard skipping-rope rhymes about AK-47s in tough sections of Berkeley.

The Opies' tracked the way that the schoolchildren themselves organized and transmitted this trove of lore, lore that often, like the K-I-S-S-I-N-G rhyme, was far too subversive to share with adults.

These practices of recess, an institution increasingly under pressure, may be far more significant and challenging for school-age children than classroom activities or the organized games and sports of after-school programs. The games, jokes, and stories are a way for each succeeding generation of children to create their own distinctive culture. In the great dance of tradition and innovation, learning about stepping on cracks and K-I-S-S-I-N-G may be far more important than anything that appears on an SAT.

But just like the infants exploring the physical world or the preschoolers exploring the psychological world, school-age children remain safely protected from the consequences of their actions. Although they can begin to genuinely contribute to the family economy, they still consume more than they produce. And however gravely eight-year-olds may prosecute snowball battles or build tree houses or create mythologies, nothing crucial hangs on those battles or projects or cultures.

At least for middle-class children, the parenting model has led to the notoriously overscheduled life of official school classes, followed by extracurriculars, followed by homework. Even children's social lives and explorations are heavily controlled and scheduled, all in the service of shaping children. Children continue to fit their own autonomous explorations into the cracks, but parents don't help. And for children who are not middle-class, the disappearance of the public spaces is even more damaging. Instead of having a safe, stable world to explore, and peer groups to experiment with, rich children live in a world of schooling and control, and poor children live in a world of chaos and neglect.

The Two Systems of Adolescence

School-age children are often models of gravity and sobriety. But there is a striking revival of plasticity, variability, and mess, both intellectual and emotional, when children reach adolescence. Indeed, some neuroscientists argue that adolescence sees a revival of the kind of neural flexibility and plasticity that is such a feature of preschool children. And adolescence, like early childhood, seems designed to be a period of innovation and change. The difference is that the agenda is no longer exploring the world in the safe context of a protected childhood. Instead, your job as an adolescent is to leave that protected context and actually make things happen yourself.

The profoundly paradoxical job of the parents of teenagers is to allow and even encourage that shift to happen. As a parent you spend years ferociously shielding your children from risk. But when they become teenagers you have to figure out how to turn them into independent people who can take risks themselves.

As with early childhood, adolescence makes the tensions inherent in the relations between parents and children particularly vivid. In other words, teenagers can drive you just as crazy as two-year-olds. What can science tell us about how teenagers think and act, and how we can deal with it?

"What was he thinking?" It's the familiar cry of bewildered parents trying to understand why their teenager acts the way he does. How does the boy who can thoughtfully explain the reasons never to drink and drive still end up in a drunken crash? Why does the girl who knows all about birth control find herself pregnant, and by a boy she doesn't even like? What happened to the gifted, imaginative child who excelled through high school but then dropped out of college, drifted from job to job, and now lives in his parents' basement?

The prevailing theoretical account of adolescence by neuroscientists is what is sometimes called a two-system theory. The crucial idea is that there are two distinct neural and psychological systems that interact to turn children into adults. The first of these systems has to do with emotion and motivation. It is very closely linked to the biological and chemical changes of puberty and involves the areas of the brain that respond to rewards. This is the system that turns generally placid ten-year-olds into restless, exuberant, emotionally intense teenagers desperate to attain every goal, fulfill every desire, and experience every sensation.

Later, after adolescence is over, this motivational system is turned down again and the restless teenagers turn into relatively placid adults. This system has a signature and somewhat sinister curve attached: as kids enter adolescence, accidents, crime, suicide, and drug-taking all go up dramatically, only to fall back to childhood levels when adolescence is over.

Studies by the neuroscientist B. J. Casey suggest that adolescents are reckless not because they underestimate risks but because they overestimate rewards—or, rather, find rewards more rewarding than adults do. The reward centers of the adolescent brain are much more active than those of either children or adults. Think about the incomparable intensity of first love, the never-to-be-recaptured glory of the high-school basketball championship.

What teenagers want most of all are social rewards, especially the respect of their peers. In one study teenagers performed a simulated high-risk driving task while lying in an fMRI brain-imaging machine. The reward system of their brains lit up much more when they thought another teenager was watching what they did—and they also took more risks.

From an evolutionary point of view, this all makes perfect sense. As we've seen, one of the most distinctive evolutionary features of human beings is our unusually long and protected childhood. But eventually we have to leave the safe bubble of family life, take what we learned as children, and apply it to the real adult world.

Becoming an adult means leaving the world of your parents and starting to make your way toward the future that you will share with your peers. Puberty not only turns on the motivational and emotional system with new force, it also turns it away from the family and toward the world of your peers.

The first system in the two-system model involves motivation. But the second system involves control; it channels and harnesses all that seething energy. In particular, the prefrontal cortex reaches out to guide other parts of the brain, including the parts that govern motivation and emotion. This is the system that inhibits impulses and guides decision-making, that encourages long-term planning and delays gratification. And this is the system, as we saw, that enables mastery.

This control system depends much more on learning. It becomes increasingly effective throughout middle childhood and continues to develop during adolescence and adulthood, as you gain more experience. You come to make better decisions by making not-so-good decisions and then correcting them. You get to be a good planner by making plans, implementing them, and seeing the results. Expertise comes with experience.

In the distant (and even the not-so-distant) past, these systems of motivation and control were largely in sync. In foraging and farming societies, children have lots of chances to practice the skills that they need to accomplish their goals as adults, and so to become expert planners and actors.

In the past, to become a good gatherer or hunter, cook or caregiver, you would actually practice gathering, hunting, cooking, and taking care of children, all through middle childhood and into early adolescence, tuning up just the prefrontal wiring you'd need as an adult. But you'd do all that under expert adult supervision, where the impact of your inevitable failures would be blunted. When the motivational juice of puberty arrived, you'd be ready to go after the real rewards with new intensity and exuberance, but you'd also have the skill and control to do it safely and effectively.

The relationship between the systems of motivation and control has changed dramatically. Today puberty arrives earlier, and the motivational system kicks in earlier, too. If you think of the teenage brain as a car, today's adolescents acquire an accelerator long before they can steer and brake.

The precise reason puberty is kicking in at an earlier and earlier age is still unknown. A leading theory points to changes in energy balance. Children eat more and move less—the same changes that are responsible for the obesity epidemic may be affecting the onset of puberty, too. Other candidates include artificial light—exacerbated by the contemporary trend toward screens at bedtime—and even hormonelike substances in the environment, particularly in sources such as plastic containers.

But other, social changes are also affecting adolescence. First with the industrial revolution and then even more dramatically with the information revolution, children have come to take on adult roles later and later. Five hundred years ago, Shakespeare knew that the emotionally intense combination of teenage sexuality and peer-induced risk could have tragic consequences— witness *Romeo and Juliet*. But, on the other hand, if not for fate, thirteen-year-old Juliet would have become a wife and mother within a year or two.

Our Juliets (as parents longing for grandchildren will recognize with a sigh) may experience the tumult of love for twenty years before they settle down into motherhood. And our Romeos may be poetic lunatics under the influence of Queen Mab until they are well into graduate school.

Contemporary children have very little experience with the kinds of tasks that they'll have to perform as grown-ups. They have increasingly fewer chances to practice basic skills like cooking and caregiving. Contemporary adolescents often don't do much of anything beyond going to school. Even the paper route and the babysitting job have largely disappeared. And the growth of the control system depends on just those sorts of experiences.

This doesn't mean that adolescents are stupider than they used to be; in many ways, they are much smarter. An ever-longer period of immaturity and dependence—a childhood that extends through college—means that young humans can learn more than ever before.

For example, there is strong evidence that IQ has increased dramatically as more children spend more time in school. IQ tests are "normed": your score reflects how you did compared with other people; it's graded on a curve. But the test designers have to keep "renorming" the tests by adding harder questions. That's because absolute performance on IQ tests, the actual number of questions people get right, has improved dramatically over the past hundred years. It's called the Flynn effect, after James Flynn, a social scientist at New Zealand's University of Otago who first noticed the phenomenon in the 1980s.

In fact, a recent study looked at scores from the 1900s, when the tests first emerged, to scores from the present day. People scored about three more points every decade, so the average score is thirty points higher than it was one hundred years ago.

The speed of the rise in scores also varied in an interesting way. The pace jumped in the 1920s and slowed down during World War II. The scores shot up again in the postwar boom, and then their growth slowed once more in the 1970s. They're still rising, but even more slowly. Adult scores climbed more than children's, which suggests that the effect involved something more than increases in nutrition and health.

The rise in IQ scores depends on a combination of factors, but clearly the rise of education and schooling has played a particularly important role. Dr. Flynn himself argues for a "social multiplier" theory. An initially small change can set off a feedback loop that leads to big effects. Slightly better education, health, income, or nutrition might make a child do better at school and appreciate learning more. That greater appreciation would motivate her to read more books and try to go to college, which would make her even smarter and more eager for education, and so on.

There is even evidence from neuroscience that higher IQ is correlated to longer frontal-lobe maturation. In studies that look at how children's brains change over time, researchers have found that children whose frontal lobes mature relatively late are likely to have higher IQs. So there may be an inverse relationship between high levels of control and wide-ranging learning.

Of course, there are different ways of being smart. IQ measures very general capacities, particularly those that are most important for doing well at school. But having a high IQ or specific kinds of knowledge, such as knowledge of physics and chemistry, is no help when making a soufflé. Wide-ranging, flexible, and broad learning, the kind we encourage in high school and college, may actually be in tension with the ability to develop finely honed, controlled, and focused expertise in a particular skill—the kind of learning that once routinely took place in human societies. For most of our history, children have started their internships at age seven, not twenty-seven.

The old have always complained about the young, of course. But this new explanation of the shift in developmental timing and its consequences elegantly accounts for the paradoxes of our particular crop of adolescents. There do seem to be many young adults who are enormously smart and knowledgeable but directionless, who are enthusiastic and exuberant, but unable to commit to a particular kind of work or a particular love until well into their twenties or thirties.

The new work on adolescence also illustrates two deeply important—and often overlooked—facts about the mind and brain. First, experience shapes the brain. People often think that if some capacity is located in a particular part of the brain, then it must be "hardwired." But in fact, the brain is so powerful precisely because it is so sensitive to experience. It's as true to say that our experience of controlling our impulses makes the prefrontal cortex develop as it is to say that prefrontal development makes us better at controlling our impulses. Our social and cultural life shapes our biology, and vice versa.

Second, development plays a crucial role in explaining human nature. The old "evolutionary psychology" picture was that genes were directly responsible for some particular pattern of adult behavior—a "module." However, there is more and more evidence that genes are just the first step in complex developmental sequences, cascades of interactions between organism and environment that in turn shape the adult brain. Even small changes in developmental timing can lead to big changes in who we become.

Fortunately, these characteristics of the brain mean that dealing with modern adolescence is not as hopeless as it might sound. Though we aren't likely to return to an agricultural life, or to stop sending our children to school, the very flexibility of the developing brain points to solutions.

The results of brain research are often taken to mean that adolescents are really just defective adults—grown-ups with a missing part. Public policy debates about teenagers often turn on the question of when, exactly, certain areas of the brain develop, and so at what age children should be allowed to drive or marry or vote—or be held fully responsible for crimes. But the new view of the adolescent brain isn't that the prefrontal lobes just fail to show up; it's that the brain isn't properly instructed and exercised through a period of mastery and apprenticeship.

Simply increasing the driving age by a year or two doesn't have much influence on the accident rate, for example. What does make a difference is having a graduated system in which teenagers slowly acquire both more skill and more freedom—a driving apprenticeship.

Instead of giving adolescents more and more school experiences—those extra hours of after-school classes and homework—we could try to arrange more opportunities for apprenticeship. AmeriCorps, the federal community-service program for youth, is an excellent example, since it provides both challenging real-life experiences and a degree of protection and supervision.

"Take your child to work" could become a routine practice rather than a single-day annual event, and college students could spend more time watching and helping scientists and scholars at work rather than just listening to their lectures. Summer enrichment activities like camp and travel, so common for children whose parents have the means, might be usefully alternated with summer jobs.

Some of the tensions in contemporary adolescence may just be inescapable. Isaiah Berlin talked about the fact that some value conflicts just can't be resolved. It may be impossible to have, at the same time, an extended period of immaturity that allows for wide-ranging learning as well as mature mastery of particular skills. We may have to settle, as we so often do as caregivers, for the usual muddles and compromises.

But a better overall vision of what we can or should accomplish might help. Just as we can try to provide a safe, stable environment for preschoolers, we can try to do the same thing at a more abstract, social level for adolescents. We can't, and shouldn't, stop adolescents from engaging in their intense and hectic experiments with adult life. But just as we can cover the plugs and gate the staircases for three-year-olds, we can adopt policies, from making condoms more available to making guns less so, that can at least make adolescent experimentation less perilous.

8. The Future and the Past: Children and Technology

They gave her the Device when she was only two years old. It had a sophisticated graphical interface, sending signals along the optic nerve that swiftly transported her brain to an alternate universe—a captivating other world. By the time she was seven, she would smuggle it into school and engage it secretly under her desk instead of listening to the teachers. By fifteen, visions from the Device—a girl entering a ballroom, a man dying on a battlefield—seemed more real than her actual adolescent life. She would sit motionless with it for hours on end, oblivious to everything around her. Its addictive grip was so great that she often stayed up half the night, unable to put it down.

When she grew up, the Device dominated her house; no room was free from it. No activity, not even eating or going to the bathroom, was carried on without its aid. Even when she made love, it was images from the Device that filled her mind. When one of her children had to go to the hospital with a concussion, her first thought was to be sure she took the Device along. Saddest of all, as soon as her children were old enough, she did everything she could to get them hooked on it, too.

Psychologists showed that she literally could not disengage from it—if the Device could reach the optic nerve, she would automatically and inescapably be in its grip. Neuroscientists demonstrated that large portions of her brain, parts that had once been devoted to understanding the real world, had been co-opted by the Device.

A tale of the dystopian technological future? No, just autobiography. The Device is, of course, the book, and I've been its willing victim all my life.

The parable of the Device addresses one of the most common recent concerns of parents. What will the new technologies of the computer and the Internet—iPhones and Google Glass, Twitter and texting and Facebook and Instagram—do to the minds of our children? And what should parents do about it?

A minor industry has developed that claims to provide answers to this question, answers that range from the apocalyptic to the utopian. The apocalyptic version inevitably has the edge (bad news is always most captivating). The simple and true scientific answer, of course, is that we simply don't know, and we won't and can't for at least another generation.

But there is a deeper question that underlies this one. What is the relationship between children and technology in general, not just the relationship between our particular children and our particular technologies?

A long tradition going back to the Romantic period envisions children as creatures who are close to a state of nature, an original innocence. This contrasts with the adult pursuit of the artificial and constructed, in the form of new technology and tools. But the evolutionary picture I've described suggests a very different view.

The two most common explanations for the evolution of human cognition are that we got much better at manipulating physical tools and that we got much better at manipulating our fellow human beings. Both these abilities involve a kind of technology, either physical or social. Our large brain and long childhood, and the distinctive learning abilities that go with them, are designed to contribute to the invention and mastery of both these kinds of technology.

Human beings are designed not only to invent new technologies, but to transmit them across generations. More than any other animal, we humans constantly reshape our environment. And our brains are rewired and shaped by experience, especially early experience. Each new generation of human children grows up in the new environment its parents have created. Each generation of brains has different early experiences and becomes wired in a unique way, which allows those new brains to reshape the environment yet again. Our minds can change radically in just a few generations.

The result is what psychologists call the cultural ratchet effect. Childhood contributes to two distinctively human complementary abilities. We can learn from the previous generation. Through observation, imitation, and testimony children can swiftly take on and re-create the skills and technologies of those who came before us. Imitating technologies is much quicker and easier than inventing them.

But if we just imitated our elders exactly, there would be no progress at all. So each generation also adds to the knowledge and expertise of the previous ones. The ratchet comes because we can take the previous generation's discoveries for granted as we pursue our own.

The ratchet also reflects the fact that we learn differently as children than we do as adults. For grown-ups, learning a new skill is painful and slow, and demands focused attention. Children, as we've seen, learn unconsciously and effortlessly. Because of this, each new generation rapidly acquires all the accumulated innovations of the past, often without even knowing it—the story of the Device is startling to my generation because we were born with print. The new generation, in turn, will consciously alter those earlier practices and invent new ones. They can take the entire past for granted as they move toward the future.

These generational shifts are the engine of cultural innovation, and they are particularly important for technological change. But generational shifts go beyond technology. They also produce entirely arbitrary changes, like the historical changes from Elizabethan language or dance or dress to the language and culture of our own time. Even in the Neolithic period, pottery decorations changed over generations. Generational change can happen at different rates in different times and places. It surely seems especially swift now, but it's a universal and pervasive feature of human development.

The fact that children learn so quickly and unconsciously, and take on cultural information so effectively, itself enables innovations to be carried on to the next generation. But some evidence also suggests that children, and especially adolescents, are often at the leading edge of technological and cultural change.

Systematic studies, as well as common observation, show that children drive linguistic change. Immigrant children quickly and effortlessly learn the language of their adopted country that their elders may never master at all. In fact, immigrant children often act as both linguistic and cultural interpreters for their parents. When people from many different language backgrounds are thrown together, they may invent very simplified pidgin languages. But the next generation of children transforms these simple communication systems into fully fledged creoles—new languages with all the complexity of natural ones. New words, grammatical rules, and even sounds often show up first in teenagers.

For example, "uptalk," the tendency to use rising intonation at the end of statements as well as questions, was once a feature of a small group of California "Valley Girl" teenagers. Uptalk first made it into the popular culture through Frank Zappa's "Valley Girl," recorded with his then fourteen-year-old daughter, more than thirty years ago. It is now pervasive in the American English of people under thirty.

People of my generation may wince when they hear those rising intonations. But in fact, contrary to popular mythology, uptalk has become a marker of status and power for this generation, rather than insecurity or uncertainty. Academic supervisors are more likely to use it with their supervisees, and bosses with their employees, than vice versa.

Young people and especially adolescents are also often at the leading edge of changes in popular culture. In the early nineteenth century, teenagers adopted a sexy, scandalous, and transgressive dance called the waltz and became obsessed with an equally sexy and scandalous new form of entertainment called the novel. In the twentieth century it was rock 'n' roll and punk and hip-hop, miniskirts and tattoos and tracksuits. (It's surely rather unfair that my baby boomer generation co-opted many of the easy forms of cultural rebellion, like long hair and guitars, and left our children with uncomfortable options like tattoos and piercing.)

Cultural innovation and transmission is relatively rare in other animals compared with human beings. But there is some evidence that when these innovations do take place, they are also invented and transmitted by the young. In one of the most famous cases of animal culture, macaque monkeys in Japan learned to dip sweet potatoes in the ocean, which both washed off grit and gave them a nicely salty taste. Scientists were there to catch the cultural change in action. The first inventor was a prepubescent female, and the practice spread first among other children—monkey early adopters—and then to the other females. (Apparently the powerful old males never got it.)

Of course, many technological and cultural innovations rely on high levels of skill, and are designed by adults. But even in these cases, the childlike predilection for novelty may change the way these innovations are adopted by the next generation. One of the paradoxes of cultural transmission is that adults tend to adopt the behaviors that we see most of our fellow adults perform— we're natural conformists. But, by definition, many innovations are going to start out as something only a few people do. The fact that younger people, particularly adolescents, are more likely to adopt a wider variety of unusual behaviors can ensure that the more eccentric inventions get preserved and passed on.

So childhood isn't really a period of innocence when children are protected from technological and cultural change—instead, childhood is the very crucible of such change. It is both the period when innovation becomes internalized and, especially in adolescence, the period in which innovation is often actually sparked.

The Reading Brain

We tend to think of the innovations of our own generation as "technology," while the innovations of past generations are just stuff. But the printed books and carpentered wooden tables in my study are just as much technologies as the computer and smartphone are—they're just a bit older.

One way we might try to predict the impact of new technologies is by considering the technologies we've already adopted and used for generations. At this very moment, all you're doing is moving your eyes over a white page dotted with black marks, and yet you feel that you are simply lost in this book. That transformation from arbitrary marks to vivid experience is one of the great mysteries of the human mind and brain. It's especially mysterious because reading is such a recent invention. Our brains didn't evolve to read.

Every time you complete a word-recognition security test on a website, you are paying unconscious homage to the sophistication and subtlety of the reading brain. The most advanced spambots can't even recognize letters as well as we can, let alone understand the significance of a book made of thousands of those letters.

Cognitive science has shown that the simplest experiences— talking, seeing, remembering—are the result of fiendishly complex computations in the brain. Transforming a series of arbitrary written symbols into ideas requires an equally clever brain. But while talking, seeing, and remembering are the result of hundreds of thousands of years of evolutionary change, the equally complex computations that are involved in reading are only a few thousand years old.

How is this possible? In order to read we reuse parts of the brain that were originally designed for other purposes. But we also reshape and create new brain areas that are dedicated to reading alone.

The shapes we use to make written letters mirror the shapes that primates use to recognize objects. After all, I could use any arbitrary squiggle to encode the sound at the start of "Tree" instead of "T." And it might seem that a Chinese scroll and this printed book have little in common. But actually the shapes of written symbols are strikingly similar across many languages; we all use combinations of crisscrossing vertical and horizontal lines, with the occasional dot or circle or half-circle added in.

It turns out that "T" shapes are important to monkeys, too. When an animal sees a "T" shape in the world, that shape is very likely to indicate the edge of an object—something the monkey can grab and maybe even eat. A particular area of the monkey's brain pays special attention to those significant shapes, those combinations of vertical and horizontal lines. There are even particular neurons that detect whether a line is vertical or horizontal.

Human brains use the same visual brain area to process letters. The brain has an innate propensity to organize the world in terms of intersecting lines and edges. We have designed our alphabets to exploit this fact.

On the other hand, the primate brain has also evolved to treat symmetrical shapes, such as the letters "p" and "q," or "b" and "d," as if they were the same. Although the monkey brain responds differently to a vertical or diagonal or horizontal line, it usually responds the same way whether the line is oriented to the right or the left. After all, in the real world we are always moving around; I will see a cup handle on the left of the cup from one perspective and the same handle on the right from another.

This explains why children and people with dyslexia have so much trouble distinguishing these symmetrical letters. It also explains our extraordinary and puzzling ability to "mirror-read" and "mirror-write." Many children spontaneously reverse not just single letters but whole paragraphs of text.

But if reading is so tightly constrained by innate brain structure, we'd expect that writers would simply never use letters such as "b" and "d." Instead, the reading brain has developed a new ability to discriminate these symmetries, even at the neural level.

A developing brain that is exposed to symmetrical letters with different meanings will rewire and overcome its natural symmetry blindness.

We rewire the brain when we learn to read. And reading hundreds of thousands of words, over many years, makes those rewired connections especially strong. Reading becomes effortless. In fact, when we learn to read at a relatively early age, reading literally becomes automatic and involuntary.

One of the best examples of this is what psychologists call the Stroop effect. Suppose I show you the word "blue" printed in red, and ask you what color it is. It will take you much longer to answer than when the word is printed in blue, and you are likely to say it is blue instead of red. This process is completely automatic. No amount of effort will let you ignore the meaning of the word and pay attention only to its color.

Damage to the parts of our brain that have become wired for reading leads to specific and characteristic reading problems. Patients who have a stroke or an accident that damages certain brain areas specifically lose the ability to read or write, even though they can still talk and see perfectly well. They can see a written text but they can't make out what it means. This also suggests that specific areas of our brains have become particularly adapted for reading.

Reading has become deeply integrated into our lives and our brains. In fact, if we didn't know the history, we could easily conclude that the reading brain is the result of hundreds of thousands of years of evolution instead of a few thousand years of culture.

If you looked at reading as if it were a new technology instead of an old one, you might be full of dread about its effects on the human mind. Cortical areas that once were devoted to vision and speech have been hijacked by print. Instead of learning through practice and apprenticeship, we've become dependent on lectures and textbooks. And look at the toll of dyslexia, attention disorders, and other learning disabilities, all signs that our brains were just not designed to deal with such a profoundly unnatural technology.

Imagine that I had learned to read at age forty instead of age four. Walking down a busy street would involve constant distractions. I'd be pulling away from the present at every moment. I would have to stop to look at those strange marks on the signs, try to recall what each one meant, decode them, and then force my attention back to the street. Driving down a highway full of billboards would be insanely dangerous.

In fact, in the past very smart people reacted to the new technology of reading in exactly this way. Socrates thought writing was a terrible idea.

In Plato's *Phaedrus*, in phrases that could come from any antitechnology *Times* op-ed, Socrates says:

> If men learn this, it will implant forgetfulness in their souls; they will cease to exercise memory because they rely on that which is written, calling things to remembrance no longer from within themselves, but by means of external marks. What you have discovered is a recipe not for memory, but for reminder. And it is no true wisdom that you offer your disciples, but only its semblance, for by telling them of many things without teaching them you will make them seem to know much, while for the most part they know nothing, and as men filled, not with wisdom but with the conceit of wisdom, they will be a burden to their fellows.

Socrates feared that reading and writing would undermine the kind of interactive, critical dialogue that was so important for reflective thought. You couldn't talk back to a written text or ask it questions, and you were far too likely to think that something was true just because it was written down.

Socrates also thought that writing would undermine the capacity for memory. In the ancient world, poets had developed an amazing ability to memorize thousands of lines of verse. Homer's epics were orally transmitted from bard to bard through memory alone. But if you had a written copy of Homer's *Iliad*, why would you go through all the trouble of memorizing it? Those impressive and hard-won memory skills would disappear.

And, of course, Socrates was completely right. Reading is different from talking; we do tend to accept things just because they're written down; and no one now knows the *Iliad* by heart. Indeed, reading reshaped many broader aspects of our culture and thought. The rise of literacy was connected to the emergence of the modern concepts of individualism and privacy, as well as the birth of Protestantism. On balance, though, most of us (or at least most of us readers) would agree that the benefits outweighed the drawbacks.

Another aspect of the literacy revolution may also be encouraging for us old readers. The much more ancient media of speech and song and theater were radically reshaped by reading and writing, but they were not supplanted. We may not memorize Homer now, but we continue to read his poems. In fact, it's hard to think of a human medium that has disappeared entirely. At least some people sing and dance, speak verse out loud in small groups at poetry slams, and cook and carpenter with as much skill and ardor as in the past. Novels didn't replace plays, and movies, those once-dreaded cultural interlopers, now strike us as a great art form about to be displaced by lesser ones.

The World of Screens

We are now immersed in another dramatic technological change. At this very moment, you may well be moving your eyes across a screen rather than a page. And you may be simultaneously clicking a hyperlink to YouTube, messaging with your friends, Skyping with your sweetheart, and checking your Twitter feed and Facebook page (or whatever new technology will take over by the time you are reading this old-fashioned book).

We are seeing a new generation of plastic baby brains reshaped by the new digital environment. Boomer hippies like my husband, cofounder of Pixar, listened to Pink Floyd as they struggled to create interactive computer graphics. Their pierced, rapping Generation Y children grew up with those graphics as second nature; this digital world was as much a part of their adolescent experience as spoken language or print. Augie's generation will take on those digital skills at an even younger age. Augie learned how to find Thomas the Tank Engine on a smartphone before he knew what the printed words "Thomas" or "Engine" meant.

There is every reason to think that these young brains will be different from our own, just as there are striking differences between the reading brain and the illiterate one. But exactly what those differences will be, how much impact they will have, and whether they will be for good or ill is another question.

The story of the Device illustrates why it's so hard to know how these new technologies will actually affect future generations. Some technologies really have reshaped our lives, minds, and societies. Almost always before the technology emerges people view it with exaggerated anxiety or anticipation, and after it's become widely accepted they barely notice it and take it for granted.

Books did change everything. But so did the telegraph—a

technology we've almost forgotten. Information had always traveled at the speed of a fast horse; suddenly it traveled at the speed of electricity, going from ten miles an hour to millions. And it was greeted with familiar dread. *The New York Times* in 1858 declared that the telegraph was "superficial, sudden, unsifted, too fast for the truth and . . . there is no rational doubt that it has caused huge injury." The train was an even more radical game changer. Until the nineteenth century no human on earth could move much faster than around twenty miles an hour. The train and the telegraph really did transform human life in a way that no recent technology can match. And yet we hardly think of telegrams and trains as technology at all.

Technological changes can lead to important cultural changes, but they do so in a way that is equally unpredictable. At the turn of the twentieth century there was extensive discussion about when and how a new, distinctively American cultural form would emerge—with much talk about the Great American Novel and the Great American Symphony. No one could have guessed that one great American art form, the movies, would actually come from Jewish immigrant businessmen and ex-vaudevilleans making popular entertainment in the wilds of Southern California with a new technology that was only a few years old.

Eden and *Mad Max*

One reason we adults tend to misjudge the impact of technological change is because the experience of change is so different for adults and children. Like many others, I feel that the Internet has made my experience more fragmented, splintered, and discontinuous. But that may well not be because of the Internet itself but because I entered the world of digital technology as an adult.

All of us learned to read with the open and flexible brains of children. No one living now will experience the digital world in the spontaneous and unself-conscious way that the children born in 2017 will experience it. They will be digital natives; we speak Digital with the painful, halting accent of a recent immigrant.

My experience of the Web feels fragmented, discontinuous, and effortful because for adults, learning a new technology depends on conscious, attentive, intentional processing. In adults, this kind of attention is a very limited resource.

This is true even at the neural level. When we pay attention to something, the prefrontal cortex—the part of our brain that is responsible for conscious, goal-directed planning—controls the release of cholinergic transmitters, those chemicals that help us learn, which travel only to certain very specific parts of the brain. The prefrontal cortex also releases inhibitory transmitters that actually keep other parts of the brain from changing. So as we wrestle with a new technology, we adults can only change our minds a little bit at a time.

Attention and learning work very differently in young brains. Young animals have much more widespread cholinergic transmitters than adults, and their ability to learn doesn't depend on planned, deliberate attention. Young brains are designed to learn from everything new, surprising, or information-rich even when it isn't particularly relevant or useful.

So children who grow up with the digital world will master it in a way that will feel as whole and natural as reading feels to us. But that doesn't mean that their experiences and brains won't be shaped by the Internet, any more than my print-soaked twentieth-century life was the same as the life of a barely literate nineteenth-century farmer.

The trouble is that the present generational transformation, the click of the ratchet, is so vivid that the long historical changes and constancies are hard to see. Inevitably, the year before you were born looks like Eden, and the year after your children were born looks like *Mad Max*.

The Technological Ratchet

Which of the effects that people, especially the digital pessimists, attribute to current technology really are radical transformations, and which are relatively small changes magnified by the ratchet effect?

The digital pessimists sometimes seem to treat minor variations in human nature like apocalyptic psychological revolutions. We won't really know the long-term effects a given technology has on our two-year-olds for many years. But we do know something about the immediate effects of smartphones and social media on teenagers. Is the teenager who comes home from school and texts her friends while she updates her Instagram page really much worse off than the one who came home and watched *Gilligan's Island* reruns? (More autobiography there.)

The media scholar Danah Boyd spent thousands of hours with teenagers from many different backgrounds, systematically observing the way they use technology and talking to them about what technology meant to them. Her conclusion is that young people use social media to do what they have always done: establish a community of friends and peers, distance themselves from their parents, flirt and gossip, bully, experiment, rebel.

In fact, contemporary teenagers may use social media to escape the pressure of their immediate families precisely because the direct route of escaping—just leaving the house by sliding down the drainpipe, climbing out the open window, or even just walking through the front door—is much less available. Much more dispersed neighborhoods and fewer means of transportation can make it literally impossible for many adolescents to leave the house by themselves. Where can you go in Los Angeles without a car? The physical spaces of lover's lane or the village square or the wilderness by the river have been replaced by the virtual spaces of the Web.

At the same time, Boyd argues that Internet technology does make a difference, just as the book, the printing press, and the telegraph did. An ugly taunt that once dissolved in the fetid locker-room air can now travel across the world in a moment, and then linger on servers forevermore. Teenagers must learn to reckon with and navigate these new aspects of our current technologies, and for the most part that's just what they do.

Madeleine George and Candace Odgers found similar results in a recent review of many scientific studies. They found that American teenagers are pervasively immersed in the digital world—they send an average of sixty texts a day, and 78 percent of them own a mobile phone that they regularly use to access the Web. But their experience in the mobile world parallels rather than supplants their experience in the physical world. Children who are popular in school are popular on the Web—the bullied and the bullies are the same in either space. Teenagers are still over-whelmingly more likely to be abused or threatened by close family members than by strangers on the Internet.

In fact, George and Odgers catalogued parents' most pervasive fears about the Internet and found little evidence to support any of them. The one genuine technological problem that did emerge was not one that most parents had even thought of, and it affects adults as much as children: the disruptive effect that LED screens have on sleep.

Although we don't know for sure, the picture that Boyd and George and Odgers paint, with far more continuity than change, is likely to apply to other digital worries as well. Some of the pessimists worry that people might interact with nonhuman simulacra—robots, for example—as if they were people, and might lose themselves in imaginary virtual worlds. But, after all, most young children communicate extensively with imaginary companions, creatures who are even more elusive than robots, since they don't exist at all. All normal children become immersed in unreal, pretend worlds. And their elders do the same. Is the child who cries over a Furby robot really all that different from the Dickensian one who weeps for a doll? Is the lonely widow who talks to a chatbot really all that different from the one who talks to her dead husband's picture? Is a romance in a virtual world all that different from a Harlequin one?

And what about the fact that we increasingly communicate through highly abstract signals, rather than face-to-face? Take texting, surely the most baffling technological success of our age; many teenagers send hundreds of texts a day. We've harnessed vast computational power to write telegrams with our thumbs. It is tempting to contrast texting nostalgically not only with live conversation but with that day-before-yesterday Eden of the telephone, a technology that once seemed equally threatening to many.

But at least since writing began, arguably even since language itself began, human beings have conducted their most intimate lives through abstract symbols. Bertrand Russell and Lady Ottoline Morrell carried on their love affair through the London post, writing several times a day, and Proust used the equally rapid and frequent pneumatic *petits bleus* of Paris. London letters were delivered twelve times a day, and a *petit bleu* arrived two hours after it was sent. The Henry James story "The Great Good Place" is a utopian fantasy about unhooking from the grid, and begins with a bitter lament at the inundation of telegrams and the overflow of obligations that will be familiar to anyone with a bulging e-mail in-box.

Another worry is that the Internet will somehow destroy our ability to pay attention. It is certainly true that by the time we're adults, attention is a limited resource, and attentional patterns are hard to change. As a result, it may be difficult for someone who has grown up with the attentional strategies that are appropriate for reading to ignore all the distractions of the Web. But as we've seen, the exaggerated, highly focused attention required by the contemporary classroom is itself a recent cultural invention, and one with costs as well as benefits.

The special attentional strategies that we require for literacy and schooling may feel natural since they are so pervasive, and since we learned them at such an early age. But at different times and places, different ways of deploying attention have been equally valuable and felt equally natural. I'll never be able to deploy the broad yet vigilant attention of a forager or hunter, though, luckily, a childhood full of practice caregiving let me master the equally ancient art of attending to work and babies at the same time.

Perhaps our digital grandchildren will view a master reader with the same nostalgic awe that we now accord to a master hunter or an even more masterly mother of six. The skills of the hyper-literate twentieth century may well disappear or at least become highly specialized enthusiasms, the way the skills of hunting, poetry, and dance are today. But if human history continues the course it has followed so far, other skills will take their place, and the earlier ones won't completely disappear.

The City of the Web

The digital pessimists may be onto something in one respect, however. Boyd's work with teenagers points to shifts that may signal genuinely important changes. It is difficult to be sure, but there is something about the Internet that seems truly different—a telegraph-like transformation. But it isn't the result of changes in the speed or character of communications. Texts and e-mails travel no faster than phone calls and telegrams, and their content isn't necessarily richer or poorer.

It does seem, though, that there is a transformative difference in how many people we interact with. There is good evidence that most of us can keep track of only about a hundred other people— a village's worth. The rise of cities led us to define that village socially instead of geographically; city dwellers learn not to acknowledge, or even see, most of the people they pass on the street, a skill that seems baffling and obnoxious to rural visitors. The post and the *petit bleu* connected a relatively small urban literary circle.

The Web expands that circle exponentially. When we do a Google search, we aren't consulting a brilliant computer but aggregating information acquired by millions of people. Facebook, which began as a way of digitally defining your social network, rapidly increases it beyond recognition. On the Web we communicate with the planet, but rely on a psychology designed for the village.

Urban children learn the skills that let you navigate a city, but we haven't yet developed similar skills for navigating the Web. Figuring out who we should talk with seems to be much harder. We can edit out the obnoxious guy on the street or ignore a ranting stranger more easily than we can filter out the anonymous inflammatory comment. On the Web, we all become small-town visitors lost in the big city, or at least so it seems now.

Still, city dwellers never entirely succeeded in turning Manhattan into Peoria, and they didn't really want to. The contradictory emotions the digital pessimists describe are the characteristic emotions of the urban world—excitement, novelty, and possibility balanced against loneliness, distraction, and alienation. Long before even the printed book, both Horace and Lady Murasaki reacted to city life by yearning for simplicity, mindfulness, and meaning. A digital version of the classical Greek pastoral retreat or the Buddhist monastery would probably do us all some good. Some very wired friends of mine have a digital Sabbath, where all the screens are turned off one day a week. But the villa and the monastery would be much less appealing if we didn't have the big city and the web of the wide world to return to.

What to Do?

These questions about technology exemplify the fundamental tensions between tradition and innovation, and dependence and independence, that are among the central paradoxes of being a parent. The puzzle is how to provide children with the rich, stable, secure context they need to grow up without expecting that we can or should be able to control how they turn out.

It may sound as if I'm recommending that grown-ups simply go with the flow, recognize the inevitability of technological and cultural change over generations, and leave their kids alone with the smartphone. But remember that the ratchet mechanism depends on both sides of the generational divide. Innovation depends on tradition. The shift to new technologies and cultures wouldn't be possible if caregivers didn't pass on their own discoveries, traditions, skills, and values to their children, even if they can't and shouldn't expect that children will simply replicate those traditions.

As caregivers, we give children a structured, stable environment, and that's exactly what allows them to be variable, random, unpredictable, and messy. We give them a world to re-create. In much the same way, it's precisely because we work so hard to pass on our traditions and skills, cultural institutions and values, that our children are able to transform them into institutions and values fit for their own time.

Because my children know how much I value books, they can go on to value screens—and I can hope, with some justification, that books will continue to be part of their lives, too. Augie knows that *Where the Wild Things Are* and *The Wizard of Oz* are the cultural touchstones of his grandmother, even if his own generation's touchstones are *Planes 2* or some as yet unidentifiable digital activity. The Yiddish traditions of my grandfather echo in my mind and the minds of my siblings in the same way, if only as a large body of terrible jokes and a taste for cream cheese and lox.

Part of the point of parents and especially grandparents is to provide a sense of cultural history and continuity. Our children's lives would be poorer without that sense of a connection to the past. To be a parent, as opposed to parenting, is to be a bridge between the past and the future.

What I can't do, and shouldn't do, is expect that my children and their children will exactly replicate my values, traditions, and culture. For good or ill, the digital generation will be their own generation and make their own world, and they, not us, will have the responsibility of figuring out how to live in it.

Of course, it is sad that after the intimacy of infancy our children inevitably end up being somewhat weird and incomprehensible visitors from the technological future. That tragedy comes with the territory. But at least one hopeful thought is that the science suggests that my grandchildren will not have the fragmented, distracted, and alienated digital experience that I have. For them the Internet will feel as fundamental, as rooted, and as timeless as a battered Penguin paperback, that apex of the literate civilization of the last century, feels to me.

9. The Value of Children

I've argued for a different picture of the relations between parents and children than the typical parenting picture. Caring for children is an absolutely fundamental, profoundly valuable part of the human project. But it isn't carpentry, it isn't a goal-directed enterprise aimed at shaping a child into a particular kind of adult. Instead, being a parent is like making a garden. It's about providing a rich, stable, safe environment that allows many different kinds of flowers to bloom. It's about producing a robust, flexible ecosystem that lets children themselves create many varied, unpredictable kinds of adult futures. It is also about a specific human relationship, a committed, unconditional love, between a specific parent and a specific child.

The parenting picture suggests that you can measure the value of caring for children by measuring the value of the adults those children become. But rather than trying to reduce the value of caring for children to other values, we should simply appreciate that the relations between parents and children are unique.

Those relations are, as philosophers say, intrinsically and not just instrumentally valuable. Caring for children is a good thing in itself, not just because it may lead to other good things in the future.

Thinking deeply about the value and morality of caring for children makes you think differently about value and morality in general. Classical philosophical approaches to morality don't apply very well to parents and children. One important approach is John Stuart Mill's utilitarianism. Utilitarians think that we should make decisions by calculating what will lead to "the greatest good for the greatest number." Another philosophical theory, Kant's "deontology," claims that there are absolute and universal moral principles all of us should follow.

But neither of these approaches captures the particular morality of caring for children. The philosopher Peter Singer is one of the leading contemporary utilitarians, and he argues, logically if controversially, that a consistent utilitarian should conclude that caring for severely disabled children, even keeping such children alive, is wrong. Any happiness such a child could experience would be outweighed by the unhappiness of the people who have to care for him. But that seems crazy to most of us.

You needn't go to this extreme length to see that utilitarian thinking doesn't naturally apply to decisions about children. Think only of the difficult decision many of us make about whether to send our children to public schools or private ones. Sending them to public schools is arguably better for everyone, but sending them to private ones is arguably better for them. The utilitarian principle of the greatest good for the greatest number should make you choose public schools. But a genuinely moral impulse to do the best for your children might lead you to private ones instead.

The Kantian picture doesn't really apply, either. Caring for children is a profound good, but it isn't and shouldn't be a universal imperative. People can care deeply for their own children but be relatively indifferent to children in general. And, of course, many people, by choice or circumstance, don't take care of children at all.

Both these ways of thinking about children run up against the paradoxes of love—the tension between the specific and the universal and between dependence and independence. Our very specific and particular love for our children is hard to capture in terms of general ethical principles like utilitarianism and Kantianism. And the classical accounts assume that moral agents are independent and autonomous decision-making creatures trying to find a way to live with one another. But the morality of being a parent is about taking a creature who isn't autonomous and can't make his own decisions, and turning him into one who can.

Another philosophical approach to morality may work better. The philosopher Isaiah Berlin argued for "value pluralism," contra both Mill and Kant. We have a multiplicity of diverse ethical values and those values are often simply incompatible. There is no way to measure or weigh them against one another, no single value that trumps the others. Justice or mercy, altruism or autonomy, what Yeats called "perfection of the life or of the work"—these values can't simply be weighed in some single objective scale. They can't be measured against each other in a way that reveals the single best thing to do. And yet often, in real life, we have to choose between them.

Berlin thought this made human life inescapably tragic, and he was right. But it is also what makes it rich and deep. Caring for children fits Berlin's picture better than Mill's or Kant's.

Even deciding to have a child in the first place is not a decision that can be made by rationally balancing the value of caring for children against other values. The philosopher L. A. Paul has argued recently that there is no rational way to decide to have children—or not to have them.

How do we make a rational decision? The classic answer is that we imagine the outcomes of different courses of action. Then we consider both the value and the probability of each outcome. Finally, we choose the option with the highest "utilities," as the economists say. Does the glow of a baby's smile outweigh all those sleepless nights? In the modern world, we assume that we can decide whether to have children based on what we think the experience of having a child will be like.

But Paul thinks there's a catch. The trouble is that there is no way to really know what having a child is like until you actually have one. You might get hints from watching other people's children. But that overwhelming feeling of love for this one particular baby just isn't something you can understand beforehand. You may not even like other people's children and yet discover that you love your own child more than anything. Of course, you also can't really understand the crushing responsibility beforehand, either. So you just can't make the decision rationally.

I think the problem is even worse. Rational decision-making assumes there is a single person with the same values before and after the decision. If I'm trying to decide whether to buy peaches or pears, I can safely assume that if I prefer peaches now, the same "I" will prefer them after my purchase. But what if making the decision turns me into a different person with different values?

Part of what makes having a child such a morally transformative experience is the fact that my child's well-being can genuinely be more important to me than my own. It may sound melodramatic to say that I would give my life for my children, but, of course, that's exactly what every parent does all the time, in ways both large and small.

Once I commit myself to a child, I'm literally not the same person I was before. My ego has expanded to include another person even though—especially though—that person is utterly helpless and unable to reciprocate. And even though—especially though—that person's desires and goals may be very different from mine. That's at the heart of the paradox of dependence and independence.

The person I am before I have children has to make a decision for the person I will be afterward. If I have kids, chances are that my future self will care more about them than just about anything else, even her own happiness, and she'll be unable to imagine life without them. But, of course, if I don't have kids, my future self will also be a different person, with different interests and values. Deciding whether to have children isn't just a matter of deciding what you want. It means deciding who you're going to be.

The Berlin picture of fundamentally incommensurable values gives us a better way of thinking about the decision not to have children, as well as the decision to have them. On either a utilitarian or a Kantian view, you might feel justified in choosing not to have children only if you could somehow argue that caring for children isn't really that valuable, after all. If caring for children really did make everybody better off or really was some kind of moral imperative, then not having children would be selfish or just wrong. And in fact, people who choose not to have children sometimes express a kind of skepticism or even an active hostility toward the value of caring for children. Phrases like "child-free" imply that caring for children is a form of oppression or a limitation.

But Berlin's tragedy is also a consolation. There are many ways to lead a life of human value, and nobody can lead them all. Someone who decides not to have children can embrace other values without rejecting the value of children. Virginia Woolf, who chose not to have children, wisely said, "Never pretend that the things you haven't got are not worth having."

And, of course, that applies to the decision to have children, too. Deciding to care for children may be incompatible with other ways of life that also have value—single-mindedly devoting yourself entirely to a particular kind of work, for example, or leading a monastic life of solitary contemplation, or even just being free to enjoy all the aesthetic pleasures life offers. But it is equally true that embracing those ways of life means that you will miss the valuable experience of caring for children.

In fact, as Paul points out, there isn't even an entirely rational way of deciding how many values you should pursue. She argues that you might have a higher-order value that living a life with more diverse goods and values and experiences is better than living a life with only a few. And one good thing about children is that they grow up—intensive care for children need only occupy a portion of your life, and can be compatible with other values before and after. It should be possible to divide your life into different periods with different values.

But even here, there is no entirely rational way to decide whether a life intensely devoted to just one value is better than a life devoted less intensely to many, or whether a life divided into different phases with different values is better than one where many values jostle with each other simultaneously.

One thing you can say is that these decisions, precisely because they are decisions about the sort of person you will become, are central to your personal autonomy, and should be made as freely as possible. This is much more true for decisions like whether to have a child than for more straightforward decisions about how to achieve particular goals.

Berlin's pluralist view of morality underpinned his defense of a pluralist liberal democracy. The freedom to work, to marry, to follow a particular religion or none at all—these are all so valuable and central to a democracy because they define who we are. Even if most people thought that a particular kind of work or marriage or religious practice really did lead to the most valuable kind of life, the very idea of a liberal, pluralist democracy is that we can't impose that value on others.

And the same is true about the value of having children. Precisely because such decisions are so morally profound and life-transforming, we should respect the freedom of individual people with individual lives to make them. It should be obvious by now that I personally place a very high value, the highest, on caring for children. That is also true for many people in religious traditions, and is often articulated as the justification for opposing contraception or abortion.

But I would argue that it's just because caring for children is so valuable, so transformative, and so morally central that contraception and abortion have to be freely available. When I was forty I unintentionally got pregnant, and decided to have an abortion. It was a difficult decision but it was, thankfully, my decision to make.

Once you have children, deciding how to balance the responsibilities you have to them, to other people, to work, and to yourself also raises profound riddles. When we care deeply for a child we are no longer just one person with one set of values and interests, values and interests we can weigh against one another and coordinate with the values and interests of others. Instead, a parent is a person whose self has been expanded to include the values and interests of another person, even when those values and interests are different from his. How do you balance and coordinate interests when the interests of the other person both are and are not your own?

The answer is that there is no simple answer. Berlin argues that in these cases of conflicting values the best we can do is muddle through and make the best decision we can given the particular context. There is no decision that is best in some absolute way, and we need to accept both the guilt and regret, and the consolations, that follow from this.

Private Ties and Public Policy

The fundamental paradoxes that underlie our moral relationship to children can also help explain some of the tensions in our policy decisions. If caring for children were just a job, another kind of work, we might feel that anyone could do it with sufficient training—in fact, we might feel that experts ought to do it, rather than parents themselves. But we don't feel that way about very young children, in particular, or even about older ones. There is something special about the relationship between parents and children, something that gives parents a special authority over, interest in, and responsibility for what happens to their children.

Usually in politics we can distinguish between views that emphasize the rights and interests of individual agents and those that emphasize the interests of larger groups—communities or states. But children are in a funny in-between position; we feel uncomfortable assuming that they are simply part of their parents' interests and equally uncomfortable assuming that they aren't.

This has consequences for many real and difficult political questions. Should education be based primarily on individual choice, giving parents the latitude to raise their children as religious fundamentalists or wild hippie progressives? Should we allow parents to determine what goes on in the public schools, which we all pay for? Should we allow parents to decide whether to spank their children? Or to vaccinate their children? Or even to decide whether to give their children medical treatment at all? Or instead should we insist that the community as a whole can decide what children should learn or how they should be treated?

To at least some extent we are willing to give people both responsibility and authority over their own lives—there is only so much we will do to protect people from their own worst impulses. But what about when those worst impulses affect their children? Our solution to this at the moment is a radically flawed foster-care system in which vulnerable children are bounced back and forth from their biological parents to badly paid foster parents or group homes. But what would be a better system? These are really hard questions, and again the Berlin principle suggests that there is no simple answer.

Finding the Money

Individual people may decide to take on caring for children or not. And it may be difficult to decide how much autonomy parents should have in making decisions about their children and how much this is also the responsibility of the community at large. But we can all agree that caring for children is important, important as a human value itself and important because of its consequences, too. And we can all agree that it takes a lot of time, energy, and money to raise children. The latest estimate is that children in the United States cost an average of $245,000 to raise, and that's not counting the cost of college.

The most urgent question of all is one we *can* answer. How do we guarantee that children get the resources they need to thrive? The fact that so many American children don't get those resources is one of those scandalous slow-motion disasters that we have come simply to take for granted. The statistics are as familiar as they are grim. In the richest country on earth more than one-fifth of the children grow up in poverty. More children are poor than people in any other age group. People who take care of children, especially young children, are paid less than almost any other group. And this disaster is getting worse: the percentage of children in poverty has actually gone up over the past ten years. Worse even than poverty itself is the fact that an increasing number of children grow up in isolation and chaos.

In a small-scale forager society, we could simply take it for granted that resources would flow to children and caregivers. As we saw in the chapters on evolution, distinctive and striking characteristics of human beings (distinctive evolutionary phenomena such as pair-bonding, grandparenting, and alloparenting) are designed to ensure that resources go to children even though— especially though—children can't produce those resources themselves. And, of course, those evolutionary impulses are still there—the drive to feed a hungry child is surely as strong and universal as any emotion we can imagine.

But that small-scale personal impulse is hard to translate into policy in a big industrial and postindustrial society. In an industrial world, there is an assumption that resources are a reward for goal-directed work (though often, of course, they are more likely to be the result of sheer luck). Getting those resources is entirely the business of each individual worker, and using those resources to support children becomes simply one more kind of consumer spending. We don't have a political way of articulating the special value of caring for children.

In this kind of world, caring for children falls into the cracks. Particularly in the United States, parents and children end up caught in a double bind—parents must either forgo work, which means forgoing exactly the resources that they need to raise a child, or else somehow find enough money out of their own paychecks to pay other people to take care of their children. Either way, this inevitably means that the people who take care of kids are among the lowest paid in the country.

For some time, of course, the solution to this problem was to link resources for children specifically to marriage. This is the classic "nuclear family" picture. Fathers exclusively gather resources at jobs outside the home, and then share them with mothers who don't work and exclusively look after children. To some people this seems like the inevitable, natural way to care for children. But, in fact, this was a very particular approach that emerged in the nineteenth and twentieth centuries with the rise of industrialization.

We talk about how women started leaving the home to work in the 1970s. But we don't recognize that fathers also started leaving the home to work only relatively recently. Until the nineteenth and even the twentieth century, most people lived and worked on farms, or in small local workshops or businesses. In 1830, 70 percent of American children lived in families with two parents who both worked on a farm; only 15 percent lived in a "nuclear family" with a working father and a stay-at-home mom. In 1930, only 30 percent of children had two farming parents, and 55 percent were in nuclear families. In the 1970s, the composition of families began to change again, and by 1989 less than a third of children were being raised in "nuclear families"—most children were raised by two parents who both worked or by a single parent who did. The percentage of children in one-parent families has continued to rise. By 2014 more than 30 percent of children were being raised by single parents.

On a farm, fathers and mothers, and families more generally, both work and care for children at the same time. It was only when home and work became separated that caregiving and work became separated as well.

The flaws of the stay-at-home-mother solution are, of course, obvious by now. Women don't get to experience the satisfactions of a career. It makes both women and children entirely dependent on fathers, and so profoundly vulnerable. And at the same time it isolates fathers from children and child-rearing. These flaws become especially apparent when divorce is widely available, as it should be for independent reasons. Children are especially likely to suffer if the only way to get them the resources they need is legal pressure on an embittered ex-husband.

Since at least the 1970s the stay-at-home-mother model has crumbled. Partly, this is the result of the women's movement, as women have rightly acted to gain more autonomy. It is also partly the result of economic forces. The average family income has been maintained only because women have gone to work. But other institutions haven't emerged to take its place.

This has had disastrous effects for children, particularly low-income children. In a foraging or farming society children had extended families to take care of them. In a traditional "nuclear family" they at least had a couple who were both dedicated to providing their resources and care. But in America right now children often end up depending on a single woman, who has to both work full-time and take care of them. In turn this leads to a vicious cycle—children who are raised in poor environments are themselves unlikely to have enough resources for their own children. This has contributed to increasing social inequality and immobility.

One set of solutions is well known and straightforward and has already been adopted in most civilized countries. This is to recognize that providing resources for children is the responsibility not only of biological mothers or even biological mothers and fathers but also of the community at large. There is no mystery about the moral advantages or the good practical consequences of policies such as universal prenatal care, home visitors and nurses, paid parental leave for men and women, universal and free preschool, and direct subsidies to parents.

These policies really do lead to better outcomes for children as a whole—in fact, this is one of the clearest results in all of social science. Multiple studies show that interventions that support parents in the early years have strong effects into adulthood. The interventions may be "home-visiting" programs where nurses provide additional care and advice to parents, or they may provide high-quality preschool, or they may give parents paid leave, or they may just give parents money. Children with this kind of support grow up to be healthier and have higher incomes, and are less likely to be imprisoned.

Is this a reason for endorsing the parenting picture—where parenting shapes a particular kind of child who becomes a particular kind of adult? Not really. These early childhood programs influence the probabilities across the whole group—it's still very hard to predict which individual children will succeed or fail.

And, often at least, these interventions actually don't influence measures like children's test scores in immediately succeeding years, as you might expect if sculpting a particular kind of child led to a particular kind of adult. Instead, there are often "sleeper" effects—the effects are only visible many years later. Early childhood interventions influence children's health and happiness as adults. But this is because providing resources early on gives children a platform that allows them to shape their own adult lives.

One particularly effective way to get resources to children is through universal, free, high-quality child care or preschool. This is one of the main children's policy issues in America now, and it is a rare example of a policy that has support from both right and left. Even here, however, there is a tension between the model of "parenting" and the model of "being a parent," the carpenter or the gardener.

Preschool teachers and child-care workers tend to have something more like a "gardener" model: kindergarten, after all, was traditionally supposed to be just what it says—a garden for children that was different from school. But they are currently caught in a kind of pincer movement between two groups who assume the "carpenter" model. One group includes the parents who want to shape their three-year-olds into Harvard freshmen. The other group includes the policy makers who want to be sure of "outcomes" in the form of high test scores. Both these groups tend to take an instrumental carpenter's approach to preschool. One New York mother sued her child's preschool because the children were just playing instead of preparing for tests. You can even see this in the way the word "preschool" has replaced "child care" in these discussions, as if caring for children is less valuable than schooling them.

But this instrumental view of preschool is misguided and even counterproductive. Preschool should be seen instead as a way of providing care for helpless children in a mobile, dispersed, and large industrial society. The facts of modern life make it difficult to support earlier ways of caring. We simply can't rely on the forager and farmer models of extended families living in the same place, or on the early industrial model of working fathers and stay-at-home mothers. Preschool is one alternative.

But preschool should be a way of providing a child's garden in which both poor and rich children can thrive. It should not be, as it sometimes seems to be for middle-class parents, the first step in the shaping process that is designed to yield successful adults at the other end. We also shouldn't think of preschool only in terms of "school readiness," as if the only point of caring for young children is to make them into older children who will do better in the particular strange institution of school.

The Old and the Young

Nothing is exactly like raising children. But rather than using other institutions, such as work or school, as a model for caring for children, we could think about caring for children as a model for other institutions. The paradoxes of love and learning that we see so clearly when we think about children also emerge in other areas of private experience and public policy.

The structure of work in an industrial society means that other kinds of care suffer in the same way that caring for children suffers. There are the same tensions between the specific commitment and love we feel toward other people and universal principles, and between respecting the independence of the people we love and recognizing that they sometimes must depend on us. Even though relationships to specific other people are at the core of our moral and emotional being, even at the core of our biology, we have no clear practical or political way to support them. Because they aren't work, they are economically and politically invisible. This is particularly true when, as with children, those relationships are asymmetrical—where we need to give more care to another person than we could ever expect to receive in return.

You can see this vividly in the way we handle aging. At about the same time that my husband, Alvy, became a grandfather, his own ninety-year-old parents began to need care themselves. His mother, crippled by arthritis and Alzheimer's, was particularly fragile. We went through the familiar litany of worrying mid-night phone calls, difficult conversations, painful decisions. Alvy's sister, who fortunately was prosperous and retired and lived in the same town as her parents, took on most of the very hard daily responsibilities. In the end, his parents moved to an "assisted living facility," where they died. Through all this, we had a sense that something was profoundly wrong about the whole process, though it was hard to know what we could do to make it better.

The way we treat the old is as much of a slow-motion invisible disaster as the way we treat the young. It's hard to visit almost any "assisted living facility" or "retirement home," no matter how dedicated and loving a child you are, and not feel your heart sink. We have spectacularly failed to provide the people we love with a good and dignified end, and we fear that this will be our fate as well.

Just as we feel a specific commitment to our children, we feel an equally specific commitment to our parents. In both cases the value of this relationship is intrinsic, not instrumental. Indeed, in the case of the aging, poignantly, there isn't even the possibility that we are shaping future adults in some important way. Our parents are already shaped and there is no way to avoid the fact that all of us end in decline and death.

The way we care for the old now is very much like the way we care for the young. To have an aging parent is a personal problem, even though, if you are middle-aged like me, it is a personal problem that almost everyone you know shares. Just as we wouldn't want to consign our children entirely to some cadre of experts, we wouldn't want to give up our personal responsibility for our parents.

What this means is that the resources we need for the very old, like the resources we need for the very young, are largely the responsibility of the carers. And, of course, for much recent history the care of the old, like the care of the young, has been the responsibility of women like my sister-in-law. This model makes sense, however, only if there is some way to systematically provide the carers with the time and money and support they need.

We end up caught in the same double bind in our care of the old that we do in our care of the young. Either we have to find the time for care by not working ourselves, or we have to find the money to pay other people to do it. And that means that the people who take care of the old, like those that take care of the young, are themselves among the lowest paid in the country.

We do, at least, have some general social mechanisms of care for the old in place, like Social Security and Medicare. In fact, we provide substantially more public support for the very old than the very young. But even there, we retain the model that this is merely a matter of individual people choosing to spend the money they earn through work on their future selves.

The myth of Medicare and Social Security is that they are savings plans. In fact, of course, they are, as they should be, a way that the current generation collectively takes care of the past generation, just as parental leave or universal preschool should be ways that the current generation takes care of the future one.

We should start thinking about caring for the people we love, young or old, as an intrinsic value, a fundamental good that deserves both recognition and support. Just as we should provide paid parental leave, we should provide paid leave for caring for the elderly. And just as we should recognize formally that the demands of work should sometimes give way to the needs of our children, we should also recognize that they should sometimes give way to the needs of our parents.

Work, Play, Art, Science

The way we think about aging reflects the paradoxes of love. The paradoxes of learning apply to other domains. The tension between play and work, tradition and innovation, isn't limited to our thinking about children. Thinking about children can inform our thinking about aging in one way, but it can inform our thinking about art and science in an entirely different way. We saw that the evolutionary purpose of childhood is to provide a protected period in which variation and innovation can thrive. Play is the most striking manifestation of that strategy. Play is, precisely, an activity with no apparent goal or purpose or outcome. Instead, play lets us explore alternatives, whether they are alternative ways of moving or acting, thinking or imagining. Play is the essence of an exploration strategy rather than an exploitation one. It's no coincidence that it's also a characteristic of childhood.

Human beings not only have an exceptionally long childhood, but even as adults we maintain many strikingly childlike characteristics, both physical and psychological. Biologists call it neoteny. Even as adults, humans have the potential for the kind of open-ended curiosity, exploration, and play that is so characteristic of children.

What's more, we have a range of adult institutions—sports, art, drama, science—that formalize play. These institutions mirror the wide-ranging exploration of movement, and the physical and the psychological world, that we see in children's play, but they combine it with the focus, drive, and purpose of adulthood.

Work is central to industrial and postindustrial society, but it lives in tension with both care and play. Work shapes the availability of resources for care, whether of the old or the young, and it also shapes the availability of resources for play. The same tensions that influence the way we treat care also influence the way we treat play.

Sometimes, we treat adult play—sport or art or science—as simply a personal indulgence, another consumer good to be bought with the proceeds of work, or the indulgence of a rich patron. At other times we treat it as a disguised form of work itself, something that has value only because it eventually leads to some practical end—physical health or moral uplift, improved machines or better medical treatments. Every scientific grant proposal has to have a section justifying it in terms of ultimate outcomes.

The irony is that over the long term, play does lead to practical benefits for both children and adults—that is certainly true of scientific exploration. But it does this precisely because the people who play, whether they are children or adults, aren't aiming at those practical benefits. The fundamental paradox of the explore/exploit trade-off is that in order to be able to reach a variety of goals in the long run, you have to actively turn away from goal-seeking in the short run.

Just as we should give children the resources and space to play, and do so without insisting that play will have immediate payoffs, we should do the same for scientists and artists and all the others who explore human possibilities.

You can see the value of this attitude to play in both post-industrial and preindustrial societies. Successful high-tech firms such as Google and Pixar, companies that require innovation and creativity, intentionally set aside time and space for play. For many years Google has had a policy in which employees have some time allotted every week to simply pursue ideas they think are interesting. The Pixar building includes secret passages and playhouses.

One of the most striking examples of the value of play, for adults and for children, that I have ever seen comes in the great 1920s silent film *Nanook of the North*. The film traces the life of an Inuit hunter, Nanook, and his family as they struggle to survive in one of the harshest climates on earth, with only their own skill at hunting and gathering to sustain them.

At one point in the movie Nanook makes a little toy sled for his adorable toddler son. Father and child have a grand romp in the snow, familiar to any Canadian parent like me. This may seem unremarkable, but think about it for a minute. Consider just how much of the gross domestic product of that barely subsisting family, in time and materials, went into building and playing with that sled. What Nanook knew, though, was that there was no better investment in a future life than the playful exploration of snow and ice. In the richest country on earth we still haven't learned that lesson.

Conclusion

Why be a parent, then? What makes caring for children worthwhile? Being a parent isn't worthwhile because it will lead to some particular outcome in the future, because it will create a particular kind of valuable adult. Instead, being a parent allows a new kind of human being to come into the world, both literally and figuratively. Each new child is entirely unprecedented and unique—the result of a new complicated combination of genes and experience, culture and luck. And each child, if cared for, will turn into an adult who can create a new, unprecedented, unique human life. That life may be happy or sad, successful or disappointing, full of pride or regret. If it's like most valuable human lives it will be all of these things. The very specific, unconditional commitment we feel to the child we care for is a way of respecting and supporting that uniqueness.

Part of the pathos, but also the moral depth, of being a parent is that a good parent creates an adult who can make his own choices, even disastrous choices. A secure, stable childhood allows children to explore, to try entirely new ways of living and being, to take risks. And risks aren't risks unless they can come out badly. If there isn't some chance that our children will fail as adults, then we haven't succeeded as parents. But it's also true that being a good parent allows children to succeed in ways that we could never have predicted or imagined shaping.

If I look back on the questions I started out with—Did I do the right thing when I raised my own children? How did I influence the way they turned out?—I am more convinced than ever that those questions were simply ill-conceived.

None of my children has replicated my life. Instead, each of them has created a uniquely valuable life of his own—a life that is a mash-up of my values and traditions, the values and traditions of the other people who have taught and cared for them, the inventions of their generation, and their own inventions. I may at times be uncomprehending or even appalled (septum piercing? gangsta rap?), but more often I am surprised and delighted (artisanal deli! eco-carpentry!). I couldn't ask for more.

The dance through time between parents and children, the past and the future, is a deep part of human nature, perhaps the deepest part. It has its tragic side. Human beings have the capacity to see ourselves in a long historical perspective. We do this in a more scientific way now, but we have always been aware of our ancestors and progenitors, and the ghosts and spirits of those who have gone before.

The myth of Orpheus and Eurydice is one of the most vivid and compelling images of our relationship with the past. As we move forward in time we leave behind the ghosts of our own departed loves. All the efforts we make to look back and keep them with us—memory, storytelling, photographs, and videos—

just serve to drive them further away into the uncapturable past. We watch helplessly as the shades of our grandparents and parents, our own youthful selves, even the beautiful and beloved faces of our young children, fade away down the long slope of the past.

But to be a parent is also to experience a kind of Orpheus effect in reverse. We parents, and grandparents even more, have to watch our beloved children glide irretrievably into the future we can never reach ourselves. It is a simple fact that I won't see Augie's life after forty, and that I can't even begin to guess what that life will be like. But there's another side to this. I won't be here but he will, and so a part of me will be, too. In the end, the human story of parents and children is surely more hopeful than sad. Our parents give us the past, and we hand on the future to our children.

Notes

Science is the cumulative result of the efforts of thousands of people, and a really complete list of references for a book as wide-ranging as this one would go on for hundreds of pages. Since this book is aimed at the general reader, I've given at least one reference for every empirical claim I make in the book, and I've also tried to direct readers to particularly accessible and useful academic books for further reading.

Introduction: The Parent Paradoxes

4 *something wrong about it*: For an excellent portrait of contemporary parents' complex attitudes, see Senior 2014.

7 *Emily Rapp*: Rapp 2011. In 2014, her book, *The Still Point of the Turning World*, was published based on her 2011 article in *The New York Times*.

1. Against Parenting

21 *"parenting"*: The Merriam-Webster dictionary says first use was in 1958. Merriam-Webster: Dictionary and Thesaurus. "parenting." Accessed October 27, 2015. http://www.merriam-webster.com/dictionary/parenting.

23 *a mug's game*: A good source outlining this research is Michael Lewis's *Altering Fate: Why the Past Does Not Predict the Future* (Lewis 1997).

24 *parenting advice and equipment*: See Paul 2008.

24 *rates of infant mortality*: Pritchard and Williams 2011.

24 *Michael Pollan*: Pollan 2006.

25 *cooking is as crucial*: See, e.g., Wrangham 2009.

25 *highest obesity rate*: Ng et al. 2014.

27 *"evolvability"*: Jablonka and Lamb 2005; Pigliucci 2008.

27 *Lyme disease*: Graves et al. 2013.

28 *risk-taking becomes important*: See, e.g., Ellis and Bjorklund 2012; Ellis et al. 2012.

28 *When you hunt*: Eisenberg et al. 2008.

29 *Karl Popper*: Popper 1959.

30 *tension between exploration and exploitation*: Cohen, McClure, and Angela 2007.

30 *One way to solve this problem*: Gopnik, Griffiths, and Lucas 2015; Lucas et al. 2014.

32 *difference between the timid and the bold*: Ebstein et al. 1996.

32 *mice who are stressed*: Weaver et al. 2004.

32 *Some children are resilient*: Frankenhuis, Panchanathan, and Belsky 2015; Boyce and Ellis 2005.

33 *Behavioral genetics*: Turkheimer 2000b. See also extended discussion in *The Philosophical Baby*, chapter 6 (Gopnik 2009).

33 *nonshared environment*: Turkheimer 2000a.

34 *more recent studies*: Bonawitz et al. 2014.

34 *As we grow older*: For information on brain development, see Cragg 1975; Giedd et al. 1999; Huttenlocher 1974, 1979, 1990. For a popular version, see Marian Diamond and Janet Hopson's *Magic Trees of the Mind: How to Nurture Your Child's Intelligence, Creativity, and Healthy Emotions from Birth Through Adolescence* (Diamond and Hopson 1999).

2. The Evolution of Childhood

40 *"extractive foraging"*: Parker and Gibson 1977; Yamakoshi 2001.

40 *grinding and cooking starches*: Revedin et al. 2010.

40 *a cooperative enterprise*: Hrdy 2009.

40 *Grandmothers*: Hawkes and Coxworth 2013.

41 *distinctively adapted to learn*: This argument with extensive supporting material can be found in *The Evolved Apprentice* (Sterelny 2012). I follow Sterelny in much of what follows.

46 *a longer childhood*: Hublin, Neubauer, and Gunz 2015.

46 *even chimpanzees and bonobos*: Kappeler and Pereira 2003.

46 *Chimpanzees are mobile*: Kaplan et al. 2000.

46 *menopause is distinctively human*: Hawkes et al. 1998.

47 *evidence from fossil teeth*: Smith et al. 2010.

47 *long period of immaturity*: Biologists often talk about this in terms of a contrast between R species and K species, a distinction originally made in *The Theory of Island Biogeography* (MacArthur and Wilson 1967).

48 *quokkas' brains*: Weisbecker and Goswami 2010.

48 *altricial and precocial birds*: Starck and Ricklefs 1998.

48 *crows are so intelligent*: Hunt and Gray 2004.

49 *crows are immature*: Holzhaider, Hunt, and Gray 2010.

50 *our brains are most active*: Kuzawa 2014.

51 *broad-based kinds of learning*: Heyes 2012.

51 *Eva Jablonka*: Jablonka and Lamb 2005.

52 *learning and cultural transmission*: Sterelny 2012; Tomasello 2009.

53 *between innovation and imitation*: Boyd and Richerson 1988; Laland, Atton, and Webster 2011; Smith et al. 2008.

53 *distinctive human cultural innovations*: Sterelny 2012.

54 *change we adapted to*: Potts 1996.

3. The Evolution of Love

59 *Sarah Blaffer Hrdy and Kristen Hawkes*: Hawkes and Coxworth 2013; Hrdy 2009.

59 *we pair-bond*: Chapais 2009.

59 *we grandmother*: Hawkes et al. 1998.

59 *we alloparent*: Hrdy 2009.

60 *what you mean by monogamy*: Reichard and Boesch 2003.

61 *Other primates*: Dixson 1998. For more on pair-bonding, see Chapais 2009, above.

63 *close to human universals*: Fisher 1992.

63 *less than 5 percent of all mammal species*: Kleiman 1977.

63 *pair-bonding and paternal investment*: For more on paternal investment, see Clutton-Brock 1991. For more on pair-bonding, see Fletcher et al. 2015.

64 *move from that to pair-bonding*: Gavrilets 2012.

65 *as human beings evolved*: Antón and Snodgrass 2012.

66 *engage in more care*: Abraham et al. 2014.

66 *more unequal societies*: Morris and Scheidel 2009.

68 *Helen Fisher*: Fisher 2004.

69 *so damn* cute: Glocker et al. 2009; Lorenz 1943.

69 *voles*: Carter, Devries, and Getz 1995; Winslow et al. 1993; Young and Wang 2004.

69 *When scientists activate those genes*: Lim et al. 2004.

69 *Oxytocin*: Donaldson and Young 2008.

71 *Grandmothers*: See Hawkes et al. 1998 and Hawkes and Coxworth 2013, above.

74 *Alloparents*: Hrdy 2009.

75 *breast-feed other moms' babies*: Hewlett and Winn 2014.

80 *problem in evolutionary theory*: Frank's 1988 account of commitment is elaborated in Sterelny 2012. The account here relies on both of those accounts.

81 *other primates*: De Waal 2008.

81 *human strengths*: Tomasello 2009.

81 *tit for tat*: Axelrod and Hamilton 1981.

84 *that warm feeling inside*: Feldman et al. 2010.

84 *decreases testosterone*: Gettler et al. 2011.

84 *applying them more generally*: Churchland 2011.

85 *less tolerant of people outside it*: De Dreu et al. 2011.

4. Learning Through Looking

90 *The Little Actors*: Wordsworth 1804.

92 *the baby will do the same*: Meltzoff and Moore 1977.

92 *startling result*: Meltzoff and Moore 1989.

93 *connects us to other people*: Ramachandran 2012.

94 *brains of living animals*: Rizzolatti, Fogassi, and Gallese 2001.

94 *undergoing brain surgery*: Keysers and Gazzola 2010.

94 *limited abilities in these areas*: Tomasello and Call 1997.

94 *can't explain our social behavior*: Hickok 2009.

95 *simple as seeing an object*: Carandini et al. 2005.

96 *simple and stable visual system*: Çukur et al. 2013.

96 *master physical tools*: Byrne 1997.

96 *Machiavellian hypothesis*: Byrne and Whiten 1989.

97 *observing the actions of others*: Laland 2004.

97 *a simple machine*: Meltzoff, Waismeyer, and Gopnik 2012.

99 *One-year-olds*: Carpenter, Akhtar, and Tomasello 1998.

99 *It has to be a person*: Meltzoff 1995.

99 *Consider another experiment*: Gergely, Bekkering, and Király 2002.

100 *In one experiment three-year-olds*: Williamson, Meltzoff, and Markman 2008.

101 *complex sequences of actions*: Buchsbaum et al. 2011.

102 *better than grown-ups do*: Lucas et al. 2014.

104 *difference between children and adults*: Gopnik, Griffiths, and Lucas 2015.

105 *Victoria Horner and Andrew Whiten*: Horner and Whiten 2005.

106 *three actions on the toy*: Buchsbaum et al. 2011.

109 *sensitive to rituals*: Legare et al. 2015.

109 *how a puzzle box worked*: Nielsen and Blank 2011.

110 *spoke a different language*: Buttelmann et al. 2013.

111 *WEIRD*: Henrich, Heine, and Norenzayan 2010.

111 *Barbara Rogoff*: Rogoff 2003.

112 *than American children were*: Correa-Chávez and Rogoff 2009.

114 *promoting social relationships*: Levitin 2011.

5. Learning Through Listening

116 *amount of conversation and language*: Hoff 2006; Hoff and Tian 2005; Hart and Risley 1995.

117 *learn from the testimony of others*: Much of the material in this chapter can be found in Paul Harris's book (Harris 2012). See also Koenig, Clément, and Harris 2004.

117 *information from a familiar caregiver*: Harris and Corriveau 2011.

117 *separated from . . . their caregivers*: Ainsworth et al. 2014.

118 *similar results with fathers and grandmoms*: Grossmann et al. 2008; Cohen and Campos 1974.

118 *result of complicated interactions*: van den Boom 1994.

118 *baby's adult love life*: Hazan and Shaver 1987.

118 *"attachment patterns"*: Corriveau et al. 2009.

119 *three-year-olds*: Vikram and Malone 2007.

119 *four-year-olds*: Koenig and Harris 2005.

119 *five-year-olds*: Lutz and Keil 2002.

119 *sensitive to consensus*: Corriveau, Fusaro, and Harris 2009.

120 *Paul Harris*: Corriveau and Harris 2010.

120 *"conformity effects"*: Asch 1956.

120 *blicket detector experiments*: For reviews of the blicket detector studies, see Gopnik 2012 and Gopnik and Wellman 2012.

121 *deal with conflict and uncertainty*: Bridgers et al. 2016.

121 *made the machine go*: Waismeyer, Meltzoff, and Gopnik 2015.

122 *how reliable someone is*: Corriveau, Meints, and Harris 2009.

123 *more vulnerable to blowhards*: For more on this topic, see Tenney et al. 2011.

127 *Jacqueline Woolley*: Estes, Wellman, and Woolley 1989; Woolley 1997.

127 *"quarantine" . . . fictional worlds*: Skolnick and Bloom 2006.

128 *the third realm*: Harris and Koenig 2006; Legare et al. 2012.

129 *explicitly mark the supernatural*: Harris and Koenig 2006.

130 *Cristine Legare*: Legare et al. 2012; Legare and Gelman 2009.

131 *look for good explanations*: See, e.g., Callanan and Oakes 1992.

131 *solicit information*: Frazier, Gelman, and Wellman 2009.

131 *young children's questions*: Chouinard, Harris, and Maratsos 2007.

132 *Young children in a poor . . . community*: Tenenbaum and Callanan 2008.

132 *details of what and where*: Davis 1932.

133 *six thousand early questions*: Chouinard, Harris, and Maratsos 2007.

133 *anomalies*: Legare, Gelman, and Wellman 2010.

134 *Tania Lombrozo*: Lombrozo 2011, 2012.

134 *when children explain things*: Legare and Lombrozo 2014.

135 *blicket detector*: Walker et al. 2014.

136 *want causal information*: Callanan and Oakes 1992.

136 *The Mayan children*: Correa-Chávez and Rogoff 2009.

137 *Susan Gelman*: Gelman 2003.

138 *looking too hard for essences*: Gelman et al. 2015.

138 *constant, invisible essence*: Gelman et al. 2008; Goldin-Meadow, Gelman, and Mylander 2005.

138 *make new predictions*: Gelman 2004.

139 *"omentum"*: Carey 1985.

139 *about all categories*: Brandone and Gelman 2013.

139 *innateness and permanence*: Gelman and Hirschfeld 1999; Johnson and Solomon 1997.

140 *essentialist views of the social world*: Gelman 2004; Taylor, Rhodes, and Gelman 2009.

140 *Zazes and Flurps*: Rhodes 2012.

140 *girls will always be girls*: Slaby and Frey 1975.

140 *more absolute about gender*: Gelman et al. 2004.

141 *Scott Atran*: Atran et al. 2001.

141 *a "carrot eater"*: Gelman and Heyman 1999.

141 *generic language*: Gelman et al. 2004; Rhodes, Leslie, and Tworek 2012.

142 *two-and-a-half-year-old Adam*: Gelman et al. 2000.

143 *"Blicks drink milk!"*: Graham, Nayer, and Gelman 2011.

143 *conversations about gender*: Gelman et al. 2004.

144 *essentialist about social categories*: Rhodes, Leslie, and Tworek 2012.

6. The Work of Play

149 *Why do animals play?*: The authoritative source is Burghardt 2005.

150 *all kinds of play share*: Burghardt 2005.

150 *rats laugh*: Panksepp and Burgdorf 2000.

151 *released to recess*: Smith and Hagan 1980.

152 *better social competence later on*: Pellegrini and Smith 1998.

152 *Young rats do, too*: Pellis and Pellis 2007, 2013.

154 *more sensitive to these chemicals later on*: Himmler, Pellis, and Kolb 2013.

154–55 *raised in "enriched" environments*: Diamond 1988.

156 *Newborn chicks*: Wood 2013.

156 *foxes and hedgehogs*: Berlin 1953.

157 *Why are foxes and hedgehogs so different?*: Macdonald 1987.

157 *the babies play*: Holzhaider, Hunt, and Gray 2010.

157 *"The Fox"*: For the Middle English version, see Perkins 1961.

158 *In one study*: Cook, Goodman, and Schulz 2011.

159 *balance beam to explore*: Bonawitz et al. 2012.

160 *Aimee Stahl and Lisa Feigenson*: Stahl and Feigenson 2015.

162 *They pretend*: Harris 2000.

162 *play varies across cultures*: Gaskins 1999.

162 *children pretend anyway*: Haight et al. 1999.

162 *they always have*: Arie 2004.

163 *Bayesianism*: Gopnik 2012.

165 *thinking about pretend play*: Weisberg and Gopnik 2013.

165 *Daphna Buchsbaum*: Buchsbaum et al. 2012.

168 *ASD children*: Baron-Cohen 1997.

168 *developing theory of mind*: For an excellent recent review, see Wellman 2014.

169 *Marjorie Taylor*: Taylor 1999.

169 *kids with imaginary friends*: Taylor and Carlson 1997.

170 *better at understanding other people*: Mar et al. 2006; Mar and Oatley 2008.

170 *In one study*: Kidd and Castano 2013.

171 *Hod Lipson*: Bongard, Zykov, and Lipson 2006.

173 *Elizabeth Bonawitz*: Bonawitz et al. 2011.

174 *three-action experiment*: Buchsbaum et al. 2011.

175 *In one study*: Fisher et al. 2013.

176 *"guided play"*: Weisberg, Hirsh-Pasek, and Golinkoff 2013.

7. Growing Up

181 *density from weight*: Smith, Carey, and Wiser 1985.

181 *biology in a new way*: Hatano and Inagaki 1994.

181 *pet fish*: Inagaki and Hatano 2006.

181 *live on a farm*: Ross et al. 2003.

181 *sarcasm*: Capelli, Nakagawa, and Madden 1990.

181 *feel sadness and happiness*: Lagattuta et al. 2015.

182 *Barbara Rogoff*: Rogoff 1990.

183 *video games*: Dye, Green, and Bavelier 2009.

183 *prefrontal area of the brain*: Zelazo, Carlson, and Kesek 2008.

183 *Other changes*: Casey et al. 2005.

184 *reshape the brain*: Markham and Greenough 2004; Ungerleider, Doyon, and Kami 2002.

184 *they still do*: Paradise and Rogoff 2009.

184 *a distinctive cycle*: Lave and Wenger 1991.

185 *Matajuro*: Reps and Senzaki 1998.

188 *for decades*: See, e.g., Bransford, Brown, and Cocking 1999; Gardner 2011.

188 *dyslexia*: Snowling 2000.

189 *mathematical calculation*: Halberda, Mazzocco, and Feigenson 2008.

189 *language at home*: Sénéchal and LeFevre 2002.

192 *children pay attention*: Posner and Rothbart 2007. For a review, see also *The Philosophical Baby*, chapter 4 (Gopnik 2009).

192 *informational "sweet spot"*: Kidd, Piantadosi, and Aslin 2012.

192 *psychedelic drugs*: Carhart-Harris et al. 2012; Carhart-Harris et al. 2014.

194 *Steve Hinshaw and Richard Scheffler*: Hinshaw and Scheffler 2014.

195 *make a difference in the long term*: Molina et al. 2009.

199 *games with rules*: DeVries 1998.

199 *"paracosms"*: Taylor et al. 2015.

200 *Peter and Iona Opie*: Opie and Opie 2000.

202 *when children reach adolescence*: Steinberg 2014. This book presents an excellent and accessible review of recent work on adolescence. I follow it in much of this section.

202 *two-system theory*: Dahl 2004; Steinberg 2004.

203 *overestimate rewards*: Casey, Jones, and Hare 2008.

203 *took more risks*: Gardner and Steinberg 2005.

206 *the Flynn effect*: Flynn 1987; Flynn 2007.

206 *a recent study*: Pietschnig and Voracek 2015.

207 *frontal-lobe maturation*: Shaw et al. 2006.

209 *driving apprenticeship*: Steinberg 2014.
209 *Isaiah Berlin*: Berlin 2013.

8. The Future and the Past: Children and Technology

213 *cultural ratchet effect*: Tennie, Call, and Tomasello 2009.
214 *never master at all*: Stevens 1999.
214 *creoles*: See, e.g., Sankoff and Laberge 1974.
215 *first in teenagers*: Kerswill 1996.
215 *"uptalk"*: Ritchart and Arvaniti 2013.
215 *marker of status*: Cheng and Martin 2005.
216 *The first inventor*: Kawamura 1959.
126 *The Reading Brain*: This section is indebted to an excellent review by Stanislas Dehaene (Dehaene 2009). Also see: Wolf 2008.
219 *the Stroop effect*: MacLeod 1991.
220 *Socrates*: Jowett 1892.
221 *rise of literacy*: Olson 1996; Ong 1988.
222 *the telegraph*: Standage 1998.
224 *the neural level*: Polley, Steinberg, and Merzenich 2006.
224 *in young brains*: Merzenich 2001; Zhang, Bao, and Merzenich 2001. For an extended discussion of this research, see *The Philosophical Baby*, chapter 4 (Gopnik 2009).
225 *Danah Boyd*: Boyd 2014.
226 *Madeleine George and Candace Odgers*: George and Odgers 2015.
229 *a village's worth*: Dunbar 1993.

9. The Value of Children

234 *utilitarianism*: Mill 2010.
234 *Kant's "deontology"*: Kant, Wood, and Schneewind 2002.
234 *Peter Singer*: Singer 2011.
235 *Isaiah Berlin*: Berlin 2002.
235 *L. A. Paul*: Paul 2014.
238 *Virginia Woolf*: Bell 1984.
241 *an average of $245,000*: United States Department of Agriculture, 2013 Annual Report (Lino 2014).
242 *poverty*: United States Census Bureau, Current Population Reports, Table B-2, pp. 68–73 (DeNavas-Walt et al. 2011).
243 *only relatively recently*: Hernandez 1994.

243 *single parents*: Livingston 2014.

245 *in all of social science*: Heckman 2006; Kirp 2009.

245 *"sleeper"* effects: Barnett 2011.

246 *New York mother sued*: Anderson 2011.

250 *neoteny*: Bufill, Agustí, and Blesa 2011; Gould 1977.

Bibliography

Abraham, Eyal, Talma Hendler, Irit Shapira-Lichter, Yaniv Kanat-Maymon, Orna Zagoory-Sharon, and Ruth Feldman. "Father's Brain Is Sensitive to Childcare Experiences." *Proceedings of the National Academy of Sciences* 111, no. 27 (2014): 9792–97. doi: 10.1073/pnas.1402569111.

Ainsworth, Mary D. Salter, Mary C. Blehar, Everett Waters, and Sally Wall. *Patterns of Attachment: A Psychological Study of the Strange Situation.* Oxford: Psychology Press, 2014.

Anderson, Jenny. "Suit Faults Test Preparation at Preschool." *New York Times*, March 14, 2011. Accessed November 8, 2015.

Antón, Susan C., Richard Potts, and Leslie C. Aiello. "Evolution of Early Homo: An Integrated Biological Perspective." *Science* 345, no. 6192 (2014): 1236828. doi: 10.1126/science.1236828.

Antón, Susan C., and J. Josh Snodgrass. "Origins and Evolution of Genus Homo." *Current Anthropology* 53, no. S6 (2012): S479–S496. doi: 10.1086/667692.

Arie, Sophie. "Dig Finds Ancient Stone Doll." *The Guardian*, August 6, 2004. Accessed November 7, 2015. http://www.theguardian.com/world/2004/aug/06/research.arts.

Asch, Solomon E. "Studies of Independence and Conformity: I. A Minority of One Against a Unanimous Majority." *Psychological Monographs: General and Applied* 70, no. 9 (1956): 1–70. doi: 10.1037/h0093718.

Atran, Scott, Douglas Medin, Elizabeth Lynch, Valentina Vapnarsky, Edilberto Ucan Ek, and Paulo Sousa. "Folkbiology Doesn't Come from Folkpsychology: Evidence from Yukatek Maya in Cross-Cultural Perspective." *Journal of Cognition and Culture* 1, no. 1 (2001): 3–42. doi: 10.1163/156853701300063561.

Axelrod, Robert, and William Donald Hamilton. "The Evolution of Cooperation." *Science* 211, no. 4489 (1981): 1390–96. doi: 10.1126/science.7466396.

Barnett, W. Steven. "Effectiveness of Early Educational Intervention." *Science* 333, no. 6045 (2011): 975–78. doi: 10.1126/science.1204534.

Baron-Cohen, Simon. *Mindblindness: An Essay on Autism and Theory of Mind.* Cambridge, Mass.: MIT Press, 1997.

Bell, Anne Olivier. *The Diary of Virginia Woolf.* London: Hogarth Press, 1984.

Berlin, Isaiah. *The Crooked Timber of Humanity: Chapters in the History of Ideas.* Princeton, N. J.: Princeton University Press, 2013.

———. *The Hedgehog and the Fox.* London: Weidenfeld and Nicolson, 1953.

———. *Liberty.* Edited by Henry Hardy. Oxford and New York: Oxford University Press, 2002.

Bonawitz, Elizabeth, Stephanie Denison, Thomas L. Griffiths, and Alison Gopnik. "Probabilistic Models, Learning Algorithms, and Response Variability: Sampling in Cognitive Development." *Trends in Cognitive Sciences* 18, no. 10 (2014): 497–500. doi: 10.1016/j.tics.2014.06.006.

Bonawitz, Elizabeth, Patrick Shafto, Hyowon Gweon, Noah D. Goodman, Elizabeth Spelke, and Laura Schulz. "The Double-Edged Sword of Pedagogy: Instruction Limits Spontaneous Exploration and Discovery." *Cognition* 120, no. 3 (2011): 322–30. doi: 10.1016/j.cognition.2010.10.001.

Bonawitz, Elizabeth Baraff, Tessa J. P. van Schijndel, Daniel Friel, and Laura Schulz. "Children Balance Theories and Evidence in Exploration, Explanation, and Learning." *Cognitive Psychology* 64, no. 4 (2012): 215–34. doi: 0.1016/j.cogpsych.2011.12.002.

Bongard, Josh, Victor Zykov, and Hod Lipson. "Resilient Machines Through Continuous Self-Modeling." *Science* 314, no. 5802 (2006): 1118–21. doi: 10.1126/science.1133687.

Boyce, W. Thomas, and Bruce J. Ellis. "Biological Sensitivity to Context: I. An Evolutionary-Developmental Theory of the Origins and Functions of Stress Reactivity." *Development and Psychopathology* 17, no. 2 (2005): 271–301. doi: 10.1017/S0954579405050145.

Boyd, Danah. *It's Complicated: The Social Lives of Networked Teens.* New Haven: Yale University Press, 2014.

Boyd, Robert, and Peter J. Richerson. *Culture and the Evolutionary Process.* Chicago: University of Chicago Press, 1988.

Brandone, Amanda C., and Susan A. Gelman. "Generic Language Use Reveals Domain Differences in Young Children's Expectations About Animal and Artifact Categories." *Cognitive Development* 28, no. 1 (2013): 63–75. doi: 10.1016/j.cogdev.2012.09.002.

Bransford, John D., Ann L. Brown, and Rodney R. Cocking. *How People Learn: Brain, Mind, Experience, and School.* Washington, D.C.: National Academy Press, 1999.

Bridgers, Sophie, Daphna Buchsbaum, Elizabeth Seiver, Thomas L. Griffiths, and Alison Gopnik. "Children's Causal Inferences from Conflicting Testimony and Observations." *Developmental Psychology* 52, no. 1 (2016): 9–18.

Buchsbaum, Daphna, Sophie Bridgers, Deena Skolnick Weisberg, and Alison Gopnik. "The Power of Possibility: Causal Learning, Counterfactual Reasoning, and Pretend Play." *Philosophical Transactions of the Royal Society B: Biological Sciences* 367, no. 1599 (2012): 2202–12. doi: 10.1098/rstb.2012.0122.

Buchsbaum, Daphna, Alison Gopnik, Thomas L. Griffiths, and Patrick Shafto. "Children's Imitation of Causal Action Sequences Is Influenced by Statistical and Pedagogical Evidence." *Cognition* 120, no. 3 (2011): 331–40. doi: 10.1016/j.cognition.2010.12.001.

Bufill, Enric, Jordi Agustí, and Rafael Blesa. "Human Neoteny Revisited: The Case of Synaptic Plasticity." *American Journal of Human Biology* 23, no. 6 (2011): 729–39. doi: 10.1002/ajhb.21225.

Burghardt, Gordon M. *The Genesis of Animal Play: Testing the Limits.* Cambridge, Mass.: MIT Press, 2005.

Buttelmann, David, Norbert Zmyj, Moritz Daum, and Malinda Carpenter. "Selective Imitation of In-Group Over Out-Group Members in 14-Month-Old Infants." *Child Development* 84, no. 2 (2013): 422–28. doi: 10.1111/j.1467-8624.2012.01860.x.

Byrne, Richard W. "The Technical Intelligence Hypothesis: An Additional Evolutionary Stimulus to Intelligence?" In *Machiavellian Intelligence II: Extensions and Evaluations,* edited by Andrew Whiten and Richard W. Byrne, 289–311. Cambridge: Cambridge University Press, 1997.

Byrne, Richard, and Andrew Whiten. *Machiavellian Intelligence: Social Expertise and the Evolution of Intellect in Monkeys, Apes, and Humans.* Oxford Science Publications, 1989.

Callanan, Maureen A., and Lisa M. Oakes. "Preschoolers' Questions and Parents' Explanations: Causal Thinking in Everyday Activity." *Cognitive Development* 7, no. 2 (1992): 213–33. doi: 10.1016/0885-2014(92)90012-G.

Capelli, Carol A., Noreen Nakagawa, and Cary M. Madden. "How Children Understand Sarcasm: The Role of Context and Intonation." *Child Development* 61, no. 6 (1990): 1824–41. doi: 10.1111/j.1467-8624.1990.tb03568.x.

Carandini, Matteo, Jonathan B. Demb, Valerio Mante, David J. Tolhurst, Yang Dan, Bruno A. Olshausen, Jack L. Gallant, and Nicole C. Rust. "Do We Know What the Early Visual System Does?" *The Journal of Neuroscience* 25, no. 46 (2005): 10577–97. doi: 10.1523/JNEUROSCI.3726-05.2005.

Carey, Susan. *Conceptual Change in Childhood.* Cambridge, Mass.: MIT Press, 1985.

Carhart-Harris, Robin L., David Erritzoe, Tim Williams, James M. Stone, Laurence J. Reed, Alessandro Colasanti, Robin J. Tyacke, et al. "Neural Correlates of the Psychedelic State as Determined by fMRI Studies with Psilocybin." *Proceedings of the National Academy of Sciences* 109, no. 6 (2012): 2138–43. doi: 10.1073/pnas.1119598109.

Carhart-Harris, Robin L., Robert Leech, Peter J. Hellyer, Murray Shanahan, Amanda Feilding, Enzo Tagliazucchi, Dante R. Chialvo, and David Nutt. "The Entropic Brain: A Theory of Conscious States Informed by Neuroimaging Research with Psychedelic Drugs." *Frontiers in Human Neuroscience* 8, no. 20 (2014): 1–22. doi: 10.3389/fnhum.2014.00020.

Carpenter, Malinda, Nameera Akhtar, and Michael Tomasello. "Fourteen-Through 18-Month-Old Infants Differentially Imitate Intentional and Accidental Actions." *Infant Behavior and Development* 21, no. 2 (1998): 315–30. doi: 10.1016/S0163-6383(98)90009-1.

Carter, C. Sue, A. Courtney Devries, and Lowell L. Getz. "Physiological Substrates of Mammalian Monogamy: The Prairie Vole Model." *Neuroscience and Biobehavioral Reviews* 19, no. 2 (1995): 303–14. doi: 10.1016/0149-7634(94)00070-H.

Casey, B. J., Rebecca M. Jones, and Todd A. Hare. "The Adolescent Brain." *Annals of the New York Academy of Sciences* 1124, no. 1 (2008): 111–26. doi: 10.1196/annals.1440.010.

Casey, B. J., Nim Tottenham, Conor Liston, and Sarah Durston. "Imaging the Developing Brain: What Have We Learned About Cognitive Development?" *Trends in Cognitive Sciences* 9, no. 3 (2005): 104–10. doi: 10.1016/j.tics.2005.01.011.

Chapais, Bernard. *Primeval Kinship: How Pair-Bonding Gave Birth to Human Society.* Cambridge, Mass.: Harvard University Press, 2009.

Cheng, Winnie, and Martin Warren. "//CAN i help you: The Use of Rise and Rise-Fall Tones in the Hong Kong Corpus of Spoken English." *International Journal of Corpus Linguistics* 10, no. 1 (2005): 85–107. doi: 10.1075/ijcl.10.1.05che.

Chouinard, Michelle M., Paul L. Harris, and Michael P. Maratsos. "Children's Questions: A Mechanism for Cognitive Development." *Monographs of the Society for Research in Child Development* (2007): i–129. doi: 10.1111/j.1540 -5834.2007.00412.x.

Churchland, Patricia S. *Braintrust: What Neuroscience Tells Us About Morality.* Princeton, N.J.: Princeton University Press, 2011.

Clutton-Brock, Tim H. *The Evolution of Parental Care.* Princeton, N.J.: Princeton University Press, 1991.

Cohen, Jonathan D., Samuel M. McClure, and Angela J. Yu. "Should I Stay or Should I Go? How the Human Brain Manages the Trade-off Between Exploitation and Exploration." *Philosophical Transactions of the Royal Society B: Biological Sciences* 362, no. 1481 (2007): 933–42. doi: 10.1098/rstb.2007.2098.

Cohen, Leslie J., and Joseph J. Campos. "Father, Mother, and Stranger as Elicitors of Attachment Behaviors in Infancy." *Developmental Psychology* 10, no. 1 (1974): 146–54. doi: 10.1037/h0035559.

Cook, Claire, Noah D. Goodman, and Laura E. Schulz. "Where Science Starts: Spontaneous Experiments in Preschoolers' Exploratory Play." *Cognition* 120, no. 3 (2011): 341–49. doi: 10.1016/j.cognition.2011.03.003.

Correa-Chávez, Maricela, and Barbara Rogoff. "Children's Attention to Interactions Directed to Others: Guatemalan Mayan and European American Patterns." *Developmental Psychology* 45, no. 3 (2009): 630–41. doi: 10.1037 /a0014144.

Corriveau, Kathleen H., Maria Fusaro, and Paul L. Harris. "Going with the Flow: Preschoolers Prefer Nondissenters as Informants." *Psychological Science* 20, no. 3 (2009): 372–77. doi: 10.1111/j.1467-9280.2009.02291.x.

Corriveau, Kathleen H., and Paul L. Harris. "Preschoolers (Sometimes) Defer to the Majority in Making Simple Perceptual Judgments." *Developmental Psychology* 46, no. 2 (2010): 435–37. doi: 10.1037/a0017553.

Corriveau, Kathleen H., Paul L. Harris, Elizabeth Meins, Charles Fernyhough, Bronia Arnott, Lorna Elliott, Beth Liddle, Alexandra Hearn, Lucia Vittorini, and Marc De Rosnay. "Young Children's Trust in Their Mother's Claims: Longitudinal Links with Attachment Security in Infancy." *Child Development* 80, no. 3 (2009): 750–61. doi: 10.1111/j.1467-8624.2009.01295.x.

Corriveau, Kathleen H., Kerstin Meints, and Paul L. Harris. "Early Tracking of Informant Accuracy and Inaccuracy." *British Journal of Developmental Psychology* 27, no. 2 (2009): 331–42. doi: 10.1348/026151008X310229.

Cragg, Brian G. "The Density of Synapses and Neurons in Normal, Mentally Defective and Ageing Human Brains." *Brain* 98, no. 1 (1975): 81–90.

Çukur, Tolga, Shinji Nishimoto, Alexander G. Huth, and Jack L. Gallant. "Attention During Natural Vision Warps Semantic Representation Across the Human Brain." *Nature Neuroscience* 16, no. 6 (2013): 763–70. doi: 10.1038/nn.3381.

Dahl, Ronald E. "Adolescent Brain Development: A Period of Vulnerabilities and Opportunities. Keynote Address." *Annals of the New York Academy of Sciences* 1021, no. 1 (2004): 1–22. doi: 10.1196/annals.1308.001.

Davidson, Natalie S., and Susan A. Gelman. "Inductions from Novel Categories: The Role of Language and Conceptual Structure." *Cognitive Development* 5, no. 2 (1990): 151–76. doi: 10.1016/0885-2014(90)90024-N.

Davis, Edith A. "The Form and Function of Children's Questions." *Child Development* 3, no. 1 (1932): 57–74. doi: 10.2307/1125754.

De Dreu, Carsten K. W., Lindred L. Greer, Gerben A. Van Kleef, Shaul Shalvi, and Michel J. J. Handgraaf. "Oxytocin Promotes Human Ethnocentrism." *Proceedings of the National Academy of Sciences* 108, no. 4 (2011): 1262–66. doi: 10.1073/pnas.1015316108.

Dehaene, Stanislas. *Reading in the Brain: The New Science of How We Read.* New York: Penguin, 2009.

DeNavas-Walt, Carmen, Bernadette D. Proctor, and Jessica C. Smith. *U.S. Census Bureau, Current Population Reports, 60-239, Income, Poverty, and Health Insurance Coverage in the United States: 2010.* Washington, D.C.: U.S. Government Printing Office, 2011.

DeVries, Rheta. "Games with Rules." In *Play from Birth to Twelve and Beyond: Contexts, Perspectives, and Meanings,* edited by Doris Pronin Fromberg and Doris Bergen, 409–15. New York and London: Garland Publishing, 1998.

De Waal, Frans B. M. "Putting the Altruism Back into Altruism: The Evolution of Empathy." *Annual Review of Psychology* 59 (2008): 279–300. doi: 10.1146 /annurev.psych.59.103006.093625.

Diamond, Marian Cleeves. *Enriching Heredity: The Impact of the Environment on the Anatomy of the Brain.* New York: Free Press, 1988.

Diamond, Marian, and Janet Hopson. *Magic Trees of the Mind: How to Nurture Your Child's Intelligence, Creativity, and Healthy Emotions from Birth Through Adolescence.* New York: Penguin, 1999.

Dixson, Alan. *Primate Sexuality: Comparative Studies of the Prosimians, Monkeys, Apes, and Human Beings.* Oxford: Oxford University Press, 1998.

Donaldson, Zoe R., and Larry J. Young. "Oxytocin, Vasopressin, and the Neurogenetics of Sociality." *Science* 322, no. 5903 (2008): 900–904. doi: 10.1126/science.1158668.

Dunbar, Robin I. M. "Coevolution of Neocortical Size, Group Size and Language in Humans." *Behavioral and Brain Sciences* 16, no. 4 (1993): 681–94. doi: 10.1017/S0140525X00032325.

Dye, Matthew W. G., C. Shawn Green, and Daphne Bavelier. "Increasing Speed of Processing with Action Video Games." *Current Directions in Psychological Science* 18, no. 6 (2009): 321–26. doi: 10.1111/j.1467-8721.2009.01660.x.

Ebstein, Richard P., Olga Novick, Roberto Umansky, Beatrice Priel, Yamima Osher, Darren Blaine, Estelle R. Bennett, Lubov Nemanov, Miri Katz, and Robert H. Belmaker. "Dopamine D4 Receptor (D4DR) Exon III Polymorphism Associated with the Human Personality Trait of Novelty Seeking." *Nature Genetics* 12, no. 1 (1996): 78–80. doi: doi:10.1038/ng0196-78.

Eisenberg, Dan T. A., Benjamin Campbell, Peter B. Gray, and Michael D. Sorenson. "Dopamine Receptor Genetic Polymorphisms and Body Composition in Undernourished Pastoralists: An Exploration of Nutrition Indices Among Nomadic and Recently Settled Ariaal Men of Northern Kenya." *BMC Evolutionary Biology* 8, no. 173 (2008). doi: 10.1186/1471-2148-8-173.

Ellis, Bruce J., and David F. Bjorklund. "Beyond Mental Health: An Evolutionary Analysis of Development Under Risky and Supportive Environmental Conditions: An Introduction to the Special Section." *Developmental Psychology* 48, no. 3 (2012): 591–97. doi: 10.1037/a0027651.

Ellis, Bruce J., Marco Del Giudice, Thomas J. Dishion, Aurelio José Figueredo, Peter Gray, Vladas Griskevicius, Patricia H. Hawley, et al. "The Evolutionary Basis of Risky Adolescent Behavior: Implications for Science, Policy, and Practice." *Developmental Psychology* 48, no. 3 (2012): 598–623. doi: 10.1037/0026220.

Estes, David, Henry M. Wellman, and Jacqueline D. Woolley. "Children's Understanding of Mental Phenomena." In *Advances in Child Development and Behavior* 22, edited by Hayne W. Reese, 41–89. San Diego: Academic Press, 1989.

Feldman, Ruth, Ilanit Gordon, Inna Schneiderman, Omri Weisman, and Orna Zagoory-Sharon. "Natural Variations in Maternal and Paternal Care Are Associated with Systematic Changes in Oxytocin Following Parent–Infant Contact." *Psychoneuroendocrinology* 35, no. 8 (2010): 1133–41. doi: 10.1016/j.psyneuen.2010.01.013.

Fisher, Helen. *Anatomy of Love: The Natural History of Monogamy, Adultery and Divorce.* New York: W. W. Norton and Co., 1992.

———. *Why We Love: The Nature and Chemistry of Romantic Love.* New York: Henry Holt and Company, 2004.

Fisher, Kelly R., Kathy Hirsh-Pasek, Nora Newcombe, and Roberta M. Golinkoff. "Taking Shape: Supporting Preschoolers' Acquisition of Geometric Knowledge Through Guided Play." *Child Development* 84, no. 6 (2013): 1872–78. doi: 10.1111/cdev.12091.

Fletcher, Garth J. O., Jeffry A. Simpson, Lorne Campbell, and Nickola C. Overall. "Pair-Bonding, Romantic Love, and Evolution: The Curious Case of *Homo sapiens.*" *Perspectives on Psychological Science* 10, no. 1 (2015): 20–36. doi: 10.1177/1745691614561683.

Flynn, James R. "Massive IQ Gains in 14 Nations: What IQ Tests Really Measure." *Psychological Bulletin* 101, no. 2 (1987): 171–91. doi: 10.1037/0033 -2909.101.2.171.

———. *What Is Intelligence? Beyond the Flynn Effect.* New York: Cambridge University Press, 2007.

Frank, Robert H. *Passion Within Reason: The Strategic Role of the Emotions.* New York: W. W. Norton and Co., 1988.

Frankenhuis, Willem E., Karthik Panchanathan, and Jay Belsky. "A Mathematical Model of the Evolution of Individual Differences in Developmental Plasticity Arising Through Parental Bet-hedging." *Developmental Science* (2015). doi: 10.1111/desc.12309.

Frazier, Brandy N., Susan A. Gelman, and Henry M. Wellman. "Preschoolers' Search for Explanatory Information Within Adult–Child Conversation." *Child Development* 80, no. 6 (2009): 1592–1611. doi: 10.1111/j.1467-8624 .2009.01356.x.

Gardner, Howard. *The Unschooled Mind: How Children Think and How Schools Should Teach.* New York: Basic Books, 2011.

Gardner, Margo, and Laurence Steinberg. "Peer Influence on Risk Taking, Risk Preference, and Risky Decision Making in Adolescence and Adulthood: An Experimental Study." *Developmental Psychology* 41, no. 4 (2005): 625–35. doi: 10.1037/0012-1649.41.4.625.

Gaskins, Suzanne. "Children's Daily Lives in a Mayan Village: A Case Study of Culturally Constructed Roles and Activities." In *Children's Engagement in the World: Sociocultural Perspectives*, edited by Artin Göncü, 25–60. Cambridge: Cambridge University Press, 1999.

Gavrilets, Sergey. "Human Origins and the Transition from Promiscuity to Pair-Bonding." *Proceedings of the National Academy of Sciences* 109, no. 25 (2012): 9923–28. doi: 10.1073/pnas.1200717109.

Gelman, Susan A. *The Essential Child: Origins of Essentialism in Everyday Thought.* New York: Oxford University Press, 2003.

———. "Psychological Essentialism in Children." *Trends in Cognitive Sciences* 8, no. 9 (2004): 404–9. doi: 10.1016/j.tics.2004.07.001.

Gelman, Susan A., Peggy J. Goetz, Barbara W. Sarnecka, and Jonathan Flukes. "Generic Language in Parent–Child Conversations." *Language Learning and Development* 4, no. 1 (2008): 1–31. doi: 10.1080/15475440701542625.

Gelman, Susan A., and Gail D. Heyman. "Carrot-Eaters and Creature-Believers: The Effects of Lexicalization on Children's Inferences About Social Categories." *Psychological Science* 10, no. 6 (1999): 489–93. doi: 10.1111/1467-9280.00194.

Gelman, Susan A., and Lawrence A. Hirschfeld. "How Biological Is Essentialism." In *Folkbiology*, edited by Douglas L. Medin and Scott Atran, 403–46. Cambridge, Mass.: MIT Press, 1999.

Gelman, Susan A., Michelle Hollander, Jon Star, and Gail D. Heyman. "The Role of Language in the Construction of Kinds." In *The Psychology of Learning and Motivation: Advances in Research and Theory*, edited by Douglas L. Medin, 201–63. San Diego: Academic Press, 2000.

Gelman, Susan A., Sarah-Jane Leslie, Alexandra M. Was, and Christina M. Koch. "Children's Interpretations of General Quantifiers, Specific Quantifiers and Generics." *Language, Cognition and Neuroscience* 30, no. 4 (2015): 448–61. doi: 10.1080/23273798.2014.931591.

Gelman, Susan A., and Ellen M. Markman. "Categories and Induction in Young Children." *Cognition* 23, no. 3 (1986): 183–209. doi: 10.1016/0010-0277(86)90034-X.

Gelman, Susan A., Marianne G. Taylor, Simone P. Nguyen, Campbell Leaper, and Rebecca S. Bigler. "Mother–Child Conversations About Gender: Understanding the Acquisition of Essentialist Beliefs." *Monographs of the Society for Research in Child Development* (2004): i–142. doi: 10.1111/j.1540-5834.2004.06901002.x.

George, Madeleine, and Candice L. Odgers. "Seven Fears and the Science of How Mobile Technologies May Be Influencing Adolescents in the Digital Age." *Perspectives on Psychological Science* 10 (November 2015): 832–51.

Gergely, György, Harold Bekkering, and Ildikó Király. "Rational Imitation in Preverbal Infants." *Nature* 415, no. 6873 (2002): 755–56. doi: 10.1038/415755a.

Gettler, Lee T., Thomas W. McDade, Alan B. Feranil, and Christopher W. Kuzawa. "Longitudinal Evidence That Fatherhood Decreases Testosterone in Human Males." *Proceedings of the National Academy of Sciences* 108, no. 39 (2011): 16194–99. doi: 10.1073/pnas.1105403108.

Giedd, Jay N., Jonathan Blumenthal, Neal O. Jeffries, F. Xavier Castellanos, Hong Liu, Alex Zijdenbos, Tomáš Paus, Alan C. Evans, and Judith L. Rapoport. "Brain Development During Childhood and Adolescence: A Longitudinal MRI Study." *Nature Neuroscience* 2, no. 10 (1999): 861–63. doi:10.1038/13158.

Glocker, Melanie L., Daniel D. Langleben, Kosha Ruparel, James W. Loughead, Jeffrey N. Valdez, Mark D. Griffin, Norbert Sachser, and Ruben C. Gur. "Baby Schema Modulates the Brain Reward System in Nulliparous

Women." *Proceedings of the National Academy of Sciences* 106, no. 22 (2009): 9115–19. doi: 10.1073/pnas.0811620106.

Goldin-Meadow, Susan, Susan A. Gelman, and Carolyn Mylander. "Expressing Generic Concepts with and without a Language Model." *Cognition* 96, no. 2 (2005): 109–26. doi: 10.1016/j.cognition.2004.07.003.

Gopnik, Alison. *The Philosophical Baby: What Children's Minds Tell Us About Truth, Love, and the Meaning of Life*. New York: Farrar, Straus and Giroux, 2009.

———. "Scientific Thinking in Young Children: Theoretical Advances, Empirical Research, and Policy Implications." *Science* 337, no. 6102 (2012): 1623–27. doi: 10.1126/science.1223416.

Gopnik, Alison, Thomas L. Griffiths, and Christopher G. Lucas. "When Younger Learners Can Be Better (or at Least More Open-Minded) Than Older Ones." *Current Directions in Psychological Science* 24, no. 2 (2015): 87–92. doi: 10.1177/0963721414556653.

Gopnik, Alison, and Henry M. Wellman. "Reconstructing Constructivism: Causal Models, Bayesian Learning Mechanisms, and the Theory Theory." *Psychological Bulletin* 138, no. 6 (2012): 1085. doi: 10.1037/a0028044.

Gould, Stephen Jay. *Ontogeny and Phylogeny*. Cambridge, Mass.: Harvard University Press, 1977.

Graham, Susan A., Samantha L. Nayer, and Susan A. Gelman. "Two-Year-Olds Use the Generic/Nongeneric Distinction to Guide Their Inferences About Novel Kinds." *Child Development* 82, no. 2 (2011): 493–507. doi: 10.1111/j.1467 -8624.2010.01572.x.

Graves, Christopher J., Vera I. D. Ros, Brian Stevenson, Paul D. Sniegowski, and Dustin Brisson. "Natural Selection Promotes Antigenic Evolvability." *PLOS Pathogens* 9, no. 11 (2013): e1003766. doi: 10.1371/journal.ppat.1003766.

Grossmann, Karin, Klaus E. Grossmann, Heinz Kindler, and Peter Zimmermann. "A Wider View of Attachment and Exploration: The Influence of Mothers and Fathers on the Development of Psychological Security from Infancy to Young Adulthood." In *Handbook of Attachment: Theory, Research, and Clinical Applications* (2nd ed.), edited by Jude Cassidy and Phillip R. Shaver, 857–79. New York: Guilford Press, 2008.

Haight, Wendy L., Xiao-lei Wang, Heidi Han-tih Fung, Kimberley Williams, and Judith Mintz. "Universal, Developmental, and Variable Aspects of Young Children's Play: A Cross-Cultural Comparison of Pretending at Home." *Child Development* 70, no. 6 (1999): 1477–88. doi: 10.1111/1467-8624.00107.

Halberda, Justin, Michèle M. M. Mazzocco, and Lisa Feigenson. "Individual Differences in Non-verbal Number Acuity Correlate with Maths Achievement." *Nature* 455, no. 7213 (2008): 665–68. doi: 10.1038/nature07246.

Harris, Paul L. *Trusting What You're Told: How Children Learn from Others.* Cambridge, Mass.: Harvard University Press, 2012.

——. *The Work of the Imagination.* Oxford: Blackwell Publishing, 2000.

Harris, Paul L., and Kathleen H. Corriveau. "Young Children's Selective Trust in Informants." *Philosophical Transactions of the Royal Society B: Biological Sciences* 366, no. 1567 (2011): 1179–87. doi: 10.1098/rstb.2010.0321.

Harris, Paul L., and Melissa A. Koenig. "Trust in Testimony: How Children Learn About Science and Religion." *Child Development* 77, no. 3 (2006): 505–24. doi: 10.1111/j.1467-8624.2006.00886.x.

Hart, Betty, and Todd R. Risley. *Meaningful Differences in the Everyday Experience of Young American Children.* Baltimore: Paul H. Brookes Publishing, 1995.

Hatano, Giyoo, and Kayoko Inagaki. "Young Children's Naïve Theory of Biology." *Cognition* 50, no. 1 (1994): 171–88. doi: 10.1016/0010-0277(94)90027-2.

Hawkes, Kristen, and James E. Coxworth. "Grandmothers and the Evolution of Human Longevity: A Review of Findings and Future Directions." *Evolutionary Anthropology: Issues, News, and Reviews* 22, no. 6 (2013): 294–302. doi: 10.1002/evan.21382.

Hawkes, Kristen, James F. O'Connell, N. G. Blurton Jones, Helen Alvarez, and Eric L. Charnov. "Grandmothering, Menopause, and the Evolution of Human Life Histories." *Proceedings of the National Academy of Sciences* 95, no. 3 (1998): 1336–39.

Hazan, Cindy, and Phillip Shaver. "Romantic Love Conceptualized as an Attachment Process." *Journal of Personality and Social Psychology* 52, no. 3 (1987): 511. doi: 10.1037/0022-3514.52.3.511.

Heckman, James J. "Skill Formation and the Economics of Investing in Disadvantaged Children." *Science* 312, no. 5782 (2006): 1900–1902. doi: 10.1126/science.1128898.

Henrich, Joseph, Steven J. Heine, and Ara Norenzayan. "The Weirdest People in the World?" *Behavioral and Brain Sciences* 33, nos. 2–3 (2010): 61–83. doi: 10.1017/S0140525X0999152X.

Hernandez, Donald J. "Children's Changing Access to Resources: A Historical Perspective." *Social Policy Report* 8, no. 1 (1994): 1–23.

Hewlett, Barry S., and Steve Winn. "Allomaternal Nursing in Humans." *Current Anthropology* 55, no. 2 (2014): 200–229. doi: 10.1086/675657.

Heyes, Cecilia. "New Thinking: The Evolution of Human Cognition." *Philosophical Transactions of the Royal Society of London B: Biological Sciences* 367, no. 1599 (2012): 2091–96. doi: 10.1098/rstb.2012.0111.

Hickok, Gregory. "Eight Problems for the Mirror Neuron Theory of Action

Understanding in Monkeys and Humans." *Journal of Cognitive Neuroscience* 21, no. 7 (2009): 1229–43. doi: 10.1162/jocn.2009.2118.

Himmler, Brett T., Sergio M. Pellis, and Bryan Kolb. "Juvenile Play Experience Primes Neurons in the Medial Prefrontal Cortex to Be More Responsive to Later Experiences." *Neuroscience Letters* 556 (2013): 42–45. doi: 10.1016/j .neulet.2013.09.061.

Hinshaw, Stephen P., and Richard M. Scheffler. *The ADHD Explosion: Myths, Medication, Money, and Today's Push for Performance.* New York: Oxford University Press, 2014.

Hoff, Erika. "Environmental Supports for Language Acquisition." *Handbook of Early Literacy Research* 2 (2006): 163–72.

Hoff, Erika, and Chunyan Tian. "Socioeconomic Status and Cultural Influences on Language." *Journal of Communication Disorders* 38, no. 4 (2005): 271–78. doi: 10.1016/j.jcomdis.2005.02.003.

Holzhaider, Jennifer C., Gavin R. Hunt, and Russell D. Gray. "The Development of Pandanus Tool Manufacture in Wild New Caledonian Crows." *Behaviour* 147, no. 5 (2010): 553–86. doi: 10.1163/000579510X12629536366284.

Horner, Victoria, and Andrew Whiten. "Causal Knowledge and Imitation/ Emulation Switching in Chimpanzees (*Pan troglodytes*) and Children (*Homo sapiens*)." *Animal Cognition* 8, no. 3 (2005): 164–81. doi: 10.1007/s10071-004 -0239-6.

Hrdy, Sarah Blaffer. *Mothers and Others: The Evolutionary Origins of Mutual Understanding.* Cambridge, Mass.: Harvard University Press, 2009.

Hublin, Jean-Jacques, Simon Neubauer, and Philipp Gunz. "Brain Ontogeny and Life History in Pleistocene Hominins." *Philosophical Transactions of the Royal Society of London B: Biological Sciences* 370, no. 1663 (2015): 20140062. doi: 10.1098/rstb.2014.0062.

Hunt, Gavin R., and Russell D. Gray. "The Crafting of Hook Tools by Wild New Caledonian Crows." *Proceedings of the Royal Society of London B: Biological Sciences* 271, Suppl. 3 (2004): S88–S90. doi: 10.1098/rsbl.2003.0085.

Huttenlocher, Peter R. "Dendritic Development in Neocortex of Children with Mental Defect and Infantile Spasms." *Neurology* 24, no. 3 (1974): 203–10.

———. "Morphometric Study of Human Cerebral Cortex Development." *Neuropsychologia* 28, no. 6 (1990): 517–27. doi: 10.1016/0028-3932(90) 90031-I.

———. "Synaptic Density in Human Frontal Cortex: Developmental Changes and Effects of Aging." *Brain Research* 163, no. 2 (1979): 195–205. doi: 10.1016/ 0006-8993(79)90349-4.

Inagaki, Kayoko, and Giyoo Hatano. "Young Children's Conception of the

Biological World." *Current Directions in Psychological Science* 15, no. 4 (2006): 177–81. doi: 10.1111/j.1467-8721.2006.00431.x.

Jablonka, Eva, and Marion J. Lamb. *Evolution in Four Dimensions: Genetic, Epigenetic, Behavioral, and Symbolic Variation in the History of Life.* Cambridge, Mass.: MIT Press, 2005.

Jaswal, Vikram K., and Lauren S. Malone. "Turning Believers into Skeptics: 3-Year-Olds' Sensitivity to Cues to Speaker Credibility." *Journal of Cognition and Development* 8, no. 3 (2007): 263–83. doi: 10.1080/15248370701446392.

Johnson, Susan C., and Gregg E. A. Solomon. "Why Dogs Have Puppies and Cats Have Kittens: The Role of Birth in Young Children's Understanding of Biological Origins." *Child Development* 68, no. 3 (1997): 404–19. doi: 10.1111 /j.1467-8624.1997.tb01948.x.

Jowett, Benjamin. *The Dialogues of Plato.* 5 vols. Oxford: Clarendon Press, 1892.

Kant, Immanuel, Allen W. Wood, and Jerome B. Schneewind. *Groundwork for the Metaphysics of Morals.* New Haven: Yale University Press, 2002.

Kaplan, Hillard, Kim Hill, Jane Lancaster, and A. Magdalena Hurtado. "A Theory of Human Life History Evolution: Diet, Intelligence, and Longevity." *Evolutionary Anthropology Issues News and Reviews* 9, no. 4 (2000): 156–85.

Kappeler, Peter M., and Michael E. Pereira, eds. *Primate Life Histories and Socioecology.* Chicago and London: University of Chicago Press, 2003.

Kawamura, Syunzo. "The Process of Sub-culture Propagation Among Japanese Macaques." *Primates* 2, no. 1 (1959): 43–60. doi: 10.1007/BF01666110.

Kerswill, Paul. "Children, Adolescents, and Language Change." *Language Variation and Change* 8, no. 2 (1996): 177–202. doi: 10.1017/S0954394500001137.

Keysers, Christian, and Valeria Gazzola. "Social Neuroscience: Mirror Neurons Recorded in Humans." *Current Biology* 20, no. 8 (2010): R353–R354. doi: 10.1016/j.cub.2010.03.013.

Kidd, Celeste, Steven T. Piantadosi, and Richard N. Aslin. "The Goldilocks Effect: Human Infants Allocate Attention to Visual Sequences That Are Neither Too Simple Nor Too Complex." *PLoS One* 7, no. 5 (2012): e36399. doi: 10.1371/journal.pone.0036399.

Kidd, David Comer, and Emanuele Castano. "Reading Literary Fiction Improves Theory of Mind." *Science* 342, no. 6156 (2013): 377–80. doi: 10.1126/science .1239918.

Kirp, David L. *The Sandbox Investment: The Preschool Movement and Kids-First Politics.* Cambridge, Mass.: Harvard University Press, 2009.

Kleiman, Devra G. "Monogamy in Mammals." *The Quarterly Review of Biology* 52, no. 1 (1977): 39–69.

Koenig, Melissa A., Fabrice Clément, and Paul L. Harris. "Trust in Testimony:

Children's Use of True and False Statements." *Psychological Science* 15, no. 10 (2004): 694–98. doi: 10.1111/j.0956-7976.2004.00742.x.

Koenig, Melissa A., and Paul L. Harris. "Preschoolers Mistrust Ignorant and Inaccurate Speakers." *Child Development* 76, no. 6 (2005): 1261–77. doi: 10.1111/j.1467-8624.2005.00849.x.

Kuzawa, Christopher W., Harry T. Chugani, Lawrence I. Grossman, Leonard Lipovich, Otto Muzik, Patrick R. Hof, Derek E. Wildman, Chet C. Sherwood, William R. Leonard, and Nicholas Lange. "Metabolic Costs and Evolutionary Implications of Human Brain Development." *Proceedings of the National Academy of Sciences* 111, no. 36 (2014): 13010–15. doi: 10.1073/pnas.1323099111.

Lagattuta, Kristin Hansen, Hannah J. Kramer, Katie Kennedy, Karen Hjortsvang, Deborah Goldfarb, and Sarah Tashjian. "Chapter Six—Beyond Sally's Missing Marble: Further Development in Children's Understanding of Mind and Emotion in Middle Childhood." *Advances in Child Development and Behavior* 48 (2015): 185–217. doi: 0.1016/bs.acdb.2014.11.005.

Laland, Kevin N. "Social Learning Strategies." *Animal Learning and Behavior* 32, no. 1 (2004): 4–14. doi: 10.3758/BF03196002.

Laland, Kevin N., Nicola Atton, and Michael M. Webster. "From Fish to Fashion: Experimental and Theoretical Insights into the Evolution of Culture." *Philosophical Transactions of the Royal Society B: Biological Sciences* 366, no. 1567 (2011): 958–68. doi: 10.1098/rstb.2010.0328.

Lave, Jean, and Etienne Wenger. *Situated Learning: Legitimate Peripheral Participation.* Cambridge: Cambridge University Press, 1991.

Legare, Cristine H., E. Margaret Evans, Karl S. Rosengren, and Paul L. Harris. "The Coexistence of Natural and Supernatural Explanations Across Cultures and Development." *Child Development* 83, no. 3 (2012): 779–93. doi: 10.1111/j.1467-8624.2012.01743.x.

Legare, Cristine H., and Susan A. Gelman. "South African Children's Understanding of AIDS and Flu: Investigating Conceptual Understanding of Cause, Treatment and Prevention." *Journal of Cognition and Culture* 9, no. 3 (2009): 333–46. doi: 10.1163/156770909X12518536414457.

Legare, Cristine H., Susan A. Gelman, and Henry M. Wellman. "Inconsistency with Prior Knowledge Triggers Children's Causal Explanatory Reasoning." *Child Development* 81, no. 3 (2010): 929–44. doi: 10.1111/j.1467-8624.2010.01443.x.

Legare, Cristine H., and Tania Lombrozo. "Selective Effects of Explanation on Learning During Early Childhood." *Journal of Experimental Child Psychology* 126 (2014): 198–212. doi: 10.1016/j.jecp.2014.03.001.

Legare, Cristine H., Nicole J. Wen, Patricia A. Herrmann, and Harvey Whitehouse. "Imitative Flexibility and the Development of Cultural Learning." *Cognition* 142 (2015): 351–61. doi: 10.1016/j.cognition.2015.05.020.

Levitin, Daniel J. *This Is Your Brain on Music: Understanding a Human Obsession.* New York: Atlantic Books, 2011.

Lewis, Michael. *Altering Fate: Why the Past Does Not Predict the Future.* New York: Guilford Press, 1997.

Lim, Miranda M., Zuoxin Wang, Daniel E. Olazábal, Xianghui Ren, Ernest F. Terwilliger, and Larry J. Young. "Enhanced Partner Preference in a Promiscuous Species by Manipulating the Expression of a Single Gene." *Nature* 429, no. 6993 (2004): 754–57. doi: 10.1038/nature02539.

Lino, Mark. "Expenditures on Children by Families, 2013 Annual Report." *U.S. Department of Agriculture, Center for Nutrition Policy and Promotion. Miscellaneous Publication,* no. 1528 (2013–14).

Livingston, Gretchen. "Less Than Half of U.S. Kids Today Live in a 'Traditional' Family." *Pew Research Center,* December 22, 2014. Accessed November 8, 2015. http://www.pewresearch.org/fact-tank/2014/12/22/less-than-half-of-u-s-kids-today-live-in-a-traditional-family/

Lombrozo, Tania. "Explanation and Abductive Inference." In *Oxford Handbook of Thinking and Reasoning,* edited by Keith J. Holyoak and Robert G. Morrison, 260–76. New York: Oxford University Press, 2012.

———. "The Instrumental Value of Explanations." *Philosophy Compass* 6, no. 8 (2011): 539–51. doi: 10.1111/j.1747-9991.2011.00413.x.

Lorenz, Konrad. "Die angeborenen Formen möglicher Erfahrung." *Zeitschrift für Tierpsychologie* 5, no. 2 (1943): 235–409. doi: 10.1111/j.1439-0310.1943.tb00655.x.

Lucas, Christopher G., Sophie Bridgers, Thomas L. Griffiths, and Alison Gopnik. "When Children Are Better (or at Least More Open-Minded) Learners Than Adults: Developmental Differences in Learning the Forms of Causal Relationships." *Cognition* 131, no. 2 (2014): 284–99. doi: 10.1016/j.cognition.2013.12.010.

Lutz, Donna J., and Frank C. Keil. "Early Understanding of the Division of Cognitive Labor." *Child Development* 73, no. 4 (2002): 1073–84. doi: 10.1111/1467-8624.00458.

MacArthur, Robert H., and Edward O. Wilson. *The Theory of Island Biogeography.* Vol. 1. Princeton: Princeton University Press, 1967.

Macdonald, David Whyte. *Running with the Fox.* London: Unwin Hyman, 1987.

MacLeod, Colin M. "Half a Century of Research on the Stroop Effect: An Integrative Review." *Psychological Bulletin* 109, no. 2 (1991): 163–201. doi: 10.1037/0033-2909.109.2.163.

Mar, Raymond A., and Keith Oatley. "The Function of Fiction Is the Abstraction and Simulation of Social Experience." *Perspectives on Psychological Science* 3, no. 3 (2008): 173–92. doi: 10.1111/j.1745-6924.2008.00073.x.

Mar, Raymond A., Keith Oatley, Jacob Hirsh, Jennifer de la Paz, and Jordan B. Peterson. "Bookworms Versus Nerds: Exposure to Fiction Versus Nonfiction, Divergent Associations with Social Ability, and the Simulation of Fictional Social Worlds." *Journal of Research in Personality* 40, no. 5 (2006): 694–712. doi: 10.1016/j.jrp.2005.08.002.

Markham, Julie A., and William T. Greenough. "Experience-Driven Brain Plasticity: Beyond the Synapse." *Neuron Glia Biology* 1, no. 4 (2004): 351–63. doi: 10.1017/s1740925x05000219.

Meltzoff, Andrew N. "Understanding the Intentions of Others: Re-enactment of Intended Acts by 18-Month-Old Children." *Developmental Psychology* 31, no. 5 (1995): 838–50. doi: 10.1037/0012-1649.31.5.838.

Meltzoff, Andrew N., and M. Keith Moore. "Imitation of Facial and Manual Gestures by Human Neonates." *Science* 198, no. 4312 (1977): 75–78. doi: 10.1126/science.198.4312.75.

———. "Imitation in Newborn Infants: Exploring the Range of Gestures Imitated and the Underlying Mechanisms." *Developmental Psychology* 25, no. 6 (1989): 954. doi: 10.1037/0012-1649.25.6.954.

Meltzoff, Andrew N., Anna Waismeyer, and Alison Gopnik. "Learning About Causes from People: Observational Causal Learning in 24-Month-Old Infants." *Developmental Psychology* 48, no. 5 (2012): 1215–28. doi:10.1037/a0027440.

Merzenich, Michael M. "Cortical Plasticity Contributing to Child Development." In *Mechanisms of Cognitive Development: Behavioral and Neural Perspectives,* edited by James L. McClelland and Robert S. Siegler, 67–95. Mahwah, N.J.: Lawrence Erlbaum Associates, 2001.

Mill, John Stuart. *Utilitarianism.* Edited by Colin Heydt. Toronto: Broadview Press, 2010.

Molina, Brooke S. G., Stephen P. Hinshaw, James M. Swanson, L. Eugene Arnold, Benedetto Vitiello, Peter S. Jensen, Jeffery N. Epstein, et al. "The MTA at 8 Years: Prospective Follow-up of Children Treated for Combined-Type ADHD in a Multisite Study." *Journal of the American Academy of Child and Adolescent Psychiatry* 48, no. 5 (2009): 484–500. doi: 10.1097/CHI.0b013e31819c23d0.

Morris, Ian, and Walter Scheidel. *The Dynamics of Ancient Empires: State Power from Assyria to Byzantium.* New York: Oxford University Press, 2009.

Nielsen, Mark, and Cornelia Blank. "Imitation in Young Children: When Who

Gets Copied Is More Important Than What Gets Copied." *Developmental Psychology* 47, no. 4 (2011): 1050–53. doi: 10.1037/a0023866.

Ng, Marie, Tom Fleming, Margaret Robinson, Blake Thomson, Nicholas Graetz, Christopher Margono, Erin C. Mullany, et al. "Global, Regional, and National Prevalence of Overweight and Obesity in Children and Adults During 1980–2013: A Systematic Analysis for the Global Burden of Disease Study 2013." *The Lancet* 384, no. 9945 (2014): 766–81. doi: 10.1016/S0140 -6736(14)60460-8.

Olson, David R. *The World on Paper: The Conceptual and Cognitive Implications of Writing and Reading.* New York: Cambridge University Press, 1996.

Ong, Walter J. *Orality and Literacy: The Technologizing of the Word.* London: Routledge, 1988.

Opie, Iona Archibald, and Peter Opie. *The Lore and Language of Schoolchildren.* New York: New York Review of Books, 2000.

Paradise, Ruth, and Barbara Rogoff. "Side by Side: Learning by Observing and Pitching In." *Ethos* 37, no. 1 (2009): 102–38. doi: 10.1111/j.1548-1352.2009 .01033.x.

Panksepp, Jaak, and Jeffrey Burgdorf. "50-kHz Chirping (Laughter?) in Response to Conditioned and Unconditioned Tickle-Induced Reward in Rats: Effects of Social Housing and Genetic Variables." *Behavioural Brain Research* 115, no. 1 (2000): 25–38. doi: 10.1016/S0166-4328(00)00238-2.

Parker, Sue Taylor, and Kathleen R. Gibson. "Object Manipulation, Tool Use and Sensorimotor Intelligence as Feeding Adaptations in Cebus Monkeys and Great Apes." *Journal of Human Evolution* 6, no. 7 (1977): 623–41. doi: 10.1016/S0047-2484(77)80135-8.

Paul, Laurie Ann. *Transformative Experience.* Oxford: Oxford University Press, 2014.

Paul, Pamela. *Parenting, Inc.: How the Billion Dollar Baby Business Has Changed the Way We Raise Our Children.* New York: Henry Holt and Company, 2008.

Pellegrini, Anthony D., and Peter K. Smith. "Physical Activity Play: The Nature and Function of a Neglected Aspect of Play." *Child Development* 69, no. 3 (1998): 577–98. doi: 10.1111/j.1467-8624.1998.tb06226.x.

Pellis, Sergio, and Vivien Pellis. *The Playful Brain: Venturing to the Limits of Neuroscience.* London: Oneworld Publications, 2013.

Pellis, Sergio M., and Vivien C. Pellis. "Rough-and-Tumble Play and the Development of the Social Brain." *Current Directions in Psychological Science* 16, no. 2 (2007): 95–98. doi: 10.1111/j.1467-8721.2007.00483.x.

Perkins, George. "A Medieval Carol Survival: 'The Fox and the Goose.'" *Journal of American Folklore* (1961): 235–44. doi: 10.2307/537636.

Pietschnig, Jakob, and Martin Voracek. "One Century of Global IQ Gains: A Formal Meta-analysis of the Flynn Effect (1909–2013)." *Perspectives on Psychological Science* 10, no. 3 (2015): 282–306. doi: 10.1177/1745691615577701.

Pigliucci, Massimo. "Is Evolvability Evolvable?" *Nature Reviews Genetics* 9, no. 1 (2008): 75–82. doi: 10.1038/nrg2278.

Pollan, Michael. *The Omnivore's Dilemma: A Natural History of Four Meals.* New York: Penguin, 2006.

Polley, Daniel B., Elizabeth E. Steinberg, and Michael M. Merzenich. "Perceptual Learning Directs Auditory Cortical Map Reorganization Through Top-down Influences." *The Journal of Neuroscience* 26, no. 18 (2006): 4970–82. doi: 10.1523/JNEUROSCI.3771-05.2006.

Popper, Karl R. *The Logic of Scientific Discovery.* London: Hutchinson and Co., 1959.

Posner, Michael I., and Mary K. Rothbart. *Educating the Human Brain.* Washington, D.C.: American Psychological Association, 2007.

Potts, Richard. "Evolution and Climate Variability." *Science* 273, no. 5277 (1996): 922s.

Pritchard, Colin, and Richard Williams. "Poverty and Child (0–14 Years) Mortality in the USA and Other Western Countries as an Indicator of 'How Well a Country Meets the Needs of Its Children' (UNICEF)." *International Journal of Adolescent Medicine and Health* 23, no. 3 (2011): 251–55. doi: 10.1515/ijamh.2011.052.

Ramachandran, Vilayanur S. *The Tell-Tale Brain: A Neuroscientist's Quest for What Makes Us Human.* New York: W. W. Norton and Co., 2012.

Rapp, Emily. "Notes from a Dragon Mom." *New York Times*, October 15, 2011. Accessed October 28, 2015. http://www.nytimes.com/2011/10/16/opinion/sunday/notes-from-a-dragon-mom.html?_r=0.

———. *The Still Point of the Turning World.* New York: Penguin, 2014.

Reichard, Ulrich H., and Christophe Boesch, eds. *Monogamy: Mating Strategies and Partnerships in Birds, Humans and Other Mammals.* Cambridge: Cambridge University Press, 2003.

Reps, Paul, and Nyogen Senzaki, compilers. *Zen Flesh, Zen Bones: A Collection of Zen and Pre-Zen Writings.* Boston: Tuttle Publishing, 1998.

Revedin, Anna, Biancamaria Aranguren, Roberto Becattini, Laura Longo, Emanuele Marconi, Marta Mariotti Lippi, Natalia Skakun, Andrey Sinitsyn, Elena Spiridonova, and Jiří Svoboda. "Thirty-Thousand-Year-Old Evidence of Plant Food Processing." *Proceedings of the National Academy of Sciences* 107, no. 44 (2010): 18815–19. doi: 10.1073/pnas.1006993107.

Rhodes, Marjorie. "Naïve Theories of Social Groups." *Child Development* 83, no. 6 (2012): 1900–1916. doi: 10.1111/j.1467-8624.2012.01835.x.

Rhodes, Marjorie, Sarah-Jane Leslie, and Christina M. Tworek. "Cultural Transmission of Social Essentialism." *Proceedings of the National Academy of Sciences* 109, no. 34 (2012): 13526–31. doi: 10.1111/1467-9280.00194.

Ritchart, Amanda, and Amalia Arvaniti. "The Use of High Rise Terminals in Southern Californian English." *The Journal of the Acoustical Society of America* 134, no. 5 (2013): 4197–98. doi: 10.1121/1.4831401.

Rizzolatti, Giacomo, Leonardo Fogassi, and Vittorio Gallese. "Neurophysiological Mechanisms Underlying the Understanding and Imitation of Action." *Nature Reviews Neuroscience* 2, no. 9 (2001): 661–70. doi: 10.1038/35090060.

Rogoff, Barbara. *Apprenticeship in Thinking: Cognitive Development in Social Context.* New York: Oxford University Press, 1990.

———. *The Cultural Nature of Human Development.* Oxford and New York: Oxford University Press, 2003.

Ross, Norbert, Douglas Medin, John D. Coley, and Scott Atran. "Cultural and Experiential Differences in the Development of Folkbiological Induction." *Cognitive Development* 18, no. 1 (2003): 25–47. doi: 10.1016/S0885 -2014(02)00142-9.

Sankoff, Gillian, and Suzanne Laberge. "On the Acquisition of Native Speakers by a Language." In *Pidgins and Creoles: Current Trends and Prospects*, edited by David DeCamp and Ian F. Hancock, 73–84. Washington, D.C.: Georgetown University Press, 1974.

Sénéchal, Monique, and Jo-Anne LeFevre. "Parental Involvement in the Development of Children's Reading Skill: A Five-Year Longitudinal Study." *Child Development* 73, no. 2 (2002): 445–60. doi: 10.1111/1467-8624.00417.

Senior, Jennifer. *All Joy and No Fun: The Paradox of Modern Parenthood.* New York: HarperCollins Publishers, 2014.

Shaw, Philip, Deanna Greenstein, Jason Lerch, Liv Clasen, Rhoshel Lenroot, N. Gogtay, Alan Evans, J. Rapoport, and J. Giedd. "Intellectual Ability and Cortical Development in Children and Adolescents." *Nature* 440, no. 7084 (2006): 676–79. doi: 10.1038/nature04513.

Singer, Peter. *Practical Ethics.* New York: Cambridge University Press, 2011.

Skolnick, Deena, and Paul Bloom. "What Does Batman Think About SpongeBob? Children's Understanding of the Fantasy/Fantasy Distinction." *Cognition* 101, no. 1 (2006): B9–B18. doi: 10.1016/j.cognition.2005.10.001.

Slaby, Ronald G., and Karin S. Frey. "Development of Gender Constancy and Selective Attention to Same-Sex Models." *Child Development* (1975): 849–56. doi: 10.2307/1128389.

Smith, Carol, Susan Carey, and Marianne Wiser. "On Differentiation: A Case Study of the Development of the Concepts of Size, Weight, and Density." *Cognition* 21, no. 3 (1985): 177–237. doi: 10.1016/0010-0277(85)90025-3.

Smith, Kenny, Michael L. Kalish, Thomas L. Griffiths, and Stephan Lewandowsky. "Theme Issue: Cultural Transmission and the Evolution of Human Behaviour." *Philosophical Transactions of the Royal Society B: Biological Sciences* 363, no. 1509 (2008).

Smith, Peter K., and Teresa Hagan. "Effects of Deprivation on Exercise Play in Nursery School Children." *Animal Behaviour* 28, no. 3 (1980): 922–28. doi: 10.1016/S0003-3472(80)80154-0.

Smith, Tanya M., Paul Tafforeau, Donald J. Reid, Joane Pouech, Vincent Lazzari, John P. Zermeno, Debbie Guatelli-Steinberg, et al. "Dental Evidence for Ontogenetic Differences Between Modern Humans and Neanderthals." *Proceedings of the National Academy of Sciences* 107, no. 49 (2010): 20923–28. doi: 10.1073/pnas.1010906107.

Snowling, Margaret J. *Dyslexia*. Malden, Mass. Blackwell Publishing, 2000.

Stahl, Aimee E., and Lisa Feigenson. "Observing the Unexpected Enhances Infants' Learning and Exploration." *Science* 348, no. 6230 (2015): 91–94. doi: 10.1126/science.aaa3799.

Standage, Tom. *The Victorian Internet: The Remarkable Story of the Telegraph and the Nineteenth Century's Online Pioneers*. London: Weidenfeld and Nicolson, 1998.

Starck, J. Matthias, and Robert E. Ricklefs, eds. *Avian Growth and Development: Evolution Within the Altricial-Precocial Spectrum*. New York and Oxford: Oxford University Press, 1998.

Steinberg, Laurence. *Age of Opportunity: Lessons from the New Science of Adolescence*. Boston: Houghton Mifflin Harcourt, 2014.

———. "Risk Taking in Adolescence: What Changes, and Why?" *Annals of the New York Academy of Sciences* 1021, no. 1 (2004): 51–58. doi: 10.1196/annals.1308.005.

Sterelny, Kim. *The Evolved Apprentice: How Evolution Made Humans Unique*. Cambridge, Mass.: MIT Press, 2012.

Stevens, Gillian. "Age at Immigration and Second Language Proficiency Among Foreign-Born Adults." *Language in Society* 28, no. 4 (1999): 555–78.

Taylor, Marianne G., Marjorie Rhodes, and Susan A. Gelman. "Boys Will Be Boys; Cows Will Be Cows: Children's Essentialist Reasoning About Gender Categories and Animal Species." *Child Development* 80, no. 2 (2009): 461–81. doi: 10.1111/j.1467-8624.2009.01272.x.

Taylor, Marjorie. *Imaginary Companions and the Children Who Create Them*. Oxford and New York: Oxford University Press, 1999.

Taylor, Marjorie, and Stephanie M. Carlson. "The Relation Between Individual Differences in Fantasy and Theory of Mind." *Child Development* 68, no. 3 (1997): 436–55. doi: 10.1111/j.1467-8624.1997.tb01950.x.

Taylor, Marjorie, Sara D. Hodges, and Adèle Koháyi. "The Illusion of Independent Agency: Do Adult Fiction Writers Experience Their Characters as Having Minds of Their Own?" *Imagination, Cognition and Personality* 22, no. 4 (2003): 361–80. doi: 10.2190/FTG3-Q9T0-7U26-5Q5X.

Taylor, Marjorie, Candice M. Mottweiler, Emilee R. Naylor, and Jacob G. Levernier. "Imaginary Worlds in Middle Childhood: A Qualitative Study of Two Pairs of Coordinated Paracosms." *Creativity Research Journal* 27, no. 2 (2015): 167–74. doi: 10.1080/10400419.2015.1030318.

Tenenbaum, Harriet R., and Maureen A. Callanan. "Parents' Science Talk to Their Children in Mexican-Descent Families Residing in the USA." *International Journal of Behavioral Development* 32, no. 1 (2008): 1–12. doi: 10.1177/0165025407084046.

Tenney, Elizabeth R., Jenna E. Small, Robyn L. Kondrad, Vikram K. Jaswal, and Barbara A. Spellman. "Accuracy, Confidence, and Calibration: How Young Children and Adults Assess Credibility." *Developmental Psychology* 47, no. 4 (2011): 1065–77. doi: 10.1037/a0023273.

Tennie, Claudio, Josep Call, and Michael Tomasello. "Ratcheting Up the Ratchet: On the Evolution of Cumulative Culture." *Philosophical Transactions of the Royal Society B: Biological Sciences* 364, no. 1528 (2009): 2405–15. doi: 10.1098/rstb.2009.0052.

Tomasello, Michael. *The Cultural Origins of Human Cognition.* Cambridge, Mass.: Harvard University Press, 1999.

———. *Why We Cooperate.* Cambridge, Mass.: MIT Press, 2009.

Tomasello, Michael, and Josep Call. *Primate Cognition.* New York and Oxford: Oxford University Press, 1997.

Turkheimer, Eric. "Three Laws of Behavior Genetics and What They Mean." *Current Directions in Psychological Science* 9, no. 5 (2000): 160–64.

Turkheimer, Eric, and Mary Waldron. "Nonshared Environment: A Theoretical, Methodological, and Quantitative Review." *Psychological Bulletin* 126, no. 1 (2000): 78.

Ungerleider, Leslie G., Julien Doyon, and Avi Karni. "Imaging Brain Plasticity During Motor Skill Learning." *Neurobiology of Learning and Memory* 78, no. 3 (2002): 553–64. doi: 10.1006/nlme.2002.4091.

van den Boom, Dymphna C. "The Influence of Temperament and Mothering on Attachment and Exploration: An Experimental Manipulation of Sensitive Responsiveness Among Lower-Class Mothers with Irritable Infants." *Child Development* 65, no. 5 (1994): 1457–77. doi: 10.1111/j.1467-8624.1994.tb00829.x.

Waismeyer, Anna, Andrew N. Meltzoff, and Alison Gopnik. "Causal Learning from Probabilistic Events in 24-Month-Olds: An Action Measure." *Developmental Science* 18, no. 1 (2015): 175–82. doi: 10.1111/desc.12208.

Walker, Caren M., Tania Lombrozo, Cristine H. Legare, and Alison Gopnik. "Explaining Prompts Children to Privilege Inductively Rich Properties." *Cognition* 133, no. 2 (2014): 343–57. doi: 10.1016/j.cognition.2014.07.008.

Weaver, Ian C. G., Nadia Cervoni, Frances A. Champagne, Ana C. D'Alessio, Shakti Sharma, Jonathan R. Seckl, Sergiy Dymov, Moshe Szyf, and Michael J. Meaney. "Epigenetic Programming by Maternal Behavior." *Nature Neuroscience* 7, no. 8 (2004): 847–54. doi: 10.1038/nn1276.

Weisbecker, Vera, and Anjali Goswami. "Brain Size, Life History, and Metabolism at the Marsupial/Placental Dichotomy." *Proceedings of the National Academy of Sciences* 107, no. 37 (2010): 16216–21. doi: 10.1073/pnas.0906486107.

Weisberg, Deena S., and Alison Gopnik. "Pretense, Counterfactuals, and Bayesian Causal Models: Why What Is Not Real Really Matters." *Cognitive Science* 37, no. 7 (2013): 1368–81. doi: doi: 10.1111/cogs.12069.

Weisberg, Deena Skolnick, Kathy Hirsh-Pasek, and Roberta Michnick Golinkoff. "Guided Play: Where Curricular Goals Meet a Playful Pedagogy." *Mind, Brain, and Education* 7, no. 2 (2013): 104–12. doi: 10.1111/mbe.12015.

Wellman, Henry M. *Making Minds: How Theory of Mind Develops.* Oxford and New York: Oxford University Press, 2014.

Williamson, Rebecca A., Andrew N. Meltzoff, and Ellen M. Markman. "Prior Experiences and Perceived Efficacy Influence 3-Year-Olds' Imitation." *Developmental Psychology* 44, no. 1 (2008): 275–85. doi: 10.1037/0012-1649.44.1.275.

Winslow, J. T., Nick Hastings, C. Sue Carter, Carroll R. Harbaugh, and Thomas R. Insel. "A Role for Central Vasopressin in Pair Bonding in Monogamous Prairie Voles." *Nature* 365, no. 6446 (1993): 545–48.

Wolf, Maryanne. *Proust and the Squid: The Story and Science of the Reading Brain.* Cambridge: Icon Books, 2008.

Wood, Justin N. "Newborn Chickens Generate Invariant Object Representations at the Onset of Visual Object Experience." *Proceedings of the National Academy of Sciences* 110, no. 34 (2013): 14000–14005. doi: 10.1073/pnas .1308246110.

Woolley, Jacqueline D. "Thinking About Fantasy: Are Children Fundamentally Different Thinkers and Believers from Adults?" *Child Development* 68, no. 6 (1997): 991–1011. doi: 10.1111/j.1467-8624.1997.tb01975.x.

Wordsworth, William. *Ode: Intimations of Immortality from Recollections of Early Childhood.* 1804.

Wrangham, Richard. *Catching Fire: How Cooking Made Us Human.* New York: Basic Books, 2009.

Yamakoshi, Gen. "Ecology of Tool Use in Wild Chimpanzees: Toward Reconstruction of Early Hominid Evolution." In *Primate Origins of Human*

Cognition and Behavior, edited by Tetsuro Matsuzawa, 537–56. Springer Japan, 2001. doi: 10.1007/978-4-431-09423-4_27.

Young, Larry J., and Zuoxin Wang. "The Neurobiology of Pair Bonding." *Nature Neuroscience* 7, no. 10 (2004): 1048–54. doi: 10.1038/nn1327.

Zelazo, Philip David, Stephanie M. Carlson, and Amanda Kesek. "The Development of Executive Function in Childhood." In *Handbook of Developmental Cognitive Neuroscience* (2nd ed.), edited by Charles A. Nelson and Monica Luciana, 553–74. *Developmental Cognitive Neuroscience.* Cambridge, Mass.: MIT Press, 2008.

Zhang, Li I., Shaowen Bao, and Michael M. Merzenich. "Persistent and Specific Influences of Early Acoustic Environments on Primary Auditory Cortex." *Nature Neuroscience* 4, no. 11 (2001): 1123–30. doi: 10.1038/nn745.

Acknowledgments

I became a parent in graduate school, at just the same time I became a scientist, so this book is the result of forty years' worth of experience, and there are far too many people to thank. The University of California at Berkeley—particularly the Department of Psychology, the Institute of Human Development, and the Institute for Brain and Cognitive Sciences—has been my home for many years. I have been deeply influenced by all my colleagues, but Tom Griffiths, Tania Lombrozo, Stephen Hinshaw, Ron Dahl, Richard Ivry, Phil and Carolyn Cowan, and Linda Wilbrecht all contributed especially to this book.

My students and post-docs, past and present, have contributed to all my work, including, especially for this book, Tamar Kushnir, Anna Waismeyer, Chris Lucas, Daphna Buchsbaum, Caren Walker, Adrienne Wente, Katie Kimura, and Azzura Ruggieri. Laura Schulz, in particular, read and discussed the play chapter, and much else. Sophie Bridgers and Rosie Aboody, my lab managers, made the research possible and were invaluable in organizing the references.

The National Science Foundation (DLS0132487, BCS-331620) has funded my research for many years, and the McDonnell Foundation, the Bezos Foundation, and the Templeton Foundation have also helped support my research. And of course, my deepest debt is to the children, parents, preschools, and museums who have been our constant collaborators.

This book was largely written thanks to a fellowship at All Souls College at Oxford in 2011, and the ideas were also very much influenced by my participation in a group there on the evolution of cognition. I am very grateful to all the participants and to Cecilia Heyes for organizing the group and inviting me to join them. Conversations with Kim Sterelny and Eva Jablonka had a particularly important influence on this book.

I must also thank a number of intellectual colleagues and good friends who have influenced my ideas for a long time: Henry Wellman, Andrew Meltzoff, Paul Harris, Clark Glymour, John Campbell, Peter Godfrey-Smith, and Jane Hirshfield. In writing this book I made two new friends and acquired two mentors in evolutionary biology, Sarah Hrdy and Kristen Hawkes, and I am very grateful to them both.

I owe a great debt to Eric Chinski, my editor at Farrar, Straus and Giroux, who had faith in the book from the start and guided it through the finish, and to Laird Gallagher, who helped fine-tune the result. Katinka Matson, my agent, was invaluable, as always.

Several passages in this book first appeared, in somewhat different form, in *The New York Times*, *Slate*, and *The Wall Street Journal*. I am very grateful to my editors there. I owe a special debt to Gary Rosen and Peter Saenger, who have gracefully edited my Mind and Matter column in *The Wall Street Journal* for the past three years.

My own parents, Myrna and Irwin, and siblings, Adam, Morgan, Hilary, Blake, and Melissa, are the foundation of everything I am and everything I do. Adam and Blake, two fellow writers, both read drafts of this book and made characteristically helpful comments.

My children, Alexei, Nicholas, and Andres, and their father, George Lewinski, taught me everything I know about being a parent, and I am very grateful.

Finally, Augustus, Georgiana, and Atticus, my grandchildren, have been the great delight of my life for the past five years. They were the true muses for this book. My greatest debt is to my co-grandparent, lover, dear companion, and first and best reader, Alvy Ray Smith. This book is dedicated to them.

Index

abortion, 239

Ache, 44

adolescence, 12, 15, 47, 201–10, 214;
  brain and, 207–209; emotion in,
  203, 204; motivation in, 202–205;
  puberty in, 203–205; social
  changes and, 205; two-system
  theory of, 202–205; *see also*
  school-age children; teenagers

aging, 247–49, 250

agriculture, 54–55, 66

AIDS, 130

Alexei (author's son), 28, 129, 142

alloparenting, 59, 74–76, 86, 242

altruism, 44, 45, 59, 73, 75–76, 80–81,
  84, 93

American culture, 223

AmeriCorps, 209

animals, 45–49, 61, 94, 115; play in,
  149–58, 170

apes, 44, 94, 155; bonobos, 46, 53, 62,
  66, 67; chimpanzees, 41, 44, 46,
  48, 53, 61–64, 66, 71, 73, 74, 94,
  97, 105, 155; gibbons, 61, 62, 66;
  gorillas, 62–64, 66, 67, 74;
  orangutans, 61

apprenticeship, 181, 184–87, 190, 209

Archilochus, 156–57

art, 250, 251

As You Like It (Shakespeare), 166,
  167

Atran, Scott, 141

attachment, 117–19, 146

attention, 191–93, 224, 228;
  classroom and, 191, 192, 228;
  Internet and, 228

attention disorders, 193–97, 220

Augie (author's grandson), 38–41,
  43–45, 50, 51–52, 58, 68, 76–79, 84,
  91, 100–101, 105, 106, 125–26, 136,
  162, 164, 167, 169, 175, 177, 189, 193,
  222, 231, 254

Autism Spectrum Disorder (ASD), 168, 169

babies, 41, 45–47; attention of, 192; breast-feeding of, 75; imitation in, 92; physical features of, 69; separation from caregivers, 117–18; weaning of, 46
balance beams, 159–60
Banzo, 185
baseball, 186, 187, 199
Bayes, Thomas, 163
Bayesianism, 163, 171
Berkeley, University of California at, 8, 78, 84, 104, 190, 198
Berlin, Isaiah, 156–57, 209, 235, 237–41
Berra, Yogi, 120
birds, 48–49, 61, 75, 83, 156; chickens, 48, 156, 157; crows, *see* crows
birth, 57, 83, 84
birthday machine, zandos in, 165–67, 171
blicket detector, 102–104, 120, 135, 158–59, 163, 165
Bonawitz, Elizabeth, 173
bonobos, 46, 53, 62, 66, 67
books, 211–12, 216–17, 222, 226, 231, 232; *see also* reading
Boyd, Danah, 225, 226, 229
brain, 50, 68, 191, 203; adolescence and, 207–209; age and, 15, 34–35, 153; cholinergic transmitters and, 153–54, 224; digital technology and, 222; energy used by, 49, 50; experience and, 34, 95, 153, 183–84, 208, 213; frontal regions of, 153, 183, 192, 204, 207–209, 224;

left and right, 93; inhibitory transmitters and, 224; innate structure in, 94–95; learning and, 95, 153–54, 224; and length of childhood, 43, 48–50; mastery learning and, 183–84; myths and misconceptions about, 93–95; neurons in, *see* neurons; plasticity of, 34, 153–55, 183, 202; play and, 153–55; psychedelic drugs and, 192–93; reading and, 216–21, 222, 224; reward centers of, 203; size of, 43, 47–50, 59, 76; social competence and, 153; specialization in, 183
breast-feeding, 75
Bridgers, Sophie, 103
Buchsbaum, Daphna, 165–67

caregiving, caregivers, 9, 16, 36, 70, 114; aging and, 247–49; alloparenting, 59, 74–76, 86, 242; babies' separation from, 117–18; early childhood programs and, 245; facultative, fathers as, 66; learning and, 88–89, 91, 146; love and, 83–84, 86–87, 113; networks of, 59; play and, 173–76; preschool and, 245–47; talking and reading to children, 116; universal child care, 245–46; work and, 242–44
carpenter model: of parenting, 4, 18, 233, 246; of schooling, 196
Casey, B. J., 203
categories, 137–44; social, 140, 143–44
causal explanations, 134–36
cause and effect, 97–99, 109, 110, 128–29

change, 15, 28, 29, 54–55, 202;
   adaptation to, 56; generational,
   213–14, 230
changing the world, 165
chickens, 48, 156, 157
CHILDES database, 131–32, 142, 146
childhood: apprenticeship in, 181,
   184–87, 190, 209; death during, 7,
   24, 71; evolution of, 37–56, 250; as
   protected period, 31, 88–89, 203,
   250; uniqueness of, 16–17
children: adolescent, *see* adolescence;
   teenagers; cost of raising, 241–43;
   decision to have, 235–38;
   dependence and independence of,
   11–12, 14, 46, 235, 237; disabled,
   234; extended immaturity of,
   45–51, 59, 65, 76, 88–89, 123, 203,
   206, 209, 250; growth of, 50;
   immigrant, 214; middle-class, 36,
   132, 201; parents' love for, 9–12, 35,
   57, 68, 70, 76, 235, 236; poor, 24,
   25, 36, 201, 242; public policies on,
   25, 208–209, 240–42; risk-taking
   in, 27–28, 33, 34, 202, 203;
   technology and, *see* technology;
   temperaments of, 32, 55, 190; value
   of, 233–54; variability in, 190–91,
   196–97
chimpanzees, 41, 44, 46, 48, 53,
   61–64, 66, 71, 73, 74, 94, 97, 105,
   155; bonobos, 46, 53, 62, 66, 67
cholinergic transmitters, 153–54, 224
C.K., Louis, 130–31, 133, 136–38,
   144–45
climate change, 54
commitment, 13, 35, 76–87, 236–37,
   247, 248; costs of, 85–86; to
   parents, 248; roots of, 83–84
community, 241–45

confirmation bias, 161
conformity effects, 120
consciousness, 192; expanded, 193
consensus, 119–20, 130
contraception, 239
control system, 204–207
conversation, 146
cooking, 24, 25, 40, 52, 204, 206, 221
cooperation, 59, 80–82, 84, 86, 199
cooperative breeding, 59, 74, 76
counterfactual thinking, 127–28,
   162–68
creativity, 27, 31, 36, 104, 105, 110, 164
creoles, 214–15
crows, 50, 97, 115, 149, 155–57; New
   Caledonian, 48–49, 155–56; tool
   use and play in, 48–49, 155–56,
   161, 165, 172, 176
cultural rebellion, 215
culture, 22, 43–44, 73, 124;
   American, 223; evolution and,
   29–30, 43–44, 91, 108, 191;
   feedback loops and, 51–54;
   generational change and, 213–14,
   230; grandparents and, 73–74, 231;
   imitation and, 111–12; innovations
   in, 53–54, 214–16; learning and,
   51–54, 110–11; play and, 176; ratchet
   effect and, 213–14, 224, 225, 230;
   reading and, 221; rituals in, *see*
   rituals; technology and, 223;
   tradition in, *see* tradition;
   transmission of, 215–16

dancing, 41, 114, 221, 228
dark energy, 164
Darwin, Charles, 161
daughters, in communities, 73, 75
decision-making, 204, 236

democracy, 24, 238–39

deontology, 234

dependence and independence, 11–12, 14, 46, 235, 237

Dickens, Charles, 148

diet, 24, 25, 177

digital environment, 222–32

disabled children, 234

discovery learning, 182–83, 191

diseases, 194–95

disorder (mess), 26–32, 35, 36, 55

divorce, 24, 244

doing things together, 112–14

dolphins, 151, 161

driving, 208–209

drugs: psychedelic, 192–93; stimulant, 195–96

ducks, 48, 83

Duck Soup, 121

dyslexia, 188, 197, 218, 220

eating rituals, 108, 109, 111

Eden, 19–20, 225

education and schools, 7, 13–14, 22, 29, 85, 88, 90, 168, 173, 175, 176, 179–81, 197; attention and focus in, 191, 192, 228; extracurricular classes and activities, 186, 201, 209; as goal-directed, 196; kindergarten, 246; learning and, 189, 190, 196–97; outside-the-classroom 197–201; parenting and, 179–80; policies on, 240; preschool and, 245–47; progressive and alternative, 189; public vs. private schools, 85, 234; scholastic skills and, 187–90, 196; teaching, 13, 56, 87, 88, 90, 106, 107, 145, 146, 173–76, 186, 187, 189;

testing in, 180, 190, 194, 196, 197, 206–207, 245, 246; and variability in children, 190–91, 196–97; *see also* learning

Eibl-Eibesfeldt, Irenäus, 62

elderly, 247–49

elephants, 75

Eliot, George, 170

emotion, in adolescence, 203, 204

empathy, 93; fiction reading and, 170

environment, 32–33, 56, 67; changing, 54–55; nomadic lifestyle and, 54; nonshared, 33–34; social, 54–55

epigenetics, 32–33

essentialism, 137–44; language and, 141

Eurydice, 253

evolution, 7, 16, 22, 23, 25–29, 37, 42–45, 86, 90, 172, 217, 242; alloparenting and, 74–76, 86, 242; of childhood, 37–56, 250; cooperation and, 80–82; cooperative breeding and, 59, 74, 76; cultural, 29–30, 43–44, 91, 108, 191; extended childhood and, 45–51, 59, 65, 76, 88–89, 123, 203; fossil record and, 43, 47, 65, 71; genes and, 53; grandmothers and, 71–74, 86; human advantage in, 96–97; of love, 57–87; pair-bonding and, 59–70, 76, 86, 242; parenting and, 55–56; paternal investment and, 64; psychology and, 43, 45, 51, 208; reading and, 217; sex and, 173; species in, 140

evolvability, 27, 29, 31–32; learning and culture and, 29–30, 191

experiments, 97–107, 109, 110, 117–22; birthday machine, 165–67, 171;

blicket detector, 102–104, 120, 135, 158–59, 163, 165; gadget, 117–19, 122, 134, 158–59; origami, 112, 191; Pop-Beads, 158–59, 163, 173; three-action, 101, 174; three lines, 120, 122; unexpected event, 160–61

exploration, 30–32, 35, 36, 180, 181, 202, 250; exploitation and, 16, 30–31, 35, 104, 182, 250, 251

exploratory play, 162, 165, 170, 172–73

Facebook, 229

false-belief test, 169

families, 243; extended, 22, 74–76, 244, 246; farming and, 243–44, 246; nuclear, 70, 243, 244; relationships in, 198–99

farms, 243–44, 246

fathers, 76; as facultative caregivers, 66; investment in children, 63–65, 70; stay-at-home mothers and, 243, 244; work and, 243, 244, 246

feedback loops, 51–54

Feigenson, Lisa, 160–61

feminism, 67, 244

fiction, 123–30, 170, 172; empathy and, 170

financial considerations, 241–43

First Communion, 181

fish, 46, 47

Fisher, Helen, 68

Flynn, James, 206, 207

Flynn effect, 206

folklorists, 200

food, 24, 25

foraging, foragers, 39–40, 44, 46, 52–53, 66, 71, 72, 75, 141, 184, 195, 204, 228, 242, 244, 246

fossil record, 43, 47, 65, 71

foster care, 241

"Fox, The," 157–58

foxes, 156–57, 161

Freud, Sigmund, 138, 198

gadget experiments, 117–19, 122, 134, 158–59

Galbraith, John Kenneth, 186–87

games, 199

gardener model, 18–20, 146, 233, 246

geese, goslings, 48, 83

Gelman, Susan, 130, 137, 143

gender, 140, 143–44

generational change, 213–14, 230

generic language, 141–46

genes, 26, 32–34, 45, 64–66, 79, 208; alloparenting and, 75; environment and, 32–33; evolution and, 53; expression of, 32; grandparents and, 71–73; pair-bonding and, 65

geometry, 175–76

George, Madeleine, 226

Georgie (author's granddaughter), 77–80, 84, 91, 177, 193

gibbons, 61, 62, 66

goals, 42–43, 110, 172, 251; in parenting, 3, 4, 18, 56, 180, 196, 233, 245–47; in schooling, 196

Google, 229, 251

gorillas, 62–64, 66, 67, 74

grandparents, 89, 242; culture and, 73–74, 231; genes and, 71–73; grandfathers, 71, 72; grandmothers, 8, 40–41, 44, 58, 59, 71–76, 86

Great Expectations (Dickens), Miss Havisham in, 148–50, 165, 166, 173

"Great Good Place, The" (James), 227–28

Griffiths, Tom, 103

Guatemalan Mayans, 111–12, 113, 136, 182, 189, 191

Haldane, J. B. S., 73, 75

harems, 66, 67

Harris, Paul, 120

Harry Potter, 116, 200

Hart, Betty, 116

Hawkes, Kristen, 59, 71–73, 76

hedgehogs, 156–57

Hinshaw, Steve, 194

Homer, 221

home-visiting programs, 245

Homo erectus, 43, 47

Homo habilis, 43

Homo sapiens, 21, 40, 42, 45, 47, 53

Horace, 230

Horner, Victoria, 105

Hrdy, Sarah Blaffer, 59, 74, 76

Hume, David, 120

hunting and hunter-gatherer cultures, 28–29, 38–40, 44, 45, 52–53, 72, 195, 204, 228

hypotheses, 163–64

hypothetical or counterfactual thinking, 127–28, 162–68

Iliad (Homer), 221

imaginary companions, 169, 170, 199, 227

imagination, 31, 124, 164, 165

imitation, 44–45, 53, 90–92, 115, 116, 136, 146, 174–75, 182, 184, 190, 213; in babies, 92; birth of, 96–97; culture and, 111–12; experiments on, 97–102, 105–107, 109, 110; imposter syndrome and, 92; intention and, 99, 101–102, 107, 110; mirror neurons and, 92–96, 98; overimitation, 105–107; rituals and, 107–11; tools and technologies and, 97–102, 213

immigrants, 132, 214, 223

imposter syndrome, 92

industrial society, 90, 187, 205, 242, 243, 247, 250, 251

infants, *see* babies

information revolution, 205

inhibitory transmitters, 224

innateness, 139

innovation, 14–15, 22, 27, 30, 36, 53, 104, 110, 197, 202, 214, 250; cultural, 53–54, 214–16; tradition and, 89, 145, 230, 250; *see also* technology

inquiry learning, 189

intentions, 99, 101–102, 107, 110

Internet, 222–30, 232

IQ tests, 206–207

Jablonka, Eva, 51

James, Henry, 227–28

Ju/'hoansi people, 124–25

kangaroos, 48

Kant, Immanuel, 234–35, 237

kindergarten, 246

knowledge, 115–16, 137, 182; confidence about, 119, 121–23; consensus and, 119–20, 130; practice and, 182–84; scaffolding and, 176; *see also* learning

!Kung, 44

language, 93, 115–16, 125, 136, 146, 227; changes in, 214–15; essentialism and, 141; generic, 141–46; pretendese, 128, 146

langurs, 74–75

learning, 15–16, 22, 34, 41–44, 50–51, 56, 59, 76, 115–16, 180, 181, 214, 224; apprenticeship and, 181, 184–87, 190, 209; attachment and, 118–19; brain and, 95, 153–54, 224; caregiving and, 88–89, 91, 146; causal, 97–99, 109, 110; cholinergic transmitters and, 153–54, 224; culture and, 51–54, 110–11, 191; discovery, 182–83, 191; evolvability and, 29–30, 191; experiments on, 117–22; explore vs. exploit, 104; feedback loops and, 51–54; hypotheses in, 163–64; inquiry, 189; mastery, 182–84, 191, 204, 209; modules and, 51; paradoxes of, 11, 13–16, 247; parenting and, 88, 90, 145; play and, 149, 168, 178; pretending and, 168; school and, see education and schools; social, 41, 53, 90; teaching and, 13, 56, 87, 88, 90, 106, 107, 145, 146, 173–76, 186, 187, 189; theory of mind and, 168–70; tool use and, 52–53; from trial and error, 97, 98, 115; types of, 149; wide-ranging, 207, 209

learning disabilities, 197, 220

learning through listening, 115–47; questions and explanations in, 130–37, 145; to stories, 123–30; to testimony, 90, 145, 182, 213

learning through observation, 88–114, 115, 136, 145–47, 182, 213;

children as better than adults at, 102–105; experiments on, 97–107; see also imitation

Legare, Cristine, 130

lemurs, 74–75

letters, in reading, 218–19

letter writing, 227

life span, 46, 47, 49, 71

Lipson, Hod, 171, 172

listening, see learning through listening

literacy, 221, 228

Lombrozo, Tania, 134

Lorenz, Konrad, 83

love, 9–11, 82, 119, 247; attachment, 117–19, 146; caregivers and, 83–84, 86–87, 113; commitment and, 76–87; evolution of, 57–87; motherly, 58; pair-bonding and, 59–70, 76, 86; paradoxes of, 11–13, 235, 247, 250; parenting and, 86–87; of parents for children, 9–12, 35, 57, 68, 70, 76, 235, 236; purpose of, 10; romantic, 68, 69, 79; sexual, 63, 68, 70; varieties of, 68–70

Lucas, Chris, 103

Lyme disease, 27

macaques, 61, 94, 215–16

Machiavellian hypothesis, 96

magic, 124, 126–30; science and, 129

marriage, 24, 63, 69, 243; divorce and, 24, 244; gay, 67

marsupials, 48

Marx, Groucho, 93

Marx Brothers, 121

mastery learning, 182–84, 191, 204, 209

Matajuro, 185, 187, 190
mathematics, 186–89, 196
Mayan Indians of Guatemala, 111–12,
    113, 136, 182, 189, 191
meadow voles, 69–70
Medicare, 249
Meltzoff, Andrew, 92, 97
memory, 221
men: reproductive interests of,
    64; *see also* fathers
menopause, 46, 59, 71
mess, 26–32, 35, 36, 55
mice, 32, 42, 94
middle class, 22, 24, 36, 89–90,
    116, 132, 177, 201, 246
Middlemarch (Eliot), 170
Mill, John Stuart, 234, 235
mirror neurons, 92–96, 98
mirror reading and writing, 218
MIT, 158
modules, 51
Molière, 142
monkeys, 51, 94, 95, 155; langurs,
    74–75; macaque, 61, 94, 215–16;
    shape recognition in, 218
monogamy, 60–63, 69
Montessori, Maria, 138
morality, 12–13, 17, 22, 86, 234,
    238–39, 247; of being a parent,
    235; philosophical approaches to,
    234–35; *see also* value
Morrell, Ottoline, 227
mothers, 5, 58; stay-at-home, 243,
    244, 246
motivation, in adolescence, 202–205
movies, 221, 223
Munro, Alice, 82, 173
Murasaki, Lady, 230; *The Tale of
    Genji*, 63
music, 114, 186

Nanook of the North, 251–52
nature vs. nurture, 32–33
Neanderthals, 40, 42, 43, 47
neoteny, 250
neurons, 95–96; connections of,
    34–35, 153, 183–84; mirror, 92–96,
    98; shape recognition and, 218
neuroscience, myths and
    misconceptions in, 93–95
New York Times, The, 223
Nicholas (author's son), 28
nicotine, 154
nomadic lifestyle, 54
nuclear family, 70, 243, 244

obesity, 25, 205
object recognition, and reading,
    217–18
observational learning, *see* learning
    through observation
octopuses, 149, 151
Odgers, Candace, 226
old, care of, 247–49
omnivore's dilemma, 24
Opie, Peter and Iona, 200
opossums, 48
orangutans, 61
origami, 112, 191
Orpheus, 253–54
oxytocin, 69–70, 84, 85

pair-bonding, 59–70, 76, 86, 242
paracosms, 199–200
parent(s): aging, 247–49; being, vs.
    parenting, 8–10, 233, 246;
    children's relationship with,
    198–99; of children who will never
    reach adulthood, 7; evolution and,

37–56; love of, for children, 9–12, 35, 57, 68, 70, 76, 235, 236; middle-class, 22, 24, 89–90, 116, 132, 177, 246; morality of being, 235; protective, 35–36; value of being, 252

parental investment, 7, 23, 26, 47–50, 55–56, 157; paternal, 63–65, 70

parenting, 3–20, 21–26, 37, 197, 233; alloparenting, 59, 74–76, 86, 242; being a parent vs., 8–10, 233, 246; carpenter model for, 4, 18, 233, 246; and dependence and independence of children, 11–12, 46, 235, 237; effects of, 23–26; evolution and, 55–56; gardener model for, 18–20, 146, 233, 246; as goal-oriented, 3, 4, 18, 56, 180, 196, 233, 245–47; how-to books on, 4–5, 22, 24, 25; learning and, 88, 90, 145; love and, 86–87; mommy wars and, 5; play and, 149; schooling and, 179–80; siblings and, 33–34; use of word, 21; value of, 252

parrots, 48

past, 253–54

paternal investment, 63–65, 70

Paul, L. A., 235–36, 238

peers, 197–201, 203, 204

Perlmutter, Saul, 164

permanence, 139

personality, 32

Phaedrus (Plato), 220

Piaget, Jean, 34, 138, 162

Pixar, 222, 251

Plato, 220

play, 13–15, 148–78, 199, 250–52; adult, 250, 251; in animals, 149–58, 170; brain development and, 155; brain plasticity and, 153–55;

caregivers and, 173–76; characteristics of, 150–51; in crows, 155–56, 161, 165, 172, 176; culture and, 176; exploratory, 162, 165, 170, 172–73; as fun, 172, 173, 177, 178; games with groups, 199; grown-ups and, 173–77; guided, 175–77; learning and, 149, 168, 178; parenting and, 149; pretend, *see* pretend play; in rats, 149–55, 161, 165, 172, 173; robots and, 171–72; rough-and-tumble, 151–55, 161, 162, 165, 170; social competence and, 152, 153; structure of, 151; with things, 154–56, 161, 173–75, 177; types of, 149; unexpected events and, 172; value of, 251; work and, 150, 250–51

playground culture, 197–201

politics, *see* public policies

Pollan, Michael, 24

polygamy, 61, 62

polygyny, 65–67

Pop-Beads, 158–59, 163, 173

Popper, Karl, 29, 35, 160, 161

poverty, 24, 25, 36, 201, 242

practice, 182–84

prairie voles, 69–70

predictions, 120–22; violations of, 160–61

pregnancy, 57, 64, 83

preschool, 245–47

pretend play, 125, 127, 128, 146, 150, 161–63, 169–70, 172, 199, 227; cognitive ability and, 167; counterfactual thinking and, 127–28, 162–68; imaginary companions in, 169, 170, 199, 227; learning and, 168; pretendese and, 128, 146

primates, 41, 46, 47, 59, 61, 75, 76, 81, 115; lemurs, 74–75; sexual patterns in, 63–66; shape recognition in, 217, 218; *see also* apes; monkeys
prisoner's dilemma, 80–82
probabilistic predictions, 120–22
Proceedings of the National Academy of Sciences, 124
protectiveness, 35–36
Proust, Marcel, 227
psilocybin, 192–93
psychedelic drugs, 192–93
psychological tools, 96–97
psychology, evolution and, 43, 45, 51, 208
puberty, 203–205; age of, 205; *see also* adolescence
public policies, 12–13, 17, 25, 29, 208–209, 240–42, 247; care of the old, 249; early childhood programs, 245
puritanism, 177

questions and explanations, 130–33; "why," 130–31, 133–37, 145
Quiché Mayan Indians of Guatemala, 111–12, 113, 136, 182, 189, 191
quokkas, 48

race, 140, 144
Rapp, Emily, 7
ratchet effect, 213–14, 224, 225, 230
rats, 149–55, 161, 165, 172, 173
ravens, 155
reading, 188, 189, 196; brain and, 216–21, 222, 224; culture and, 221; mirror, 218; Socrates's views on,

220–21; as technology, 211–12, 216–17, 219–20; *see also* fiction
reasoning, 100
rebellion, 215
religion, 86, 124, 126, 128–30, 239
reproduction, 64, 173
rewards, 203, 205
risk-taking, 27–28, 33, 34, 202, 203, 253
Risley, Todd, 116
rituals, 41, 107–11, 112–13; coming-of-age, 181; eating, 108, 109, 111
robots, 170–72, 227
Rogoff, Barbara, 111–12, 136, 182, 191
romantic love, 68, 69, 79
Romantic period, 27, 212
Romeo and Juliet (Shakespeare), 205
rooks, 155
rough-and-tumble play, 151–55, 161, 162, 165, 170
Rowling, J. K., Harry Potter stories of, 116, 200
Russell, Bertrand, 227

Santa Claus, 129
Sayings of the Philosophers, 157
scaffolding, 176
Scheffler, Richard, 194
school-age children, 179–210; attention deficit disorder in, 193–97; peers and, 197–201, 203, 204; schoolyard culture and outside-the-classroom learning, 197–201; *see also* adolescence; education and schools
Schulz, Laura, 158, 163
science, 186–87, 250, 251; magic and, 129
Sendak, Maurice, 68

sex, 62–63, 65–67, 173, 177; feminism and, 67; love and, 63, 68, 70; pair-bonding and, 59–70, 76, 86; primates and, 63–66; reproduction and, 64, 173

sexism, 143–44

Shakespeare, William: *As You Like It*, 166, 167; *Romeo and Juliet*, 205

shapes, geometrical, 175–76

siblings: caregiving and, 75; parenting and, 33–34

Singer, Peter, 234

smartphones, 222, 225, 226, 230

Smith, Alvy Ray (author's husband), 247–48

social categories, 140, 143–44

social competence, 152, 153

social environment, 54–55

social learning, 41, 53, 90

social media, 222, 225–26, 229

social organization, 54–55, 66

social pressure, 119–20

social problems, 194–95

social rewards, 203

Social Security, 249

social skills, 181

social technologies, 108–109, 213

Socrates, 220–21

species, 140

spirituality, 86, 124

sports, 186, 250, 251

Stahl, Aimee, 160–61

stories, 123–30

Stroop effect, 219

summer enrichment activities, 209

supernatural, 126, 128–30

swans, 61

swordsmanship, 185–87

symbols, 217–18, 227

Tale of Genji, The (Murasaki), 63

talking and reading to children, 116

Taylor, Marjorie, 169

teaching, 13, 56, 87, 88, 90, 106, 107, 145, 146, 173–76, 186, 187, 189; schools and education, 7, 13–14, 22, 29, 85, 168, 173, 175, 176; *see also* learning

technology(ies), 14, 29, 211–32; books and reading as, 211–12, 216–17, 219–20; culture and, 223; Device story and, 211–12, 214, 222; digital, 222–32; imitation of, 213; long-term effects of, 225; predicting impact of, 216–17, 223; social, 108–109, 213; teenagers and, 225; *see also* tools

teenagers: cultural transmission and, 215, 216; driving and, 208–209; public policies and, 208–209; rebellion in, 215; risk-taking in, 202; social media and, 225–26; social rewards and, 203; technology and, 225; *see also* adolescence; school-age children

telegraph, telegrams, 222–23, 226, 227, 229

telephone, 227

temperament, 32, 55, 190

testimony, learning from, 90, 145, 182, 213

testosterone, 84

texting, 227, 229

theory of mind, 168–70

three-action experiment, 101, 174

three-lines experiment, 120, 122

tit-for-tat strategy, 81–83

Tolkien, J.R.R., 200

tools, 52–53, 96–97, 108, 109, 111, 212; crows' use of, 48–49, 155–56, 165, 172, 176; imitation and, 97–102;

tools (*cont.*)
  psychological, 96–97; *see also*
  technology
Tooth Fairy, 129
toys, 154–56, 173–75, 177
tradition, 14–15, 22, 24–25, 90,
  230–31; innovation and, 89, 145,
  230, 250; rituals, *see* rituals
trains, 223
trial and error, 97, 98, 115
triple threat, 59–60
"T" shapes, 218
turkeys, 48

United States, 24, 162, 241, 242–43
University of California at Berkeley,
  8, 78, 84, 104, 190, 198
uptalk, 215
utilitarianism, 85, 86, 234, 235, 237

"Valley Girl" (Zappa), 215
value(s), 234, 238, 239; of children,
  233–54; conflicts in, 239–40;
  pluralism of, 235; *see also* morality
variability, 54–55
vasopressin, 69, 70
voles, 69–70

Waismeyer, Anna, 97
wallabies, 48
WEIRD cultures, 111
whales, 71
Whiten, Andrew, 105

"why" questions, 130–31, 133–37, 145
wide-ranging learning, 207, 209
Wiessner, Polly, 124
Wired, 177
Wittgenstein, Ludwig, 25
women: grandmothers, 8, 40–41, 44,
  58, 59, 71–76, 86; menopause in,
  46, 59, 71; pelvis size in, 47;
  reproductive interests of, 64;
  working, 243; *see also* mothers
women's movement, 67, 244
Woolf, Virginia, 238
Woolley, Jacqueline, 127
Wordsworth, William, 90–91, 92
work, 13, 14, 22, 247, 250;
  apprenticeship and, 181, 184–87,
  190, 209; fathers and, 243, 244,
  246; play and, 150, 250–51;
  puritanism and, 177; and
  resources for caring for children,
  242–43; separation of home from,
  243–44; taking your child to, 209;
  women and, 243
Would-be Gentleman, The (Molière),
  142
writing, 185–89, 196; mirror, 218;
  Socrates's views on, 220–21;
  symbols in, 217–18

Yeats, William Butler, 235

zandos, in birthday machine,
  165–67, 171
Zappa, Frank, 215